THE LITTLE GUIDES

# FLOWERS

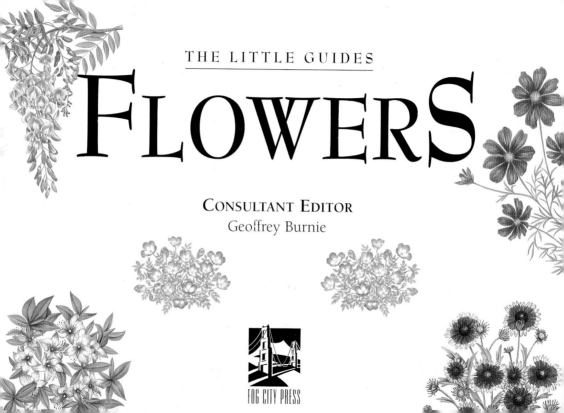

THE LITTLE GUIDES

# FLOWERS

**CONSULTANT EDITOR**
Geoffrey Burnie

FOG CITY PRESS

Published by Fog City Press
814 Montgomery Street
San Francisco, CA 94133 USA
Reprinted 2000 (twice), 2001 (twice)

Chief Executive Officer: John Owen
President: Terry Newell
Publisher: Lynn Humphries
Managing Editor: Janine Flew
Art Director: Kylie Mulquin
Editorial Coordinator: Tracey Gibson
Production Manager: Martha Malic-Chavez
Business Manager: Emily Jahn
Vice President International Sales: Stuart Laurence

Project Editor: Klay Lamprell
Designer: Emma Seymour
Consultant: Geoffrey Burnie

A catalog record for this book is available from
the Library of Congress, Washington, DC.

ISBN 1 875137 75 0

Color reproduction by Bright Arts Graphics (S) Pte Ltd
Printed by LeeFung-Asco Printers
Printed in China

A Weldon Owen Production

# CONTENTS

# PART ONE

# LEARNING ABOUT YOUR LANDSCAPE

# UNDERSTANDING YOUR SOIL

One of the great joys of flower gardening comes from mixing all kinds of annuals, biennials and bulbs with perennials, trees, shrubs and vines to create eye-catching combinations. Whatever kinds of flowers you choose to grow, a key to success is knowing your soil. Even if you've lived in the same house for years, you may never have thought about what kind of soil you have—but this will have a large effect on which flowering plants will thrive for you. The information in this chapter will help you to understand what soil conditions your yard has to offer. By learning about your site and summarizing what you've learned into a permanent plot plan, you will be able to have flowers in your garden throughout the year.

# STUDYING YOUR SOIL

Your hands, a trowel and a simple soil test kit are all you need to get a basic picture of what's going on in the earth beneath your feet. Then you can prepare the soil to make it more suitable for the flowers you want to grow. There isn't any practical way to change the texture of your soil. You can, however, improve the soil's structure.

**COLORFUL HYDRANGEAS**
Hydrangeas flourish in deep, moist, well-drained soil. The color of their flowers depends on the amount of pH present in the soil.

**What's up down below**  Until now, you may have thought that all soil was pretty much the same. But when you start looking at it more closely, you'll find that even soils that look the same can have very different traits. These traits determine which flowering plants, trees, shrubs and vines will thrive on a particular site.

**Soil texture**  Soil is made up of three basic mineral components: sand grains, smaller silt particles and fine clay particles. The relative amounts of these three mineral particles determine the texture of your soil. Take a handful of moist soil, squeeze it and check it for these characteristics: If the soil won't stay in a clump in your open hand, it's on the sandy side. If the soil forms a loose clump that breaks apart when you tap it

*Sandy soil easily loses water and nutrients.*

*Loamy soil has a fertile balance.*

*Clayey soil drains slowly.*

lightly with your finger, it's a loam—a balanced mixture of sand, silt and clay that's ideal for many garden plants. If the soil forms a sticky lump that you can mold into various shapes, it's high in clay. Soils that contain lots of sand are said to be light or sandy. Light soils lose water and dissolved nutrients quickly, so they tend to be dry and infertile. Loamy soils

usually drain quite well but hold enough water and nutrients for good plant growth. Heavy (clayey) soils tend to hold a lot of water and nutrients, but they are apt to become waterlogged when wet and hard when dry.

**Soil structure** Structure refers to how the sand, silt and clay particles in your soil stick together.

Many small clumps create ample space for the air and water that roots need to grow well. Tight, compacted soils have little or no structure, making them hard for you to dig and hard for the roots of your perennials to force their way through. Loose, sandy soils with little structure lose water and nutrients quickly. Adding organic matter will restructure your soil.

13

# ORGANIC MATTER

Organic matter is the dead material that gets added to the soil, such as fallen leaves and grass clippings. As soil organisms feed on the organic matter, they break it down into nutrients for the plants and humus. Humus is the material that forms loose connections between the soil particles and gives soil a good crumbly structure.

**GARDEN GOLD MINE**
Fallen leaves are an excellent base matter from which to make a rich, organic mulch to add to your soil.

**Knowing about nutrients**
Soil with lots of organic matter is called rich because it holds ample reservoirs of nutrients. The big three plant nutrients are nitrogen (N), phosphorus (P) and potassium (K). Plants need nitrogen to grow healthy green leaves and to regulate the use of other nutrients. Phosphorus helps form healthy roots and flowers; it also strengthens resistance to pests. Potassium also promotes strong roots and general resistance, but it's important in photosynthesis as well. Plants need several other nutrients, such as calcium and iron, in smaller quantities. Soils with ample amounts of organic matter usually contain enough nutrients to keep many kinds of flowers thriving. But you'll also need to make sure your soil is at the right pH, so that those

nutrients are available to your plants. A soil test can tell you whether your soil is acid or alkaline and whether the supply of different nutrients is adequate for flowering plants. The results of a professional soil test will also tell you exactly what to add to correct any nutrient deficiencies.

**Puzzling out pH**  Nutrients tend to be most available to roots when the soil pH is near neutral (around 6.5 to 7). When the soil is either very acid (with a lower pH) or alkaline (with a higher pH), chemical compounds are formed that make nutrients unavailable to your plants. A home test kit (which you can buy at a garden center) or a professional soil test can tell you the pH of your soil. Balance acid soils by adding lime, and alkaline soils by adding sulfur. Your test kit or soil test results sheet should tell you how much to

**IMPROVING PEONIES**
Peonies, showy perennials beloved for their huge, fragrant flowers, grow best in soil that has been enriched with organic matter.

apply. In general, adding ample quantities of organic matter—in the form of compost, chopped leaves or similar materials—will help to improve just about any kind of soil without altering the pH balance.

**Using compost**  If you intend to enrich your soil by using compost, work it in as you dig a new bed. In an established garden, use your compost as a mulch. Cover the bed with about 2 inches (5 cm) a year to maintain a fertile soil. Use more if you are growing moisture-loving perennials like astilbes or if you want to control weeds.

**CHOP FIRST, THEN SPREAD**
Chopped leaves will decompose more quickly than whole leaves.

# MAKING AND USING COMPOST

Compost is a balanced blend of recycled garden, yard and household wastes that have broken down into dark, crumbly organic matter. The time you spend making compost and applying it to your garden will be more than returned by improved soil and plant health.

**IN THE BIN**

If you're concerned that a loose compost pile would be unattractive, you can contain it in a bin. A circular bin of woven wire is easy to make and use. The large stick helps direct water to the center of the pile.

**Creating your own compost**

Making compost is a lot like cooking; you mix together the ingredients, stir them up and let them cook. The source of the heat is decomposer organisms like bacteria and fungi that live in soil and break down dead plant and animal tissues. These organisms work best when given warmth, moisture, plenty of oxygen and a balance of carbon and nitrogen. Vegetable scraps from the kitchen, grass clippings, fallen leaves and soft plant trimmings are all appropriate. If you have access to manure from chickens, rabbits, cows or horses, you can add that also. Avoid fats, bones and meat scraps, which are likely to attract scavengers to your pile. Also avoid composting manure from humans, dogs and cats—this material can carry disease organisms.

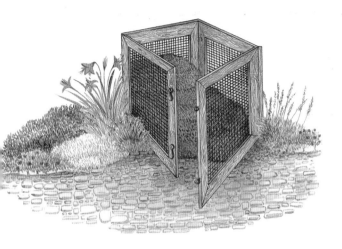

**COMPOST CONTAINED**

A wood and wire bin with a door is another good way to keep your compost contained but easily accessible. If possible, choose a shady, well-drained spot close to your garden for convenience.

**Hot composting** This type of composting will provide you with quality compost in just weeks. To create a hot compost pile, blend one part soft, green plant scraps, like lawn clippings, lettuce scraps and dandelion leaves, with two parts tough, brown scraps, like fallen leaves and woody flower stalks. The moist items provide the decomposers with the nitrogen they consume as they break down the tough, high-carbon materials. Chop the material and pile it about 3 feet (90 cm) high and wide. Add water to keep the pile evenly moist, and turn it with a pitchfork every week for oxygen. When most of the materials are unrecognizable, it is ready to use.

**Cold composting** Though it takes longer to break down, a cold compost is easier to make. Just choose a shady, well-drained place to drop your organic scraps. Let them build up to a pile about 3 feet (90 cm) high and wide and then begin again in a new location. In a year or so, the materials should be decomposed. Cold compost won't heat up enough to kill seeds or disease organisms, so don't add mature weeds or diseased plant material to the pile.

# CLIMATE
## AND
# TOPOGRAPHY

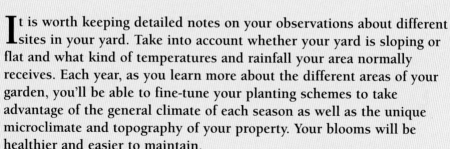

It is worth keeping detailed notes on your observations about different sites in your yard. Take into account whether your yard is sloping or flat and what kind of temperatures and rainfall your area normally receives. Each year, as you learn more about the different areas of your garden, you'll be able to fine-tune your planting schemes to take advantage of the general climate of each season as well as the unique microclimate and topography of your property. Your blooms will be healthier and easier to maintain.

# CONSIDER YOUR CLIMATE

If you've lived in the same area for many years, you already know a lot about your climate, even if you've never applied it to gardening. If you are new to an area, you'll have to ask local gardeners or do a bit of research to find out about the conditions in your region. It's worth making a little effort, since you'll save yourself the time, money and aggravation of coping with poorly adapted plants.

**Understanding hardiness zones** You'll find a plant hardiness zone map on page 311. This map divides the country into zones based on average yearly minimum temperatures. Each plant is assigned a range of zones. This tells you the lower and upper temperatures within which the plant will thrive most successfully. For example, if a plant is assigned a rating of Zones 5–8, winters in zones below Zone 5 may kill the plant, and winters in zones above Zone 8 may not be cold enough for the plant to thrive.

### Learning about local weather

Hardiness zones are helpful for narrowing down your plant choices, but they aren't foolproof guidelines. If you live in a large town or city, for instance, your area may be significantly warmer than the hardiness map would predict. Higher elevations and open, exposed areas may get a little colder than other properties in the same zone. In cold areas, consistent snow cover provides insulation and may allow you to grow plants from warmer zones. If you want plants that won't demand regular watering, it's very important to know when and how much it rains in your area.

### Windy weather
Wind can make your climate more severe than you think. As you spend time in your yard, observe which direction the wind usually comes from. Is your yard exposed to strong winds, or is it reasonably sheltered by trees, buildings or hills? Strong winds may quickly dry out plants and erode bare soil. When it's cold, windy weather can draw water out of exposed plant tops and roots faster than it can be replaced, leading to severe damage or death. But wind can be an asset in very humid climates, where good air circulation is important to prevent the development of plant diseases.

**EVER HARDY PLANTS**
Hostas are durable, dependable flowering perennials that can adjust to either warm or cold climates.

**WINTER INTEREST**
Evergreen perennials, such as bergenias, bloom in spring but their red-green foliage continues to offer winter interest.

# MANAGING MICROCLIMATES

Now that you understand your local climate, look at your yard to see what different microclimates it contains. A microclimate is simply a relatively uniform climate in a small area.

**WESTERN EXPOSURES**
In west-facing sites, consider plants that can tolerate both sun and partial shade, like coneflowers.

### Examine your exposure

Exposure refers to the amount of sun and shade your yard receives throughout the day. The exposure of different parts of your property can vary widely, depending on where each garden is in relation to the house and to other shade-casting features such as trees and fences. Identifying the directions in which the different parts of your property face will give you a general idea of the growing conditions at your disposal. But unless you have a flat, featureless lot, you'll also have to consider the shade cast by trees, shrubs, fences, hedges, trellises, buildings and other structures.

### Identifying microclimates

How do you tell if a given spot has full sun, partial shade or full shade? Watch the spot regularly over the course of a day (check on it every hour or so), and note each time you look whether the spot is sunny or shady. Any site with less than six hours of direct sunlight is shady. Plants that prefer full sun need six hours or more of direct sunlight to grow well. A site that receives a few hours of morning or late afternoon sun, but no direct midday sun, is described as having partial shade. Many flowering plants that prefer full sun will tolerate partial shade. A generally bright site that receives little direct sun but lots of filtered or reflected light is said to have light or dappled shade. Typically, this kind of shade occurs beneath deciduous trees with high branches

**Seasonal changes** Keep in mind that shade changes during the year, both because the angle of the Sun changes in the sky and because deciduous trees grow and shed their leaves. A site that seems sunny in July may be shaded by a nearby tree or building in April or October, when the Sun is much lower in the sky. The deep shade under a maple or oak disappears

**NORTHERN EXPOSURE**
Flowering and foliage perennials, like foamflowers, favor north-facing sites.

that don't cast solid shadows. Full, dense or deep shade is darker, and fewer flowering plants grow well in it. The area under hemlocks or other evergreens is in deep shade all year long. Plants growing under maples, beeches and other densely branched deciduous trees are in full shade most of the summer.

**EASTERN EXPOSURE**
Plants that enjoy afternoon shade, like geraniums, thrive in east-facing gardens.

**SOUTHERN EXPOSURE**
South-facing gardens receive maximum light. In areas with long, hot summers, try heat-resistant plants like yarrows.

when the tree loses its leaves, and the ground below can stay bright until late spring. Many spring wildflowers, including bluebells and foamflowers, have adapted to take advantage of this temporary sun and bloom before the overhead trees leaf out.

# THINK ABOUT TOPOGRAPHY

Is your yard flat or on the side of a hill? Or does it contain gradual ups and downs that you only notice when you're pushing a lawn mower? The shape of your land will affect your growing conditions and landscaping options.

**USING YOUR TOPOGRAPHY**
Flat and sloping sites offer a wealth of different planting opportunities. In flat areas, plan for outdoor activities, like dining or playing. On slopes, use terraced planting beds or a mix of shrubs and groundcovers to stop soil erosion.

**Gardening on flat sites**  If your yard is completely flat or at the bottom of a slope, check for drainage problems. After a heavy rain, do puddles always form in the same spot? Puddles indicate poor drainage that you'll need to correct by adding lots of organic matter or building raised beds. Or you may choose to turn those sites into moist meadows or bog gardens designed around plants that like wet feet.

**Coping with slopes**  Gentle slopes are an asset in planting and maintaining an attractive landscape. They drain well, add visual interest, and are generally easy to garden on. Steep slopes are hard to plant, weed and mow, and bare soil tends to wash off them in heavy rains. If you have to garden on a steep slope, consider building terraces to create a stepped series of level areas.

**Creating a site map**  The easiest way to record everything you've learned about your site is by making a site plan. The more accurate your plan, the more useful it will be. Start with a survey map of your property. If you don't have one, draw a rough outline of the yard to scale, marking 1 square inch (2.5 cm$^2$) on graph paper for each 4 square feet (1.2 m$^2$) of garden space. Locate north with a compass or from a local street map and indicate it on your map. Draw outlines of your house, driveway, paths and patios, sheds or garages, plus fences, hedges and existing gardens. Include low areas (and whether or not they are wet) and hilltops as well as large boulders. Note which direction slopes face and whether slopes are gentle or steep. Include trees and large shrubs on your map. Note any other areas that get less than six hours of direct sun, and whether they have light, partial or dense shade. Also note areas that may be sunny in spring and shady once the trees leaf out. Finally, mark down views you'd like to preserve and views you want to screen out.

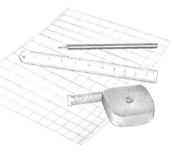

**PLAYING WITH YOUR PLAN**
Make several photocopies of your finished site map, so you'll be able to sketch in different landscaping ideas and plan how they will look.

# PART TWO

# FLOWERING ANNUALS
# AND BIENNIALS

# ANNUALS
## IN YOUR
# GARDEN

Annuals and biennials offer particularly exciting opportunities for creative gardeners because they only last a short time. Annuals germinate, grow, flower, set seed and die all in one season. Biennials do the same within two years. Part of the pleasure of growing these plants lies in their versatile natures. No matter where you live or what growing conditions you have to offer, you can find annuals and biennials that will thrive where you plant them. And you can change them periodically.

# TRUE ANNUALS

**As with all plants, the single goal of annuals and biennials is to reproduce themselves. The good news for the gardener is that most of these short-lived plants will flower like mad to achieve this goal. Better still, they can often be tricked into extending their seasons.**

*Self-sowing annuals such as delphiniums provide constant surprises in a flower garden.*

**Versatile and easy** The greatest feature of true annuals and biennials can be summed up in one word: versatility. Take a popular, easy-to-grow annual like the marigold. Individual plants can add spots of cheerful color to a window box, patio planter or hanging basket. A mass of marigolds in its own bed creates an eye-catching landscape feature. A row of marigolds creates a tidy edging for a walkway or provides a steady supply of fresh flowers for a cutting garden. A small group can sparkle near a doorway, brighten a foundation planting of dark evergreens or highlight an important garden feature, such as a birdbath or statue. Marigolds can even accent established perennial plantings with season-long color, fill in around new perennials while they're getting established or cover bare soil left by fading bulbs.

**Tricks of the trade** Some of the best known annuals, like marigolds, have achieved their popularity because of their easily flowering nature. If you use tricks such as deadheading (removing spent flowers) to prevent seed formation, many annuals will step up flower production and bloom well for an extended period, until cold weather arrives.

### Perennial annuals

It's not always enough to know just what a plant's natural life cycle is: It also helps to know how the plant grows in your climate. You may be surprised to discover that some of the most popular annuals are actually perennials! These plants are grown as annuals in most climates, but they can live for years in mild or frost-free areas. They include: wax begonia, China pink, English daisy, Madagascar periwinkle, wallflower, marguerite, coleus, prairie gentian, treasure flower, heliotrope, impatiens, four-o'clock, zonal geranium and gloriosa daisy. Gardeners in cold-climate areas must treat these warm-climate perennials as annuals, and grow them from seed each year.

*Add vibrant color to your garden with four-o'clocks.*

### Starting from transplants

Starting an annual flower bed from transplants is a good idea if you have specific plant groupings in mind. Placing transplants just where you want them gives you the most control over which colors and plant heights are next to each other. If you plan to plant different annuals in separate drifts, you could also start from seed sown directly in the garden.

**RESEEDING ANNUALS**

Many gardeners count on self-sowing annuals for perennial pleasure. Far from being a nuisance, these reliable repeaters delight many gardeners with their perseverance and their ability to pop up in the most unexpected places. Exactly which plants will self-sow depends on your region, but the ones listed below are some of the most dependable reseeders.

- ✿ hollyhock
- ✿ love-lies-bleeding
- ✿ pot marigold
- ✿ cornflower, bachelor's button
- ✿ feverfew
- ✿ cleome
- ✿ rocket larkspur
- ✿ calliopsis
- ✿ cosmos
- ✿ foxglove
- ✿ California poppy
- ✿ common sunflower
- ✿ annual candytuft
- ✿ garden balsam
- ✿ morning glory
- ✿ sweet alyssum
- ✿ honesty
- ✿ four-o'clock
- ✿ forget-me-not
- ✿ flowering tobacco
- ✿ love-in-a-mist
- ✿ corn poppy
- ✿ rose moss
- ✿ creeping zinnia
- ✿ Mexican sunflower
- ✿ nasturtium
- ✿ mullein
- ✿ narrow-leaved zinnia
- ✿ zinnia

# KINDS OF ANNUALS

Annuals are sometimes further separated into three groups—hardy, half-hardy and tender—based on their cold tolerance. It's useful to know which kind of annuals you're growing so you'll know how soon you can get away with planting the annuals in the spring. The catalog, seed packet or plant tag should tell you whether your plant is hardy, half-hardy or tender.

**Hardy annuals** Hardiness is the quality that enables plants to survive climatic extremes, especially cold, heat and dryness. Hardy flowering annuals include snapdragons, forget-me-nots, pansies and other plants that withstand freezing temperatures.

*Marigolds are generally classified as half-hardy annuals. They prefer warm weather, but can take a light frost fall.*

Most of these plants perform best during cool weather. They are often planted in early spring by gardeners in cold-winter areas or in winter by gardeners in the south and west. Some hardy annuals, such as ornamental kale, are also associated with cool fall weather.

**Half-hardy annuals** Annuals that are referred to as half-hardy fit somewhere midway between hardy and tender. They will often withstand a touch of frost near the beginning or end of the gardening season. Many of the most popular annuals fit into this category. A half-hardy designation is like yellow on a traffic signal: You will have to use your judgment to decide when you can plant safely. If your spring has been on the warm side and you're itching to plant—even though your average frost-free day has not yet arrived— you might just get away with planting half-hardy annuals. If you do, though, be prepared to cover them if cold night temperatures are predicted. One option is to hedge your bets by planting out only a small proportion of your half-hardy seeds or transplants at one time; then wait a week or two to plant the rest.

**Tender annuals** Tender annuals, originally from tropical or subtropical climates, can't stand a degree of frost. More than that, they often grow poorly during cold weather and may be stunted if they are exposed to temperatures below 50°F (10°C) for extended periods. For the best results when growing seedlings or established plants, wait until late spring to plant tender annuals.

*Shirley poppies are hardy annuals. You can sow them in early spring or fall in mild areas.*

# ANNUALS FOR BEDS AND BORDERS

**Flower beds are traditionally one of the most popular ways to display annuals. Some gardeners like to showcase their annual flowers in separate beds; others enjoy mixing annuals with bulbs, perennials, herbs, grasses and other plants. Either way, the possibilities for creating exciting plantings are virtually endless.**

*Some gardeners like to plant annuals, such as petunias, on their own.*

**Annuals alone** Setting aside separate beds for annual flowers is an easy way to go. Since you start with an empty area each year, spring soil preparation is a snap; you simply clean up any debris left in the bed, scatter some compost over the top to add nutrients and organic matter, and dig or till to loosen the top layer of soil.

**Annuals with other plants** Although they look wonderful by themselves, annuals also have a lot to offer in groupings with other plants. In borders predominantly planted with perennials, bulbs and shrubs, you can use annuals as a formal or informal edging, suggesting a flowering necklace around the border. While the other plants come in and out of bloom, the annual edging adds consistent color through most of the season. Repeating the same annual edging along different beds, perhaps in the front yard as well as the back yard, is an excellent way to link separate beds into a complete garden picture.

**Marvelous meadow gardens** If you enjoy the look of meadow gardens but don't want to wait years for perennial plants to get established, try planting an annual meadow. Many catalogs are now selling seed mixes of meadow annuals, containing a variety of colorful, easy-care plants like corn poppy, cornflower, calliopsis and

**ORNAMENTAL BEDS**
Try a colorful planting of low-growing annuals as a groundcover around new tree and shrub plantings.

*Though many meadow annuals, such as cosmos, will reseed themselves, the second year seldom rivals the beauty of the first. Sowing a fresh mix of seed each year will provide the best results.*

California poppy. Choose a site with as much sun as possible and prepare the soil as you would for any other annual garden. It's smart to prepare the site in the fall so it will be ready for planting the next spring. Hoe the surface to clear off any weeds that have sprouted, then scatter the seed evenly over the surface. Rake the bed lightly to scratch the seed into the soil, and water the area well with a light spray. Keep the soil moist for two or three weeks, until the seedlings start growing. Established annual meadows don't need much care; just hand pull any weeds you see. At the end of the season, mow the plants to the ground.

35

# FORMAL AND INFORMAL GARDENS

When you are planning and planting annual flower beds, you need to decide if you want a formal look or an informal look. The style you choose will determine how many different annuals you'll plant and how you'll arrange the garden beds.

**Formal gardens** Formal flower beds tend to have a simple, geometric shape—such as a square, rectangle or circle—and a limited number of different plants. The simplest may contain a mass of just one annual, such as marigolds or geraniums. For a little more variety, you could combine two or three different annuals, planted in straight rows or patterns. If you grow different annuals together, pick those with varying heights. Select one that's low and spreading—such as sweet alyssum or edging lobelia—for the outer edge. The plants for the

### DRAWING THE EYE
Add some excitement to beds of low annuals by including a taller focal point, such as a fuchsia trained as a standard. The eye will naturally be drawn to this point.

inside of the bed should be somewhat taller, usually no more than about 24 inches (60 cm). If the bed is in a spot where you can see it from all sides, you might want to include a taller focal point annual, such as castor bean or love-lies-bleeding, as a dramatic accent in the center. The key to success with a formal bed is uniformity: You want the plants to be evenly spaced and evenly developed. If you're growing a bed of just one kind of annual—all marigolds, let's say—you could sow seed over the prepared bed, thin the seedlings to an even spacing and expect fairly uniform results. In most cases, though, you'll get the best results by starting with transplants. All of the plants will be at the same stage, so they'll start blooming at the same time and you can set them out at the proper spacing to get a nice, even look.

**BORDER BOUQUETS** if you don't want to set aside an area just for cut flowers, you can snip blooms from beds and borders as needed.

**Informal gardens** If you prefer your garden to have a more casual look, an informal planting may be more your style. Informal gardens can be any shape you like; they often have a flowing outline that curves around the base of shrubs, trees or garden structures. Informal plantings usually include at least three or four different annuals. As with formal plantings, the plants you choose for informal beds should be of varying heights to provide visual interest. But you need not feel limited to planting informal beds in masses or rows. You can set your plants out in whatever drifts or groupings look good to you.

# ANNUALS FOR CONTAINER GARDENS

**Annuals make perfect container plants. They grow quickly, flower profusely and provide a long season of good looks. Some also offer distinctive foliage, while others perfume the air with their sweet scents. Consider displaying your colorful annuals in window boxes and hanging baskets.**

**Picking annuals for containers** As with any kind of garden, the first step to planning successful container plantings is to choose plants that have similar growth needs. If you have a shady area, impatiens, monkey flower and other shade-lovers are your best bets. Sunny spots can support a wider range of colorful annuals, including treasure flower, mealy-cup sage and narrow-leaved zinnia. When planning a container

*Treasure flowers add country charm.*

garden—whether it is a window box, hanging basket, or planter or pot—you also need to consider the ultimate height of the annuals you select. As a general guideline, try to choose annuals that are the same height or smaller than the height of the container; otherwise, the planting may look top-heavy.

**Mixed and single plantings** Plantings of single annuals in containers can be pleasing, but mixed plantings of three or four different annuals are even more exciting. While the choice of the exact plants to grow together is up to you, there are some basic guidelines you can follow to create a successful container planting. First, select a focal plant. Base your container

**PRETTY POTS**

A large container can support a pleasing mixture of bushy and trailing plants. Misting or watering with liquid fertilizer will keep the plants vigorously growing throughout the season.

## WONDERFUL WINDOW BOXES

Nothing adds "country charm" like lush window boxes cascading with colorful flowers and foliage. While the general principles of container planting apply, there are a few tips to keep in mind in planning and maintaining great-looking window boxes:

**Consider the site** Make sure you can reach your window boxes easily to water and maintain them. Because they are so visible, it's especially important to keep them well groomed.

**Stick with short plants** Window boxes are usually planted to be seen from the outside, but the view from the inside is also important. It's generally best to stick with plants no taller than about 8 inches (20 cm); taller plants can block your view.

**Choose compatible colors** Look for flower and foliage colors that complement those of the house and the trim. Silvers and whites look crisp and cool against warm-toned brick, for instance, while blues and purples look pretty against cream colors.

planting around one focal plant— perhaps a bushy marguerite daisy, a free-flowering tuberous begonia or a bold ornamental cabbage. Then choose supporting plants to complement the star plant and fill out the container. Try one or two with bold leaves or an upright habit—such as coleus or dusty miller—and one or two that sprawl or trail—such as edging lobelia or creeping zinnia.

*Pots of pink and yellow plants can add life to the somber gray siding of a house.*

# CARING FOR CONTAINER ANNUALS

Groups of containers create charming spots of movable color; large planters can showcase a stunning mix of colorful annuals in a relatively small space. However, container plants share closer quarters than garden plants, so they need some special care to stay lush and lovely.

### Choosing a container

The first step to successful container growing is choosing a good container. Large pots tend to provide the best conditions for growth, since they hold more soil, nutrients and water, but they are also quite heavy if you need to move or hang them. Pots or baskets about 8 inches (20 cm) deep can usually hold enough soil for good growth without getting too heavy. If you don't plan to move the planter, it can be as big as you want; containers as large as half-barrels will give you ample planting space for a wide variety of annuals. You need to allow a good amount of space for these plants to fill in as they mature, so don't overplant the pot.

**Potting mixes** Fill your container with a general potting mix from your local nursery or garden center. Straight garden soil is generally not suitable for containers, since it will pack down with repeated watering; the plant roots will not have enough room to establish themselves. Commercial potting mixes are easy to use and they can support a variety of different plants. Set your plants gently into the container soil, firm them in, and water by hand or with a sprinkler system to keep the soil moist throughout the season.

**Critical watering** Container gardens dry out quickly, so you may need to water every day during hot weather. Very small pots, clay containers of all sizes

**CONTAINER CARE**
Keep your container flowers in peak condition by regularly removing spent flowers and old or yellowed leaves.

and hanging baskets dry out especially quickly; you may have to water these as often as twice a day. If a pot or basket dries out completely, you still may be able to save the plants. Set the pot or basket in a larger container filled with water, let it sit there for an hour or two and then set the pot or basket in a shady spot for a few hours until the plants start to perk up again. Then move the pot or basket back to its original spot, but be extra careful to keep the plants well watered from then on. Damage may have been done to the cellular structure of the plants, and they may be fragile for the rest of the season.

**Fertilizing** As well as regular watering, the other key to successful, lush-looking container plants is regular fertilizing. Give them a boost by watering them with diluted fish emulsion or compost tea (made by soaking a shovelful of finished compost in a bucket of water for about a week, then straining out the soaked compost). Start in late spring by feeding once every two weeks, then judge the containers in midsummer. If plants look lush but aren't flowering well, change to fertilizing once every three weeks. If the plants look somewhat spindly, start fertilizing every week. If the plants seem to be growing and flowering well, stick with the two-week schedule.

**MULCHING BENEFITS**
Potted flowering plants can benefit from mulch. Use enough to cover the soil early in the season.

# ANNUALS AS FILLERS

**When you start any new garden, one of the hardest parts of the process is waiting for plants to fill in. This is especially true with perennial beds, since these plants can take years to really get established. In the meantime, a planting of annuals can help out.**

**Annuals as a mulch alternative** While mulch can suppress weeds, it doesn't add much excitement to a new planting. That's where filler annuals come in handy. A few seed packets of quick-growing annuals can provide welcome color and excitement for minimal cost. Sweet alyssum, flowering tobacco and cornflower are a few great filler annuals that can quickly cover the soil and deprive weed seeds of the light they need to grow. Many annuals may also self-sow to provide cover in succeeding years, gradually yielding space to expanding perennials.

**Fillers for flower beds** If you're looking for annuals to fill in around new perennial plantings,

**SOIL SAVERS**
New gardens can look bare the first year or two before the perennials establish themselves. Annuals will cover the soil, making the garden look good and keeping weeds away.

*Baby-blue-eyes make a colorful filler.*

choose those with a similar range of heights and colors as the perennials will have. Select a few short or trailing annuals for the front of the border, a few plants of medium size for the middle of the border and a few tall annuals for the back. While you could sow annual seed directly into the ground around the perennials, it's often easier to start with annual transplants. Some good filler annuals, like cleome and cornflower, will drop seed and come back year after year. If your annuals do reseed, thin the seedlings to allow the perennials room to develop.

### Filler plantings for groundcovers

Annuals that are low-growing, such as sweet alyssum and rose moss, can be excellent fillers for young groundcover plantings. Stick with one kind of annual for a uniform effect. Scatter the seed around the groundcover plants or set out annual transplants in the available spaces. While many low-growing annuals will self-sow, you may want to scatter some fresh annual seed over the planting for the first few springs until the groundcover fills in and becomes established.

### Fillers for foundations

New foundation plantings also benefit from annuals during the first few years as they develop. Shrubs and groundcovers will take over their allotted space in a few years, but a carpet of annuals is useful in the meantime. Sprinkle a few market packs of your favorite annuals, and the resulting flowers and foliage will provide infinitely more interest than a dull covering of bark chips.

*Annuals provide colorful fillers in a newly planted foundation garden.*

# ANNUALS FOR SCREENS

**Not all flowering annuals are as compact as marigolds and petunias. Some fast-growing annuals can reach the height of a small tree in a single season. There are also annual vines, the twining stems of which quickly cover trellises for welcome shade and privacy.**

*Black-eyed Susan vine climbs quickly to cover fences or trellises with bright blooms.*

**Tall annuals** Grow tall annuals in your yard to block or cover unattractive features, such as dog runs, alleys or clothesline poles. Or plant a row or mass of tall annuals to create a temporary fence that delineates your property line or separates different areas of your garden. Some top-notch tall annuals include castor bean, summer cypress, hollyhocks, sunflowers and Mexican sunflower.

**Annual vines** A leafy curtain of annual vines is an ideal way to ensure privacy on a porch or patio. Flowering vines also add a quaint, old-fashioned touch to the most ordinary support. A cloak of morning glories or a mass of scarlet runner bean will accent any arch, liven up a lamppost or make a feature of a garden shed. Most annual vines cover territory in a

*Foxglove is an easy-to-grow tall annual.*

**Scents and shapes** Morning glories are beloved for their heart-shaped leaves and trumpet-shaped flowers. The closely related moonflower is popular for its large, white, heavily fragrant flowers that open in the night. Besides being covered with clusters of colorful blooms, scarlet runner bean has the added bonus of edible beans.

hurry. You can easily train them to climb a trellis or even strong twine. Tall wooden or bamboo stakes also make effective supports. While annual vines are usually lighter than woody vines (such as wisteria or trumpet creeper), they can put on a lot of growth in one season, so supply a sturdy support. Unlike clinging vines such as ivy, annual vines mostly climb with tendrils or twining stems, so they will not be able to climb bare wall.

*Colorful morning glory climbs quickly.*

# ANNUALS FOR COLOR THEME GARDENS

There's no denying that we all have a favorite color or two. So why not indulge yourself and plant a whole garden dedicated to your most cherished colors? Annual displays designed around a particular color are fun to plan, and the results can be delightful.

**Color considerations**  If you're not sure exactly which color to choose, think about the time of day you'll usually view the garden and what kind of weather prevails in your area. If your climate tends to be cloudy and misty, consider using whites, yellows and pastels to add a bright touch to your yard. White flowers also tend to glow luminously in twilight or moonlit gardens. If sun shines down on your garden for most of the season, consider bright colors for your theme. You can continue your theme inside the house, with potpourris (fragrant mixtures of dried plant material) made from the petals in your garden. Try rose petals and lavender flowers, or geraniums and marigolds.

*Blues and purples look best where you can see them up close.*

**Wonderful white** A white garden is always elegant, and crisp whites will brighten up any dull areas. Many common annuals that are available in a range of colors—including petunias, cosmos and cleome—are also available in white. Choose cultivars that have been selected for white flowers, or buy plants in bloom to make sure they are white.

**Pretty pastels** Soft pinks, yellows and baby blues planted together tend to have a calm, soothing look. To keep the garden from looking too washed out, consider adding a little spark by planting some bright whites or a deeper hue of one of the colors—perhaps pure yellow marigolds or bright pink verbena.

*Blues often need a contrasting color so that they don't fade into the lighter green shades of their foliage.*

# ANNUALS FOR CUTTING GARDENS

If you enjoy having fresh cut flowers to display indoors but dislike denuding your carefully planned flower beds, consider starting a cutting garden. It doesn't need to be anything fancy. It could be part of an existing vegetable or herb garden or any place with at least a half-day of sun, an accessible water source and average, workable soil. A few rows of annuals for cutting can provide a generous supply of fresh flowers for much of the growing season.

*You could make this beautiful posy from your own garden.*

## Creating a cutting garden

If you already have a garden area where other plants grow well, the conditions are probably ideal for a cutting garden. If you're converting an existing lawn area, you'll need to strip off the sod and dig in some compost to loosen and enrich the soil. You can sow annual seeds or set out transplants just as you would for any garden, but don't worry about grouping specific heights and colors; just plant them in rows. It's important to mulch between the rows with a loose organic material (such as straw or shredded leaves) to discourage weeds, keep the soil moist and prevent soil from splashing up on the flowers. Water the garden as needed to keep the soil evenly moist for the best possible growth. Do not overwater, as you will drown the roots.

**ANNUALS FOREVER**
"Everlasting" annuals, like strawflowers and statice, produce papery flowers or showy seedpods that hold their color when they dry. They can be used in either fresh or dried arrangements. To keep the stems straight and stiff for easy arranging, separate them into groups of six to eight stems, secure the stems with a rubber band and hang them upside down. A dark, dry place is best for drying, since those conditions help to preserve the colors.

**Handling cut flowers** The best time to collect cut flowers is in the morning, before it gets too hot and before they are fully open. If you select blooms that are just opening, you will have a longer bloom from the plant once it is cut. Using shears or a sharp knife, cut the bloom stalks at whatever point will provide enough stem for your arrangement. It is always good to gather some foliage to use as a filler and as a backdrop for the flowers. Have a pail of lukewarm water at hand and put the cut stems immediately into it. When you are finished cutting, take your flowers indoors and pull the leaves off the bottom part of the stems. At this point, you can arrange your flowers right away or return the stems to the pail of water and set the flowers in a cool, dark place overnight until you're ready for them.

*Sunflowers are ideal for fresh arrangements.*

# ANNUALS FOR FRAGRANCE

To some gardeners, having fragrant flowers is just as important as having particular colors or kinds of plants. If you're a fragrance fanatic, there are some wonderfully scented annuals that you just shouldn't be without.

*Stock has a rich, spicy fragrance.*

**Scented blooms** For fragrant flowers, consider sweet William or China pinks, two carnation relatives noted for their spicy scents. Sweet alyssum is a common and easy-to-grow annual that is loved for its honeylike fragrance. Mignonette is very much an old-fashioned favorite with small, insignificant flowers but a powerful and delightful fragrance. A few annuals withhold their scents until the Sun sets, then release their sweet perfume on the evening breeze. Night-scented stock, sweet rocket and flowering tobacco carry remarkably potent night scents.

**Fragrant foliage** Of course, flowers aren't the only source of garden scents; some annuals have fragrant leaves as well. Scented geraniums are noted for their aromatic leaves. When you rub them, they release scents resembling those of peppermint, lemons, roses and many other plants. Annual herbs such as basil, anise and dill also offer fragrant foliage as well as small blooms.

*Sweet pea is fragrant and hardy.*

**Choosing a fragrance** The real key to choosing a fragrance for your garden is that you smell the plants before you buy them. The fragrance that a friend raves about may be undetectable or even unpleasant to you. Visit nurseries or public gardens when the plants you want are blooming and sniff the flowers or foliage to see what you think. Different cultivars of the same plant may vary widely in their scents, so smell them all before you choose. Just as a bed of many different flower colors can look jumbled, a mixture of many strong fragrances can be distracting or even repulsive. As you plan your garden, try to arrange it with just one or two scents at any given time. That way, you can enjoy different fragrances all through the season without being deluged by too many at once. To get the most pleasure from your fragrant plants, grow them where you will walk, sit or brush by them often.

# ANNUALS FOR HERB GARDENS

**Besides adding colorful flowers and handsome foliage to your garden, some annuals and biennials can add flavor to your food and provide gifts for friends! These herbs are easy to grow and they'll produce generous quantities of tasty leaves or seeds to spice up your favorite dishes.**

*Potpourri made from dried garden material.*

**Basil** What would a cook's garden be without basil? A traditional part of pesto and tomato dishes, it's also a snappy addition to salads, poultry, pasta, rice, eggs and vegetable dishes. For best growth, give basil a site with full sun and rich, drained soil. Snip the leaves as you need them. For extra interest, look for the basil cultivar with purple leaves; it's ornamental as well as edible and can be used, dried, in potpourris. White blooms, carried on green spikes at terminal buds, flower from midsummer on.

**Coriander** The leaves of this annual plant have a powerful odor and a flavor that combines sage and citrus. The leaves and the roots are popular in many cuisines for use in salads, sauces and relishes. The citrus-flavored seeds are a nice addition to herbal teas or desserts. Sow seeds every two to three weeks until late summer for a continuous supply of fresh leaves. Pick the leaves as needed; harvest the seeds when they begin to fall from the flower heads. Coriander flowers from spring to late summer, depending on when it was sown, with tiny white flowers in umbels.

**Dill** Grow dill for its lacy green leaves and flavorful seeds. The fresh leaves are a popular addition to fish dishes as well as vegetable dishes, sauces and salads. Dill seed is most commonly used as a pickling spice. Sow the seed outdoors in spring in full sun and rich, well-drained soil. Snip the leaves as needed; collect the seeds when they turn brown and begin to drop. Dill produces yellow-green flowers through summer and fall.

**SUNNY SAFFLOWERS**
The fresh flowers of the safflower plant make a bold, bright bouquet. The dried flowers can be used in crafts and for making yellow and red dyes, and an oil is extracted commercially for general cooking use.

*Potted herbs make a tasty and colorful ornament.*

# GROWING ANNUALS

With some basic care, annuals and biennials can provide a long season of color and beauty. Whether you buy them as plants from your local garden center or start your own transplants from seed, annuals and biennials are a fairly inexpensive way to fill your garden with flowers. And when you provide a good growing site, plant them properly and give them a little routine maintenance, their beautiful blooms will give you a big return for your money.

# GROWING ANNUALS FROM SEED

**Growing your own annual plants from seed is great fun—and easier than you might think. A single packet of seeds can produce dozens, or even hundreds, of plants for a fraction of the cost of buying transplants. Some annuals grow best when started indoors; others are tough enough to be planted right in the garden where you want them to grow.**

**Earlier blooms** Many annuals—including dwarf morning glory and strawflowers—grow equally well when sown indoors or out, but they'll begin blooming earlier if you start them indoors. This saving in time is important in northern gardens and especially at high elevations, where growing seasons are short. When you're not sure if you should start a particular plant indoors, check the seed catalog description or seed packet, or just sow a few and see what happens.

**Choosing a container** While suitable containers come in a wide variety of shapes and sizes, they generally fall into two types: open trays that can hold many seedlings, or pots that hold just a few seedlings each. Both types work well, but if you're sowing small quantities of several different annual seeds, you may find it easier to keep track of them in individual pots. Buy commercially made pots or trays (often called flats), or recycle common materials, such as milk cartons

*If seedlings are crowded, move them to a larger container.*

and margarine tubs. Just about any container will work, as long as it has drainage holes in the bottom. For really easy transplanting, try preformed peat pots (available from most garden centers). At transplanting time, you can set the whole plant—pot and all—in the

*Sow seeds in pots or trays at the depth indicated on the packet.*

*Give seedlings plenty of light to promote compact, bushy growth.*

ground. The pot walls will break down, allowing the roots to spread out with no transplant shock. Peat pots are useful for starting seeds that are difficult to transplant, such as rocket larkspur and morning glories, but sow only one seed in each peat pot.

**Picking a growing mix** For the best results, buy a bag of commercial growing mix. Some gardeners select standard potting soil; others prefer mixes created specifically for seed starting. These mixes contain a balanced mixture of disease- and weed-free materials that will hold a good supply of moisture while letting excess water drain freely.

**Dealing with damping-off**

Damping-off is a disease that can strike young seedlings. Affected seedlings tend to topple over, since their stems are damaged at the soil level. This disease can quickly spread so prevention is best. Always use fresh seed-starting mix. If you're reusing old pots or trays, knock out the old soil, dip the containers in a solution of one part household bleach to nine parts water and dry the containers well. You can also sprinkle a thin layer of milled sphagnum moss on top of newly planted seeds and improve air circulation with a small fan set to blow lightly just over the tops of the seedlings. If damping-off strikes outdoor-sown seeds, wait until the weather warms up and sow again.

**57**

# GROWING ANNUALS FROM SEED continued

**Choosing a spot** For good growth, your seedlings will need the right temperatures and adequate light. Most annuals will sprout and grow well at average indoor temperatures (between 60° and 75°F [16° and 24°C]), so warmth usually isn't a problem. Finding a spot with enough light can be tricky, though. If your house is blessed with a sunroom or deep, sunny window sills, you can get good results growing seedlings there without providing extra light. Otherwise, you'll need to set up a simple light system to

**A GOOD START**
Start your garden by setting out indoor-grown transplants, then plant direct-sown seeds around them.

keep your seedlings happy and healthy. Garden centers and garden-supply catalogs sell lights in a variety of sizes and prices. Four-foot (1.2-m) fluorescent shop lights sold in home centers also provide excellent results, and they're generally much less expensive than grow lights.

**Knowing when to sow** You can sow most annual seeds indoors in early spring, about six to ten weeks before your last frost date, although some need to be started earlier or later. When you're ready to sow (or, even better, the night before), dump your seed-starting mix in a large bucket or tub and add some warm water to moisten it. Start with a few cups of water and work the mix with your hands to help it absorb the moisture. Keep adding several cups of water at a time and work it into the mix until the mix

*Some annuals, such as globe amaranths, can be started indoors; they are still easy to maintain once they are taken outside.*

feels evenly moist but not soggy. (If you squeeze a handful of mix and water runs out, it's too wet; add some more dry mix to get the balance right.)

Once the mix is moist, you can fill your chosen containers. Scoop the mix into each container and level it out to about 1/4 inch (6 mm) below the upper edge of the container. Don't pack down the mix; just tap the filled container once or twice on your work surface to eliminate air pockets.

**Figuring out your last frost date** Sowing guidelines often advise to plant well before or after your last frost date, but how do you work that date out? You can't know exactly when your last spring frost will occur in a given year. But you can find out the average date of the last frost in your area by asking gardening friends or neighbors or local gardening centers. Pay close attention to weather forecasts around this time and be prepared to protect tender plants if late frosts are predicted.

# SOWING ANNUAL SEEDS

Starting seed indoors takes some time and space, but it also gives the best results for many annuals. Tender annuals, such as impatiens and globe amaranth, need the warm conditions to get a good start in life. If you don't have the time or space to raise seedlings indoors, you can still grow a wide variety of annuals from seed. Many popular annuals grow just as well from seed sown outdoors as from seed sown indoors. Some even grow better from direct-sown seed because they prefer cool outdoor temperatures or because they don't respond well to transplanting.

**Sowing inside** When you're sowing large seeds, use a pencil to make individual holes about 1 inch (25 mm) apart. For small seeds, use a pencil to make shallow rows, and sow as evenly as possible into the rows. Fine seeds, such as those of petunias and begonias, can be hard to sow directly from the packet. To distribute tiny seeds more evenly, mix them with a spoonful of dry sand and scatter the mixture over the surface of the mix with a saltshaker. If the seeds should be buried (as indicated on the seed packet), sprinkle the needed amount of dry mix over the seed. Fine seeds are usually not covered; you can just press them lightly into the surface of the mix with your fingers or the back of a spoon. After sowing, moisten gently using a fine mist.

### PERENNIAL PANSIES
Pansies are actually short-lived perennials which are usually grown as hardy annuals or biennials. For best growth, sow the seeds outdoors in a nursery bed in late spring and move the plants to the garden in mid-fall.

**Sowing outside** Direct-sowing is simple. First, get the soil ready for planting. Sow large seeds individually or scatter them evenly over the surface. It's best to try to space them 1 inch (25 mm) apart. If you have very small seeds, mix them with a handful of dry sand and distribute them over the seedbed. Cover the seeds with a thin layer of fine soil or sand. If you're dealing with fine seeds, just pat them into the soil. Make sure the seedbed stays moist until the seedlings are visible. If rainfall is lacking, water gently with a watering can or fine hose spray. Covering the seedbed with a layer of floating row cover helps to keep the soil moist and protects the seed from drying winds, heavy rain and birds. (Remove the cover once the seedlings emerge.) If seedlings are crowded, you'll need to thin them out for good growth. Dig up and carefully transplant extra seedlings, or use scissors to cut off the stems of unwanted seedlings at ground level.

**Beds for biennials** Like annual flowers, biennials have a limited life span. They germinate, flower, set seed and die within two years. During their first year they produce plenty of foliage and strong root systems. They flower and make seed in their second season just before they die. Biennial plants, such as foxgloves and forget-me-nots, need a slightly different growing approach. Most biennials will sprout well when sown outdoors, so that part is easy. But if you sow them directly into the garden, their leafy, first-year growth will take up room without adding much interest to your flower display. The best approach is to set aside a temporary growing

*Forget-me-nots sprout best when sown in a nursery bed.*

area (called a nursery bed) where your biennials can grow through the summer. Prepare your nursery bed just as you would any garden area, but site it in an out-of-the-way spot. Sow the biennial seeds in spring or summer and thin as needed. Dig the plants and move them to their final garden spots.

# BUYING HEALTHY PLANTS

Who can resist the parade of brilliant blossoms for sale at every garden center each spring? It's sometimes difficult to be a smart shopper when faced with such floral extravagance. The key is to look beyond the flowers and make a close inspection of the plants themselves.

*Avoid plants with yellowed leaves or brown tips or those with holes in the leaves.*

*If you buy plants in bloom, pinch off the flowers when you plant.*

### Smart shopping strategies

When you shop, look for plants that are fairly uniform and seem healthy. Avoid those that are wilted, as well as those with visible problems. While wilted plants usually recover when watered, repeated wilting can stunt their growth and make them less likely to perform well in your garden over the season.

Another thing to consider is whether or not the plants are in bloom. If you're looking for specific flower colors, you may want to buy plants that already have some blooms. In most cases, though, you'll get the best growth from plants that aren't yet blooming. If you can buy only transplants that are already flowering, pinch off the flowers at planting time. It seems

*Only buy plants that are already blooming if you want specific colors.*

### HEALTHY PLANT CHECKLIST

**Peruse the plant** The plant should be similar in size and color to other plants of the same type. Avoid plants that seem stunted or off-color.

**Look at the leaves** Steer clear of plants with yellowed leaves or brown tips (signs of improper watering). Carefully turn over a few leaves and check the undersides for signs of pests. Don't buy plants with tiny white insects that fly up when you move the leaves (whiteflies); clusters of small, pear-shaped insects (aphids); or yellow-stippled leaves with tiny webs underneath (caused by spider mites).

**Check the stems** Stems should be stocky and evenly colored, with no visible cuts, bruises or pest problems.

**Inspect the roots** It's okay if a few roots are coming out of the drainage holes at the bottom of the pot, but masses of tangled roots indicate that the plant is long overdue for transplanting. Overgrown plants can be saved if you remove some of the matted roots at transplanting time, but it's better to start with younger plants.

hard to do, but it will help your plants in the long run. They'll put their energy into making new roots and then quickly start producing bushy new growth and dozens of new flower buds. It's easy to overlook quality in the quest for getting the perfect plant. But as you choose, keep in mind that bringing home a stressed, diseased, or pest-infested plant is a recipe for disappointing results. Before you pay for your purchases, take a minute to check them over.

# CARING FOR ANNUALS

**While most annuals can grow just fine without much help from you, providing some basic care through the season will keep your plants looking their best.**

**Mulching** Wait until early summer to put mulch into your garden, when the soil has had a chance to warm up and your annual and biennial seedlings or transplants are at least 4 inches (10 cm) tall. Then apply a 2-inch (5-cm) layer of mulch over the soil. Keep the mulch at least 1 inch (2.5 cm) from the base of the stems. As the mulch breaks down, add more once or twice during the summer to keep it at the right depth. You can till or dig the mulch into the soil at the end of the season.

**Weeding** Since the soil in annual gardens gets turned every year, perennial weeds such as dandelions and thistles usually don't have much chance to get established. But digging the soil does bring up buried weed seeds, so annual weeds can be a problem. To catch problems early, try preparing the soil for planting and letting it sit for a week or two; then hoe out any

**CONSTANT CARE**
Take a walk through your garden each day and remove weeds as soon as you see them to keep them from reseeding and spreading.

sprouting weeds before planting your annuals. Hoe or hand weed around the plants again in early summer, then mulch. After that, check beds every week or two and hand pull any weeds that pop through the mulch.

**Watering** The easiest way to handle watering is to not do it at all. If summer rains are unreliable in your area, consider sticking with annuals that are naturally adapted to somewhat dry conditions. Choosing appropriate plants and maintaining soil moisture with mulch reduces watering chores. Container gardens dry out quickly, so you may need to water every day (or even twice a day) during hot weather. For plants in the ground, how often you water depends on how dry the soil is. Before you decide to water, pull back the mulch and feel the soil surface;

if it's moist, wait a day or two and test again. If the surface is dry, dig a small hole with a trowel. Irrigate until the top few inches of soil are moist. Watering with sprinklers isn't very efficient, since much of the water is lost to evaporation. Plus, it wets the plant leaves,

providing ideal conditions for disease development. If you can afford a drip irrigation system, it's an easy and effective way to get water right to the soil, where the roots need it.

*Choosing appropriate plants will go a long way toward reducing your watering chores.*

## CARING FOR ANNUALS continued

**Fertilizing** Annuals grow quickly, so they need an ample supply of nutrients for good flowering. In early spring, scatter a 2-inch (5-cm) layer of compost over the bed and dig it in as you prepare the bed for planting. Or, if you're tucking annuals and biennials around perennials and other permanent plants, mix a handful of compost into each planting hole. If you don't have compost, you could also use a general organic garden fertilizer. Once or twice during the season, pull back the mulch and scatter more compost or fertilizer around the base of each plant; then replace the mulch. For most annuals and biennials, this will provide all the nutrients they need. For plants that appreciate extra fertility, such as wax begonias and sweet peas, or for those that are

looking a little tired by midsummer, a monthly dose of liquid fertilizer can provide a quick nutrient boost. Spray the leaves or water the plants with diluted fish emulsion or a tea made from soaking a shovelful of finished compost in a bucket of water for about a week, then straining out the soaked compost.

**Deadheading** Annual flowers are genetically programmed to quickly produce seed for a new generation of plants. When you pinch off spent flowers before they can form seed (a technique called deadheading), the plants will produce more flowers in an attempt to make more seed. If your annuals have leafy stems, cut

**SMALL SUPPORT**
Tall annuals are easily staked, but smaller annuals can be more difficult. Try pushing short pieces of twiggy brush or branches into the soil around the plants when they're young.

*Deadheading forces the plants to produce more flowers.*

or pinch off the spent blooms or bloom stalks just above the top set of leaves. Cut leafless stems back to a main shoot or to the base of the plant. If you plan to save seed, stop deadheading by late summer to allow some seeds to form.

**Preparing for winter** Before the first frost, take cuttings from or dig up any plants you want to take inside for the winter. Also collect any seeds you want to save. After the first hard frost, tender and half-hardy annuals usually turn brown; pull these out and toss them in the compost pile. Hardy annuals like alyssum may keep blooming through several frosts; you can either pull them out in fall or wait until early spring. Foxgloves, honesty and other biennials usually make it through winter just fine, but a protective layer of mulch applied after the ground is frozen can help in severe-winter areas.

**Staking** Many annuals are bred or selected for compact growth, so staking usually isn't much of a problem. It's useful, though, for a few plants, such as hollyhocks, tall snapdragons and castor beans. Choose stakes that are about three-quarters of the mature height of the plant. Put them in place early—before planting seed in the garden or as you set out transplants. As the plants grow, attach their stems loosely to the stake with string, twine or plastic ties.

*Take plants inside for winter before the first frost.*

# HANDLING PEST AND DISEASE PROBLEMS

**Annuals are among the most trouble-free garden plants you can grow. If you choose annuals that are suited to your growing conditions, buy healthy plants and give them regular care, pest and disease problems seldom become serious enough to require action on your part.**

**Preventing problems** Most annuals grow best when they aren't overcrowded. Crowding leads to competition for water and nutrients, so plants are weaker and prone to problems. It also interferes with air circulation and provides ideal conditions for diseases to develop. Besides spacing plants properly, watering correctly—by wetting the soil, not the leaves—will also prevent disease problems. Ideally, use a soaker hose or irrigation system that will ooze water onto the soil, where it will go right to the roots. If you must water plants from the top, at least do it in the morning so plants will dry quickly.

*When diseases appear, pinch off the damaged leaves and spray the rest with commercial fungicidal soap, or dust every two weeks with sulfur.*

**Easy organic controls** To catch any problems that slip past your defenses, walk through your garden at least once or twice a week. Look over each planted area and inspect at least two or three plants in each area closely. Check the upper and lower leaf surfaces, the stems and buds or flowers. If you notice any damage or discoloration, act quickly. Look the symptoms up in a book or talk to your local garden center.

**Sprays and dusts** Sometimes controlling pests is as simple as spraying them with water. This can knock small pests like mites and aphids right off the plants. Pinching or cutting off infected or infested plant parts is another easy way to remove problems. If you're not squeamish, you can even handpick large pests like slugs, caterpillars and beetles and drop them into soapy water.

*Japanese beetles eat the flowers of host plants.*

*Aphids feed on leaves, turning them yellow.*

*Whiteflies suck the juices from new growth.*

*Mites feed on leaves and roots, covering them in a fine web.*

**SIMPLE SOLUTION**

A simple soap spray will handle many pest problems. You can buy insecticidal soap, or make your own by mixing 3 teaspoons of liquid dish soap in 1 gallon (4 L) of water. Test it on a few leaves and wait three days. If you don't notice any damage, spray the whole plant. Repeat the spraying three days later.

# A GUIDE
## TO
# ANNUALS

This is a guide to the more common flowering annuals. Each entry has a color photograph to show you what the plant looks like, as well as a description, the height and spread, best site, growing guidelines and suggested landscape uses. The plants are listed alphabetically according to their botanical names because some plants have more than one common name. Skim through the entries to find plants that you'd like to grow, or look up specific plants to find out how to care for them. For more information, talk to your local garden center.

# LOVE-LIES-BLEEDING

*Amaranthus caudatus* Amaranthaceae

Love-lies-bleeding is lovely in fresh or dried arrangements.
To preserve the flowers, stand the cut stems in a heavy
bucket so the tassels hang naturally as they dry.

*Amaranthus caudatus*

**Description** This unusual tender annual produces thick, sturdy, branched stems with large, oval, pale green leaves. Long clusters of tightly packed, crimson flowers dangle from the stem tips from midsummer until frost. The ropy, tassel-like clusters can grow to 18 inches (45 cm) long in optimum conditions.

**Height and spread** Height 3–5 feet (90–150 cm); spread to about 2 feet (60 cm).

**Best site** Full sun; average, well-drained to dry soil. Shelter from strong winds is essential as the tall stems are easily bent or blown over.

**Growing guidelines** Sow seed indoors, ⅛ inch (3 mm) deep, four to six weeks before your last frost date. Set plants out 18 inches (45 cm) apart when the weather is warm, about two to three weeks after the last frost date. Seed also germinates quickly in warm soil, so you could sow it instead in the garden in the last weeks of spring.

**Landscape uses** Makes a striking accent in flower beds and borders and in cottage gardens. Add a few plants to the cutting garden, too.

**Cultivars** 'Viridis' is similar but has green flower clusters. 'Pygmy Torch' has upright, crimson clusters above purplish leaves on 18–24-inch (45–60-cm) tall stems.

**Other species** Joseph's coat is grown for its large, green leaves that are splashed with yellow and bright red. The sturdy, 3-foot (90-cm) tall plants make striking accents in flower borders. Use the same guidelines for planting and growing Joseph's coat as for love-lies-bleeding.

## SNAPDRAGON

*Antirrhinum majus* Scrophulariaceae

A mass planting of snapdragons makes an eye-catching landscape accent. Pinch the stem tips of dwarf types once after transplanting to promote branching.

**Description** These tender perennials are usually grown as hardy or half-hardy annuals. The plants may be low and mound-forming or tall and spiky. Slender stems carry narrow, bright green leaves and are topped with velvety flowers that bloom in every color except blue through summer.

**Height and spread** Height ranges from 1 foot (30 cm) for dwarf types to 2 feet (60 cm) for intermediate types and up to 4 feet (1.2 m) for tall types. Spread ranges from 8–18 inches (20–45 cm).

**Best site** Full sun to light shade (especially in hot-summer areas); average, well-drained soil.

**Growing guidelines** Buy transplants in spring, or start your own by planting seed indoors six to eight weeks before the last frost date. Keep the soil evenly moist. Pinch or cut off spent spikes to promote more flowers. They can survive mild winters but are prone to rust, a fungal disease that shows up as brownish spots on leaves. The best prevention is to grow snapdragons as annuals and pull the plants out in fall.

**Landscape uses** Snapdragons have a spiky form that makes them excellent companions for rounded flowers, like daisies. Use the low-growing cultivars as edging plants for annual beds. Use the tall-stemmed snapdragons as a central focus in fresh arrangements.

**Cultivars** 'Magic Carpet Mixed' grows 6 inches (15 cm) tall in a range of colors. 'Royal Carpet Mixed' is bright and rust-resistant with 8-inch (20-cm) stems.

*Antirrhinum majus*

# SWAN RIVER DAISY

*Brachycome iberidifolia* Compositae

If Swan River daisy plants get floppy after the first flush of
bloom, shear them back by half and water well to promote
compact growth and flowers until frost.

**Description** This half-hardy
annual forms bushy mounds of
thin stems and lacy, finely cut
leaves. From midsummer until
frost, plants bear many 1-inch
(2.5-cm), rounded, daisy-like
flowers in shades of blue, purple,
pink and white. The delicately
scented blooms may have a black,
deep purple or yellow center.

**Height and spread** Grows to
1 foot (30 cm) tall; spreads to
18 inches (45 cm).

**Best site** Full sun; average,
well-drained soil with added
organic matter.

**Growing guidelines** For the
earliest blooms, buy flowering
plants and set them out after your
last frost date. You can also start
Swan River daisy from seed
planted indoors or outdoors. Sow
indoors six to eight weeks before
your last frost date. Scatter the
seed over the surface, lightly press
it into the soil, and enclose the pot
in a plastic bag until seedlings
appear. Set the plants out after
the last frost date or sow the
seed directly into the garden in
late spring. Once they've sprouted,
thin the plants so they are spaced
6–8 inches (15–20 cm) apart. This
will form a solid carpet of flowers.

**Landscape uses** Swan River
daisy makes an unusual edging for
beds and borders. Its trailing habit
is ideal for window boxes, large
pots and hanging baskets. Mix
colors or plant in blocks of color.

**Cultivars** 'Blue Star' has
purplish blue, black-centered
flowers with spiky-looking petals.
'White Splendour' has white
flowers with black centers. 'Purple
Splendour' has purple blooms.

*Brachycome iberidifolia*

# ORNAMENTAL CABBAGE

*Brassica oleracea* Cruciferae

Ornamental cabbages add a showy accent to late-season gardens. They withstand frost and can look good until late fall or even early spring.

**Other common names**
Flowering cabbage.

**Description** This is a biennial plant that is grown as an annual for its rosettes of colorful fall foliage. The smooth, glossy, blue-green leaves are marked with pink, purple, cream or white. As temperatures get cooler in fall, the leaves in the center of the rosette become much more colorful, usually with a deeper purple or crimson; green is often only visible around the edge and sometimes not visible at all. It can be mistaken for ornamental kale, which is very similar; the leaves of the kale are more frilly.

**Height and spread** Height 12–18 inches (30–45 cm); spread to 18 inches (45 cm).

**Best site** Full sun to light shade; average, well-drained soil.

**Growing guidelines** In hot-summer areas, sow seed indoors; elsewhere, sow outdoors in pots or a nursery bed. Plant seed ¼ inch (6 mm) deep in midsummer. Move plants to the garden in fall. Set in holes 12 inches (30 cm) apart and deep enough to cover the stem up to the lowest leaves. Pick caterpillars off by hand or spray the leaves with the water from boiled garlic.

*Brassica oleracea*

**Landscape uses** Ornamental cabbage and kale add color to fall flower beds and borders as other annuals are finishing for the season. They are also showy in containers or large window boxes.

**Cultivars** 'Cherry Sundae Mixed' is an ornamental cabbage with white, pink or purplish markings. The final colors are not always obvious in the seedling.

# CHINA ASTER

*Callistephus chinensis* Compositae

China asters bloom from late summer to frost in white, cream, pink, red, purple or blue. To minimize disease problems, plant them in a different spot each year.

**Description** This tender annual is grown for its showy blooms. The stems carry broadly oval, toothed, green leaves and are topped with daisy-like or puffy, single or double flowers up to 5 inches (12.5 cm) wide.

**Height and spread** Height 12–24 inches (30–60 cm); spread 12–18 inches (30–45 cm).

**Best site** Full sun; average, well-drained soil with added organic matter.

**Growing guidelines** For late-summer bloom, buy transplants in spring or sow seed indoors, ⅛ inch (3 mm) deep, before the last frost date, when the weather is warm. For fall bloom, sow seed directly into the garden after the last frost date. Space plants or thin seedlings of most types to stand 10–12 inches (25–30 cm) apart; leave 18 inches (45 cm) between tall-stemmed cultivars. Pinch off stem tips once in early summer to promote branching. Stake tall cultivars. Remove spent flowers. Control aphids with soap sprays or garlic sprays to prevent the spread of aster yellows, which causes yellowed, stunted growth; destroy infected plants. Remember that repeated use of soap sprays can

*Callistephus chinensis*

harm plants, so use only as necessary and don't use on surrounding plants unless they are affected. Aster wilt is a soil-borne disease that causes plants to droop; destroy infected plants.

**Landscape uses** Grow in masses or mix with other plants in beds, borders and planters for late-season color. China asters produce many flowers and last well indoors so it is worth growing even a few.

# CANTERBURY BELLS

*Campanula medium*  Campanulaceae

Plan ahead for next year's flowers by starting seed during the summer, or buy overwintered container-grown plants in spring for blooms the same year.

**Description**  Canterbury bells form leafy rosettes of toothed, lance-shaped leaves during their first year. In the second year, they send up slender stalks topped with loose spikes of bell-shaped blooms in white, pink or purple-blue. The spring to early-summer flowers may be single or surrounded by a larger cup.

**Height and spread**  Height 18–36 inches (45–90 cm); spread 12 inches (30 cm).

**Best site**  Full sun; average, well-drained soil.

**Growing guidelines**  Sow seed outdoors in summer in pots or a nursery bed. Cover the seed lightly and keep the soil moist with a spray until seedlings appear. Move the plants to their permanent flowering positions in fall or early spring. Space the seedlings about 12 inches (30 cm) apart. Pinching off the spent blooms will encourage prolonged flowering. Pull out the plants that have finished blooming.

**Landscape uses**  Canterbury bells are naturals for cottage gardens, alongside winding paths or as a foundation planting next to a picket fence. In beds and borders, grow them in small clumps with later-blooming annuals and perennials that can fill in the space left when you remove spent plants in midsummer. Use it in containers and cutting gardens, too.

**Cultivars**  'Cup and Saucer Mixed' has double-cupped blooms on 30-inch (75-cm) stems. 'Russian Pink' has pink flowers on 15-inch (37.5-cm) stems; it will bloom the first year.

*Campanula medium*

# CORNFLOWER

*Centaurea cyanus* Compositae

Stick brushy prunings into the ground around young cornflower plants to support the stems as they grow. Pinching off spent blooms can prolong the flowering season.

**Other common names**
Bachelor's buttons.

**Description** This is a dependable, easy-care, hardy annual. The bushy plants have

*Centaurea cyanus*

narrow, lance-shaped, silvery green leaves and thin stems topped with fluffy flower heads. The 1–2-inch (2.5–5-cm) flowers bloom through the summer in white or shades of blue, purple, pink or red.

**Height and spread** Height 12–30 inches (30–75 cm); spread to 12 inches (30 cm).

**Best site** Full sun; average, well-drained soil.

**Growing guidelines** Grows easily from seed sown directly into the garden in early fall (in mild-winter areas) or early spring. Plant seed ⅛ inch (3 mm) deep.

To extend the flowering season from an early-spring planting, sow again every two to four weeks until midsummer. Other ways to establish cornflowers include buying transplants in spring or starting the seed indoors about eight weeks before your last frost date. Set plants outdoors about two weeks before the last frost date. Space or thin plants to stand 8–12 inches (20–30 cm) apart. Cornflowers will self-sow.

**Landscape uses** Cornflowers are charming in meadow gardens and flower beds. They are also excellent for the cutting garden as they make an excellent fresh bouquet and are long-lasting dried flowers. Try compact cultivars in container gardens.

**Cultivars** 'Jubilee Gem' has deep blue flowers on slim, 1-foot (30-cm) stems.

# WALLFLOWER

*Cheiranthus cheiri* Cruciferae

The fragrant blooms of wallflowers are normally orange or yellow, but they also bloom in shades of red, pink or creamy white. The flowers are ideal for spring arrangements.

**Description** This perennial can live for years in mild or frost-free areas but is commonly grown as a half-hardy annual or biennial for spring color; they can withstand a touch of frost early in the season. The bushy clumps of slender green leaves are topped with clusters of 1-inch (2.5-cm) wide flowers from midspring to early summer.

**Height and spread** Height 12–24 inches (30–60 cm); spread to 12 inches (30 cm).

**Best site** Full sun to partial shade; average to moist, well-drained soil, ideally with a neutral to slightly alkaline pH.

**Growing guidelines** To grow as annuals, sow outdoors in early spring or indoors about eight weeks before your last frost date. Plant seed ¼ inch (6 mm) deep. Set plants out 8–12 inches (20–30 cm) apart around the last frost date. In frost-free areas, grow wallflowers as biennials. Sow seed in pots or in a nursery bed in early summer; move plants to their flowering position in early fall. Water during dry spells to keep the soil evenly moist. Pull out the plants when they have finished blooming.

**Landscape uses** Grow in masses or in flower beds for spots of early color. One traditional combination is orange wallflowers underplanted with blue forget-me-nots. Wallflowers also combine beautifully with tulips and full-bodied perennials such as lavender.

**Cultivars** 'Tom Thumb Mixed' blooms in a range of colors on 6–9-inch (15–22.5-cm) plants. and yarrow; giant onions make an unusual contrast in summer.

*Cheiranthus cheiri*

79

# CUP-AND-SAUCER VINE

*Cobaea scandens* Polemoniaceae

The bell-shaped flowers of cup-and-saucer vine open light green and age to purple or white; mature flowers have a sweet, honey-like fragrance.

**Other common names**
Cathedral bells, Mexican ivy.

**Description** This vigorous, tender perennial climber is grown as a half-hardy annual. It has compound leaves, as well as tendrils that help the stems climb. From late summer until frost, inflated buds on long stalks open to 2-inch (5-cm) long, mauve, bell-shaped flowers. Short, green, petal-like bracts surround the base of each bell.

**Height and spread** The vines can grow to 10 feet (3 m) or more; the ultimate height and width depends on the size of its support.

**Best site** Full sun (or afternoon shade in hot-summer areas); average to moist, well-drained soil with added organic matter.

**Growing guidelines** Before planting, make sure you have a sturdy support in place for the vines to climb on. Sow seed indoors eight to ten weeks before your last frost date. Soak the flat seeds in warm water overnight, then plant them on their side in peat pots. Sow two or three seeds ¼ inch (6 mm) deep in each pot. Once seedlings emerge, clip off extras to leave one per pot. Set plants out 1 foot (30 cm) apart after the last frost date.

*Cobaea scandens*

**Landscape uses** This is a super screening plant for quick shade or privacy. It can be trained easily to climb a wooden or wire trellis and makes a wonderful background plant for cottage gardens. Use this vine to create an attractive block or cover for the less attractive features of your yard, such as garden and tool sheds.

**Cultivars** 'Alba' has green-tinted white flowers.

# COLEUS

*Coleus x hybridus* Labiatae

Keep favorite coleus plants from year to year by taking cuttings in summer; they'll root quickly in water. Pot up the cuttings for winter; then put them outdoors in spring.

**Description** These tender perennials are grown as bushy, tender annuals. Their sturdy, square stems carry showy, patterned leaves with scalloped or ruffled edges. Each leaf can have several different colors, with zones, edges, or splashes in shades of red, pink, orange, yellow and cream.

**Height and spread** Height 6–24 inches (15–60 cm); spread 8–12 inches (20–30 cm).

**Best site** Partial shade; average to moist, well-drained soil with added organic matter.

**Growing guidelines** Buy transplants in spring, or start your own by sowing seed indoors eight to ten weeks before your last frost date. Don't cover the seed; just press it lightly into the soil and enclose the pot in a plastic bag until seedlings appear. Set plants out 8–12 inches (20–30 cm) apart after the last frost. During the summer, water during dry spells. Pinch off the spikes of the pale blue flowers to promote more leafy growth.

**Landscape uses** Flowers aren't the only source of color in a garden; coleus are great for adding warm-season color to beds, borders and container plantings.

*Coleus x hybridus*

Groups of mixed leaf patterns can look too busy when combined with flowering plants, so grow them alone in masses, or consider sticking with a single leaf pattern. Coleus looks great grown with other shade-loving annual companions, such as fibrous begonias, browallia, impatiens and wishbone flower.

**Cultivars** 'Rainbow Mixed' has scalloped leaves in a variety of colors on 20-inch (50-cm) stems.

# CALLIOPSIS

*Coreopsis tinctoria* Compositae

Calliopsis grows easily from direct-sown seed and needs little fussing. Shearing the plants back by one-third in mid- to late-summer can prolong the bloom season.

*Coreopsis tinctoria*

**Description** Calliopsis is a colorful, fast-growing, hardy annual. Its wiry stems carry narrow, green leaves and 1–2-inch (2.5–5-cm) wide, single or double, daisy-like flowers. The flowers, with their ragged-edged petals, are usually golden yellow with maroon centers, but may also be all yellow or all orange. Plants can bloom from midsummer until frost.

**Height and spread** Height 24–36 inches (30–90 cm) depending on the cultivar; some are smaller. Can spread to about 12 inches (30 cm).

**Best site** Full sun; average, well-drained, weed-free soil. Caliopsis will tolerate hot weather and drought.

**Growing guidelines** Grows quickly from seed sown directly into the garden in early- to mid-spring. You can also sow seed ⅛ inch (3 mm) deep indoors about six weeks before your last frost date. Set plants out around the last frost date. Space transplants or thin seedlings to stand about 8 inches (20 cm) apart. Push twiggy brush into the soil around the young plants of tall-growing cultivars to support the stems as they grow. Pinch off the dead flowers to promote and prolong flowering.

**Landscape uses** Calliopsis adds fast, easy-care color to beds and borders. It also looks wonderful in meadow gardens; scatter the seed or buy it as part of a commercially available meadow mix. Grow some in the cutting garden for fresh arrangements. Try the compact cultivars in containers or use them to form the solid geometric shapes of a formal garden.

# COSMOS

*Cosmos bipinnatus* Compositae

Use fast-growing cosmos to fill spaces left by early-blooming annuals and perennials. Pinch off spent flowers to encourage more bloom; leave a few to self-sow.

**Description** These popular half-hardy annuals are grown for their colorful blooms. The bushy plants bear many finely cut, green leaves. In late summer and fall, the stems are topped with white, pink or rosy red flowers; some varieties have two or more colors in the one plant. The single or semidouble, daisy-like blooms can grow up to 4 inches (10 cm) across.

*Cosmos bipinnatus*

**Height and spread** Height 3–4 feet (90–120 cm); spread to 18 inches (45 cm).

**Best site** Full sun is best, although plants can take partial or dappled shade; average to moist, well-drained soil.

**Growing guidelines** For earliest blooms, buy transplants in spring or start seed indoors three to four weeks before your last frost date. Plant seed ¼ inch (6 mm) deep. Set plants out 12 weeks after the last frost date. You can also sow seed directly into the garden around the last frost date. Space transplants or thin seedlings to stand 6–12 inches (15–30 cm) apart. Pinch off stem tips in early summer to promote branching and more flowers. Push sturdy twigs into the soil around young plants to support the stems as they grow, or stake individual stems as needed. Or just let plants sprawl; they'll send up more flowering stems.

**Landscape uses** Cosmos adds height to the back of flower beds and borders; spread seeds in large expanses of lawn to add color. Grow a few in the cutting garden for fresh arrangements. Use white cosmos to brighten up dull areas of the yard.

# CHINA PINK

*Dianthus chinensis* Caryophyllaceae

China pinks look equally lovely in beds, borders and container plantings. Pinching off spent flowers is time-consuming, but it will prolong the bloom season.

*Dianthus chinensis*

**Other common names** Rainbow pink.

**Description** This biennial or short-lived perennial is usually grown as an annual for its pretty flowers. Plants form tufts of narrow, green leaves. The upright stems bear 1-inch (2.5-cm) wide, flat flowers with broad, fringed petals. The white, pink or red flowers bloom through summer. They have also been hybridized to produce more colorful flowers over a longer season.

**Height and spread** Height 8–12 inches (20–30 cm); spread to 12 inches (30 cm).

**Best site** Full sun (afternoon shade in hot-summer areas); average, well-drained soil.

**Growing guidelines** Buy plants in spring, or start seed indoors six to eight weeks before your last frost date. (Just barely cover it with soil or potting mix). You can also sow seed directly into the garden two to three weeks before the last frost date. Thin seedlings or set the transplants to stand 6–8 inches (15–20 cm) apart.

**Landscape uses** China pinks are a natural choice for cottage gardens. They also make colorful edgings for flower beds and walkways. Try a few in container gardens, too. As a relative of the carnation, China pink has a spicy scent that is noticeable in fresh arrangements.

**Cultivars** 'Telstar' blooms from summer into fall in a range of white, pinks, reds and bicolors on 6–8-inch (15–20-cm) tall stems. 'Snowfire' grows to 8 inches (20 cm) tall and has white, fringed flowers with a red center.

## COMMON FOXGLOVE

*Digitalis purpurea* Scrophulariaceae

Cut down the spent flower stems of common foxgloves after bloom to keep the garden tidy, or allow the seeds to form so plants can self-sow.

**Description** This beautiful biennial or short-lived perennial is grown for its showy blooms, especially in border plantings. During the first year, plants form mounds of broad, velvety, grayish green leaves. In early- to midsummer of the following year, the rosettes send up long, graceful spikes topped with thimble-shaped flowers. The 2–3-inch (5–7.5-cm) blooms may be white, cream, pink or pinkish purple and often have contrasting spots on the inside of the flower.

**Height and spread** Height 3–5 feet (90–150 cm); spread to 2 feet (60 cm) from the base of the plant to the bottom of the bloom.

**Best site** Full sun to partial shade (afternoon shade in hot-summer areas); average, well-drained soil with added organic matter.

**Growing guidelines** Grow most foxgloves as biennials by sowing outdoors in pots or in a nursery bed in late summer. Sow the seed on the soil surface, press it in lightly, and keep the soil moist until seedlings appear. Move plants to the garden in fall. Space them about 12 inches (30 cm) apart. Tall cultivars may need staking.

**Landscape uses** Grow them in the back of borders, where other plants will fill the space left in midsummer. The tall spires also look super in masses in lightly shaded woodlands. Use foxglove to block a poor view while a hedge grows or until you put in a fence.

**Cultivars** 'Foxy Mixed' blooms the first year from seed on 3–4-foot (90–120-cm) tall stems.

*Digitalis purpurea*

# SNOW-ON-THE-MOUNTAIN

*Euphorbia marginata* Euphorbiaceae

Shrubby snow-on-the-mountain forms showy clumps of white-marked leaves by late summer. Use this old-fashioned favorite as a filler or accent plant in beds and borders.

**Description** This half-hardy annual is grown for its showy foliage. Young plants produce upright stems with oblong to pointed, green leaves. In mid- to late-summer, the stems begin to branch more, and the leaves produced on the upper parts of the branches are edged with white. At the branch tips, clusters of tiny flowers are surrounded by pure white, petal-like bracts.

**Height and spread** Height 24–48 inches (60–120 cm); spread 12–18 inches (30–45 cm).

**Best site** Full sun; average, well-drained soil.

**Growing guidelines** For earliest color, start seed ½ inch (12 mm) deep indoors four to six weeks before your last frost date. Set plants out after the last frost date. Or sow seed directly into the garden around the last frost date. Thin seedlings or space transplants to stand 12 inches (30 cm) apart. Plants may lean or flop by late summer; prevent this by staking plants in early- to mid-summer, while they're still young. Plants often self-sow.

**Landscape uses** Use as a shrubby filler or accent in flower beds and borders. Use it to contrast smaller, colorful plantings in front, and taller plantings behind. The showy leaves are especially lovely in fresh arrangements, so include a few plants in the cutting garden. Handle cut stems carefully because they will leak a milky sap that can irritate your skin, eyes and mouth.

**Cultivars** 'Summer Icicle' grows to a compact 18 inches (45 cm) tall; taller in some conditions.

*Euphorbia marginata*

# Prairie Gentian

*Eustoma grandiflorum* Gentianaceae

Prairie gentian looks lovely planted in masses with shrubs or alone in a container. The gorgeous blooms can last several weeks in fresh arrangements.

**Description** This beautiful but slow-growing biennial is generally grown as a half-hardy annual. Its slender, upright stems carry oblong, gray-green leaves and are topped with pointed buds. The buds unfurl to produce long-lasting, single or double flowers that resemble poppies or roses. The 2–3-inch (5–7.5-cm) flowers bloom in white and shades of cream, pink, rose and purple-blue.

**Height and spread** Height usually 12–24 inches (30–60 cm); spread to 12 inches (30 cm).

**Best site** Full sun to partial shade; average, well-drained soil.

**Growing guidelines** You'll get the quickest results by buying transplants in spring. If you want to try raising your own, sow them indoors in January. Scatter the seed over the pot surface, press it lightly into the soil, and enclose the pot in a plastic bag until seedlings appear. Set transplants out three months after your last frost date. Space them about 6 inches (15 cm) apart in clumps of three or more plants. Pinching off stem tips once or twice in early summer will promote branching and more blooms. Remove spent blooms to prolong flowering.

**Landscape uses** Prairie gentian is an elegant addition to any flower bed or border. It is especially useful in color theme gardens; blues and purples can be planted close to the house or next to paths where they can be seen easily; the white blooms reflecting the light from the moon at night.

**Cultivars** 'Double Eagle Mixed'; double flowers in a range of colors on 24-inch (60-cm) tall stems.

*Eustoma grandiflorum*

# GLOBE AMARANTH

*Gomphrena globosa* Amaranthaceae

Globe amaranth is generally trouble-free. Grow it in the cutting garden for use in fresh or dried arrangements; try the compact cultivars as edgings or in containers.

**Description** This tender annual is grown for its long-lasting flower heads, which begin blooming almost as soon as the seedlings are set outside. The oblong to elliptical green leaves grow in pairs along sturdy stems; both the stems and the leaves are covered with fine hairs. Tiny, yellow flowers peek out from between layers of colorful, papery bracts that make up the clover-like flower heads. The magenta, pink or creamy white, 1-inch (2.5-cm) wide flower heads bloom from midsummer until frost.

**Height and spread** Height 8–18 inches (20–45 cm); spread 8–12 inches (20–30 cm).

**Best site** Full sun; average, well-drained to dry soil.

**Growing guidelines** Buy transplants in spring, or start your own by sowing seed indoors four to six weeks before your last frost date. Plant the seed ⅛–¼ inch (3–6 mm) deep. For quickest germination, place the pots in a warm place (about 75°F [24°C]) until seedlings appear; then move them back to room temperature. Set transplants out two to three weeks after the last frost date. If your area has a long, warm growing season, you can also sow seed directly into the garden after the last frost date, when the soil is warm. Space transplants or thin seedlings to stand 8–10 inches (20–25 cm) apart.

**Landscape uses** Globe amaranth is popular as a dried flower, since the flower heads keep their color well, especially when air-dried. Tuck a few plants into beds and borders for a colorful accent in the garden.

*Gomphrena globosa*

# ANNUAL BABY'S-BREATH

*Gypsophila elegans* Caryophyllaceae

Sowing seed of annual baby's-breath every two to three weeks from early to late spring can extend the bloom season well into summer.

**Description** This hardy annual is grown for its airy sprays of dainty flowers. Plants form loose clumps of slender stems with pairs of narrow, gray-green leaves. Loose clusters of many five-petaled flowers bloom atop the stems for up to two months in spring and early summer. The 1/4–1/2-inch (6–12-mm) wide flowers are usually white or light pink.

**Height and spread** Height 18–24 inches (45–60 cm); spread 6–12 inches (15–30 cm).

**Best site** Full sun (or afternoon shade in hot-summer areas); average, well-drained soil.

**Growing guidelines** Plant seed directly into the garden or container where you want plants to grow; cover it with 1/8 inch (3 mm) of soil. Sow seed in early spring (or in fall in mild-winter areas). Thin seedlings to stand about 6 inches (15 cm) apart. Push twiggy brush into the soil around young plants to support the stems as they grow. Pull out plants that are done flowering.

**Landscape uses** Makes a nice filler for flower beds and borders in late spring and early summer. It looks especially charming in masses with other cool-loving annuals, such as rocket larkspur

*Gypsophila elegans*

and sweet peas. Follow these early bloomers with summer-flowering annuals to keep the show going. Baby's-breath is a classic in fresh and dry arrangements; it makes a lovely contrast for bunches of foliage and is charming in bouquets of white flowers.

**Cultivars** 'Covent Garden White' has white flowers on 18-inch (45 cm) tall stems.

# COMMON HELIOTROPE

*Heliotropium arborescens* Boraginaceae

The violet, purple-blue, or white flowers of common heliotrope may have a vanilla- or cherry-like scent. Sniff the flowers before you buy to find the most fragrant ones.

**Other common names**
Cherry pie.

**Description** This perennial is usually grown as a tender annual. Produces shrubby clumps of sturdy stems and hairy, deep green, heavily veined, oval leaves. Clusters of ¼-inch (6-mm) wide, tubular blooms in summer.

**Height and spread** Height usually 24–36 inches (60–90 cm); spread 12–24 inches (30–60 cm).

**Best site** Full sun (to afternoon shade in hot-summer climates); average, well-drained soil with added organic matter.

**Growing guidelines** Easiest to start from nursery-grown or overwintered plants. If you want to grow your own, sow seed indoors 10 to 12 weeks before your last frost date. Seed may take several weeks to germinate. Set plants out 12 inches (30 cm) apart, two to three weeks after the last frost date. Pinch off the stem tips in early summer to promote branching and more flowers. To overwinter plants, cut them back, then dig them up before the first fall frost; remove the leaves from the lower half of the cutting and insert the stem in potting soil. Enclose in plastic bag til well-rooted; put pot in sunny place.

*Heliotropium arborescens*

**Landscape uses** Grow in flower beds and borders or containers. It is commonly grown for its pleasant fragrance; a nice addition to pots on decks and patios, and to garden beds alongside walkways, under windows and near entryways.

**Cultivars** 'Marine' has deep purple, dense, rounded flower heads and purplish green leaves; fragrance is variable.

# ANNUAL CANDYTUFT

*Iberis umbellata* Cruciferae

Annual candytuft needs little care and tends to self-sow. In hot-summer areas, pull out plants after bloom and replace them with summer- to fall-blooming annuals.

**Other common names** Globe candytuft.

**Description** This dependable, hardy annual forms mounds of narrow, green leaves on many-branched stems. The mounds are covered with dense, slightly rounded flower clusters about 2 inches (5 cm) across from late spring through midsummer. Each cluster contains many ¼–½ inch (6–12 mm) wide, four-petaled blooms. Flowers may be white, pink, pinkish purple, rose or red.

**Height and spread** Height 8–12 inches (20–30 cm); spread 8–10 inches (20–25 cm).

**Best site** Full sun to partial shade; average, well-drained soil.

**Growing guidelines** For the earliest flowers, sow seed indoors six to eight weeks before your last

*Iberis umbellata*

frost date. Plant seed about ¼ inch (6 mm) deep. Set plants out around the last frost date. Annual candytuft also grows easily from seed sown directly into the garden. Make the first sowing in early- to mid-spring. Sowing again every three to four weeks until early summer can extend the bloom season until fall if your summer temperatures don't get much above 90°F (32°C). Thin seedlings or space plants to stand 6–8 inches (15–20 cm) apart.

**Landscape uses** Annual candytuft makes a colorful edging or filler for flower beds. Use in fresh arrangements.

**Cultivars** 'Dwarf Fairyland Mixed' grows to 8 inches (20 cm) tall with white, pink, crimson or purplish blooms.

## IMPATIENS

*Impatiens wallerana* Balsaminaceae

A mixed planting of impatiens makes a colorful annual groundcover under trees and shrubs. For good growth, they need moist soil; mulch them and water during dry spells.

*Impatiens wallerana*

**Other common names** Busy Lizzie, patient Lucy, patience.

**Description** Impatiens are tender perennials grown as tender annuals. Plants form neat, shrubby mounds of succulent stems; lance-shaped, green or bronze-brown leaves have slightly scalloped edges. Plants are covered with flat, spurred flowers up to 2 inches (5 cm) wide from late spring until frost. The single or double blooms may be white, pink, red, orange or lavender; some have swirls of contrasting colors. Flowers are followed by ribbed seedpods that burst open when ripe, flinging seeds far and wide.

**Height and spread** Height is 6–24 inches (15–60 cm); similar spread in most cultivars.

**Best site** Partial to full shade; average to moist, well-drained soil with added organic matter.

**Growing guidelines** Transplants of these popular annuals are usually available for sale in spring in a variety of plant heights and flower colors. You can also start your own by sowing seed indoors eight to ten weeks before your last frost date. Don't cover the seed; just press it lightly into the soil surface. Enclose the pot in a plastic bag and keep it in a warm place until seedlings appear. Young seedlings tend to grow slowly. Set transplants out about two weeks after your last frost date. Space compact types 6–8 inches (15–20 cm) apart and tall cultivars 12–18 inches (30–45 cm) apart. Mulch plants to keep their roots moist and water during dry spells. Other than that, these low-maintenance plants don't need much care to keep blooming throughout the season.

# MOONFLOWER

*Ipomoea alba* Convolvulaceae

The heavily scented blooms of moonflowers open in the evening. Before planting this climber, set up some kind of support, such as vertical wires or a trellis.

*Ipomoea alba*

**Description** This tender perennial vine is usually grown as a tender annual. The stems produce heart-shaped leaves and pointed buds that unfurl into funnel-shaped to flat, white blooms up to 6 inches (15 cm) across. These highly fragrant summer flowers open in the evening and may stay open through to the next morning. The thin vine twists around its support.

**Height and spread** Height to 10 feet (3 m) or more; ultimate Height and spread depend on the size of the support the vine is climbing on; it will grow well regardless of poor conditions.

**Best site** Full sun; average, well-drained soil.

**Growing guidelines** For earliest flowers, start seed indoors four to six weeks before your last frost date. Soak seed in warm water overnight, then plant it about 1 inch (2.5 cm) deep in peat pots (two or three seeds per pot). When seedlings appear, keep the strongest one in each pot and cut off the others in the same pot at the soil surface. Set plants out 12 weeks after the last frost date. If you have a long, warm growing season, you could instead sow seed directly into the garden after the last frost date, when the soil is warm. Set plants or thin seedlings to stand 12 inches (30 cm) apart. Other than watering during dry spells, moonflowers need little care.

**Landscape uses** Use as a fast-growing screen for shade or privacy. Its night-blooming habit makes it an excellent choice for planting around decks, patios and garden settings where you might sit on summer evenings.

## SWEET PEA
*Lathyrus odoratus* Leguminosae

Dozens of sweet pea cultivars are available in a range of heights and colors. Many modern cultivars aren't very fragrant; check catalog descriptions to find scented types.

*Lathyrus odoratus*

**Description** These old-fashioned hardy annuals are grown for their charming flowers. Plants produce leafy vines that climb by tendrils. Foliage is a bright, pale green. Dainty, pea-like flowers to 2 inches (5 cm) long bloom on long, slender flower stems from midspring into summer. Flower colors are usually bright or pastel shades of pink, red or purple; it can also produce white flowers. The petals are often slightly crimped or ruffled.

**Height and spread** Height usually 4–6 feet (1.2–1.8 m); spread 6–12 inches (15–30 cm).

**Best site** Full sun (or afternoon shade in hot-summer areas); loose, evenly moist soil enriched with ample amounts of organic matter.

**Growing guidelines** Before planting, set up some sort of string or netting trellis for the vines to climb. Start seed indoors six to eight weeks before your last frost date. Soak seed in warm water overnight, then plant ½ inch (12 mm) deep in peat pots. Set plants out in midspring, after danger of heavy frost. Or sow seed directly into the garden in early spring. Set transplants or thin seedlings to stand 4–6 inches (10–15 cm) apart. Mulch to keep the roots cool and moist. Water during dry spells. Pull the vines out when they stop blooming.

**Landscape uses** Train sweet peas to climb a tripod of stakes as an early-season accent for beds, borders and cottage gardens. Include them in the cutting garden for fresh cut flowers. Train it on a trellis to provide an attractive screen or a backdrop.

## ANNUAL STATICE

*Limonium sinuatum* Plumbaginaceae

Annual statice is a natural for fresh or dried arrangements. To dry it, pick stems when the clusters are about three-quarters open; hang them in a dark, airy place.

**Other common names**
Sea lavender.

**Description** This biennial or tender perennial is usually grown as a half-hardy annual. Plants form low rosettes of wavy-edged, green leaves that send up sturdy, winged stems in summer. The loosely branched stems are topped with flattened clusters of ¼-inch (6-mm) wide white flowers, each surrounded by a papery, tubular calyx—the colorful part of the flower head. Annual statice comes in a rainbow of colors, including white, pink, peach, red, orange, yellow, purple and blue. It is native to the Mediterranean area.

**Height and spread** Height 12–24 inches (30–60 cm); spread to 12 inches (30 cm).

**Best site** Full sun; average, well-drained soil.

**Growing guidelines** Buy transplants in spring, or start your own by sowing seed indoors six to eight weeks before your last frost date. Plant the seed ¼ inch (6 mm) deep. Move seedlings to individual pots when they have two or three sets of leaves. Plant them in the garden around the last frost date, or sow seed directly into the garden after the last frost date. Space transplants or thin

*Limonium sinuatum*

seedlings to stand 8–10 inches (20–25 cm) apart. Established plants need little care, other than to water when conditions are dry. It tolerates seaside conditions but will rot in soil that remains wet.

**Landscape uses** Annual statice is an unusual and attractive filler for flower beds and borders. Try the compact types in container gardens. Some cultivars dry nicely and retain their color.

# HONESTY

*Lunaria annua* Cruciferae

Honesty is a hardy biennial grown for its pretty flowers and showy dried seedpods. Leave a few plants in the garden to self-sow; harvest the rest for arrangements.

**Other common names**
Money plant, silver dollar.

**Description** First-year plants form clumps of coarse, heart-shaped, hairy, green leaves. In

*Lunaria annua*

the second spring, the clumps send up loosely branched stems topped with elongated clusters of ½-inch (12-mm) wide, four-petaled flowers. The lightly fragrant, purple-pink blooms are followed by flat, circular seedpods with papery outer skins and a satiny white central disk.

**Height and spread** Height 18–36 inches (45–90 cm) in bloom; spread to 12 inches (30 cm).

**Best site** Partial shade; average, well-drained soil. Added organic matter is a plus; use a commercial mix if you do not make compost.

**Growing guidelines** Buy and set out nursery-grown plants in early spring for bloom the same year, or start your own from seed for bloom next year. Sow seed directly into the garden, ⅛–¼ inch (3–6 mm) deep, in spring or late summer. Set transplants or thin seedlings to stand about 12 inches (30 cm) apart. It will tolerate wet and dry conditions.

**Landscape uses** The flowers add color to spring beds and borders. The white-flowered forms look especially nice in woodland gardens. Honesty is also a traditional favorite in cutting gardens for its dried seedpods. When the seedpods turn beige, cut the stems off at ground level and bring them indoors. Once seedpods feel dry, gently peel off the outer skins to reveal the silvery center membrane.

# Virginia Stock

*Nalcomia maritima* Cruciferae

Virginia stock can bloom in as little as four weeks from seed sown directly into the garden. Sow every three to four weeks through midsummer to have flowers from summer until frost.

*Nalcomia maritima*

**Description**  The upright, branching stems of this fast-growing hardy annual carry small, pointed, grayish green leaves. Flat, four-petaled, lightly fragrant flowers bloom in loose clusters atop the stems. The purple, pink or white flowers are ¼–½ inch (6–12 mm) wide. Most cultivars have yellow centers.

**Height and spread**  Height 6–8 inches (15–20 cm); spread to 4 inches (10 cm).

**Best site**  Full sun to partial shade (in hot-summer areas); average, well-drained soil.

**Growing guidelines**  Grows best from seed sown directly in the garden. For the longest bloom season, sow at three to four week intervals from early spring through midsummer. (In mild-winter areas, you can sow in fall for even earlier spring bloom.) Rake the seedbed to cover the seed lightly, then keep the soil moist until seedlings appear. Thin seedlings to stand 3–4 inches (7.5–10 cm) apart.

**Landscape uses**  Virginia stock makes a nice edging annual for flower beds and borders and will perfume a garden throughout summer. Use it to fill areas where seedling perennials have been planted. The flowers are very popular with honeybees so plant near fruit and vegetable crops to promote good pollination. Cut large bunches of stock for fresh indoor arrangements.

# FOUR-O'CLOCK

*Mirabilis jalapa*  Nyctaginaceae

Four-o'clocks have fragrant flowers that open in late afternoon. They tend to close the next morning, unless the weather is cloudy. Grow them in the garden or in pots.

**Other common names**
Marvel-of-Peru.

**Description**  These tender perennials are usually grown as half-hardy annuals. The bushy, fast-growing plants have branching stems and oval to lance-shaped, deep green leaves. Trumpet-shaped, 1-inch (2.5-cm) wide flowers bloom from midsummer until frost in white or shades of pink, magenta, red and yellow; sometimes different colored blooms appear on the same plant.

**Height and spread**  Height usually 24–36 inches (60–90 cm); spread to 24 inches (60 cm).

**Best site**  Full sun to partial shade; average, well-drained soil.

**Growing guidelines**  Four-o'clocks are gratifyingly easy to grow from seed. For earliest bloom, start them indoors four to six weeks before your last frost date. Soak the seed in warm water overnight, then plant it ¼–½ inch (6–12 mm) deep in peat pots. Transplant seedlings to the garden about two weeks after the last frost date, when the soil is warm. You can also sow seed directly into the garden after the last frost date. Space transplants or thin the seedlings to stand 12–18 inches (30–45 cm) apart.

*Mirabilis jalapa*

**Landscape uses**  Plant clumps in the middle of new perennial flower beds and along borders for a colorful filler. Grow a few around an outdoor sitting area, where you can enjoy the flowers and gentle fragrance after a long day. Four-o'clock does well in containers, so use it on patios and decks or plant it in window boxes and hanging pots; make sure there is drainage.

# FORGET-ME-NOT

*Myosotis sylvatica* Boraginaceae

Forget-me-not blooms are often sky blue with white or yellow centers, but they can also be pink or white. They are ideal companions for spring bulbs and other early annuals.

**Description** These short-lived perennials are usually grown as hardy biennials or annuals. Plants form dense clumps of narrow, lance-shaped, hairy leaves. Sprays of many ⅓-inch (8-mm) wide

*Myosotis sylvatica*

flowers bloom over the leaves from midspring through early summer.

**Height and spread** Height usually 12–18 inches (30–45 cm); spread 8–10 inches (20–25 cm).

**Best site** Partial shade; average to moist, well-drained soil with added organic matter.

**Growing guidelines** To grow forget-me-nots as biennials, sow seed outdoors in pots or in a nursery bed in spring or summer. Plant seed ⅛ inch (3 mm) deep. Move plants to the garden in early fall. For bloom the same year, buy plants in early spring; set plants out

12 weeks before the last frost date. Or start seed indoors four to six weeks before your last frost date. Space plants or thin seedlings to stand 6 inches (15 cm) apart. Water during dry spells. Shearing off spent flowers often promotes rebloom. Plants often self-sow freely, so thin regularly if you want to contain the planting within a specific area.

**Landscape uses** Forget-me-nots are invaluable for spring color in shady gardens. Try them as an early-season groundcover under shrubs, or grow them in beds and borders with short tulips and other spring bulbs for stunning color combinations. In past times, forget-me-nots were considered the flowers of true love, and used in bouquets given by lovers.

**Cultivars** 'Blue Ball' has blue flowers on compact, 6-inch (15-cm) tall plants.

# FLOWERING TOBACCO

### Nicotiana alata Solanaceae

Hybrids and red-flowered types of flowering tobacco often have little or no scent, but old-fashioned, white-flowered types tend to be quite fragrant, especially at night.

Nicotiana alata

**Description** This tender perennial is usually grown as a half-hardy annual. Plants form lush rosettes of broad, oval to pointed, green leaves and many-branched stems; both the stems and leaves are sticky and hairy. Trumpet-shaped flowers grow to about 2 inches (5 cm) across from midsummer until frost. It flowers in a range of colors, including white, pink, purple and red.

**Height and spread** Height usually 18–36 inches (45–90 cm); spread to 12 inches (30 cm).

**Best site** Full sun to partial shade; average to moist, well-drained soil with added organic matter.

**Growing guidelines** Buy transplants in spring, or grow your own by starting seed indoors six to eight weeks before your last frost date. Don't cover the fine seed; just press it into the soil and enclose the pot in a plastic bag until seedlings appear. Set seedlings out 10–12 inches (25–30 cm) apart after the last frost date. Water during dry spells. Cut out spent stems to prolong flowering. Plants may self-sow. Grow with marigolds to repel insects such as nematodes. Do not grow with rye crops.

**Landscape uses** Excellent as a filler or accent in beds and borders. Grow some in the cutting garden for fresh flowers. Plant fragrant, white-flowered types around outdoor sitting areas for evening enjoyment. Try compact types in containers.

**Cultivars** 'Sensation Mixed' has fragrant flowers in many colors, on 36-inch (90-cm) tall stems.

# LOVE-IN-A-MIST

*Nigella damascena* Ranunculaceae

Sowing every three to four weeks from early spring to early summer can extend the bloom season of love-in-a-mist through the summer and possibly into fall.

**Other common names** Fennel flower, devil-in-the-bush.

**Description** A fast-growing, hardy annual that forms bushy mounds of slender stems and thread-like, soft, bright green leaves. Single or double, 1–2-inch (2.5–5-cm) wide flowers are nestled into the leaves at the tops of the stems. The blue, pink, mauve or white flowers have dark centers with long, green stamens; they are followed by striped seedpods with pointed horns.

**Height and spread** Height 18–24 inches (45–60 cm); spread 6–8 inches (15–20 cm).

**Best site** Full sun to partial shade; average, well-drained soil.

**Growing guidelines** For the earliest flowers, you could start seed indoors six to eight weeks before your last frost date. Sow seed (just barely cover it with soil) in peat pots. Keep moist and warm. Move plants to the garden after the last frost date. In most cases, though, you'll get better results by sowing directly into the garden, starting in early spring in cold-winter areas, or in winter in areas with a moderate climate. Space transplants or thin seedlings to stand 6 inches (15 cm) apart. Established plants are care-free.

*Nigella damascena*

**Landscape uses** Grow as a filler in beds, borders and cottage gardens. It's also a natural for the cutting garden. Use some of the flowers in fresh arrangements to add interesting shapes; leave the rest to mature into the puffy seedpods. Cut the stems at ground level and hang them upside down to dry in a dark, airy place. Use the seedpods in potpourri and dried flower arrangements.

## ZONAL GERANIUM

*Pelargonium* x *hortorum* Geraniaceae

Colorful and dependable, zonal geraniums are a mainstay of summer flower gardens. You can also bring them indoors in the fall and enjoy their flowers through the winter.

**Description** These tender perennials are usually grown as tender annuals for their attractive leaves and colorful flowers. The sturdy, branched stems carry hairy, rounded, bright to dark green leaves with scalloped margins. The pungent leaves are often marked with dark green or brown, curved bands (zones). Plants produce thin but sturdy stems topped with clusters of many 2-inch (5-cm) wide flowers. The flowers bloom from late spring until frost in white or shades of red and bicolors.

**Height and spread** Height 12–24 inches (30–60 cm); spread usually 12–18 inches (30–45 cm).

**Best site** Full sun to partial shade; average, well-drained soil.

**Growing guidelines** Plant seedlings in spring. Sow seed indoors eight to ten weeks before your last frost date. Set in a very warm place (about 80°F [27°C]) until seedlings appear, then move to individual pots. Set plants out after the last frost date. Space 12–18 inches (30–45 cm) apart. Deadhead to promote rebloom.

**Landscape uses** Grow alone in masses, or tuck into beds and borders with other annuals and perennials as accents or fillers. Great in container gardens.

*Pelargonium* x *hortorum*

**Cultivars** 'Orbit' series blooms in white and shades of red, pink and orange on 18-inch (45-cm) tall stems; 'Apple Blossom Orbit' is a selection of white, pinks and red blossoms on compact, 10-inch (25-cm) tall plants; 'Big Red' has large, scarlet flower clusters on 14-inch (35-cm) tall stems. 'Ben Franklin' is raised from cuttings and has white-edged leaves and its flowers are magenta through to pink.

# PETUNIA

*Petunia x hybrida* Solanaceae

Petunias are tender perennials usually grown as half-hardy annuals. They may self-sow, but the seedlings seldom resemble the parent plants.

**Description** Plants form clumps of upright or trailing stems with oval, green leaves; both the leaves and stems are hairy and somewhat sticky. Funnel-shaped, single or double flowers bloom from early summer until frost in nearly every color of the rainbow; some have stripes, streaks or bands of contrasting colors. Petunias are usually divided into groups, based on their flower forms. Grandifloras have the largest flowers, growing up to 5 inches (12.5 cm) across. They are very showy but tend to be damaged easily by heavy rain. Multifloras have smaller flowers (usually 2 inches [5 cm] across) but produce many durable blooms on each plant. Floribundas are an intermediate type, with 3-inch (7.5-cm) wide flowers on fast-growing plants.

**Height and spread** Height usually 6–10 inches (15–25 cm); spread to 12 inches (30 cm).

**Best site** Full sun (can take light shade); average to moist, well-drained soil.

**Growing guidelines** Petunias are among the most popular annuals, and many types are sold as transplants each spring. You can also grow your own from seed, although the fine, dust-like seed can be hard to handle and often produces poor results.

**Landscape uses** Multiflora and floribunda types are favorites for flower beds and borders. They are excellent for filling in gaps left by spring-flowering annuals and bulbs. Grandiflora types look great spilling out of pots. They drop their lower leaves by late summer; grow them with other bushy plants to cover their bare ankles.

*Petunia x hybrida*

# ROSE MOSS

*Portulaca grandiflora* Portulacaceae

Rose moss comes in many vibrant colors, including white, pink, red, orange, yellow and magenta. The flowers tend to close by afternoon and stay closed on cloudy days.

**Description** A low-growing, tender annual, rose moss forms creeping mats of fleshy, reddish, many-branched stems with small, thick, almost needlelike leaves. Single or double, 1-inch (2.5-cm) wide flowers bloom from early summer through fall.

**Height and spread** Height to 6 inches (15 cm); spread 6–8 inches (15–20 cm).

**Best site** Full sun; average, well-drained to dry soil.

**Growing guidelines** For earliest bloom, buy transplants in spring, or start your own by sowing seed indoors six to eight weeks before your last frost date. For easy transplanting later, sow the seed in cell packs or small pots. Do not cover the seed; just press it lightly into the soil and enclose the containers in a plastic bag until seedlings appear. Set plants out 12 weeks after the last frost date, when the soil is warm; space them about 6 inches (15 cm) apart. You can also sow the fine seed directly into the garden after the last frost date; keep the soil moist until seedlings appear. Thin seedlings only if they're crowded. Established plants may self-sow. It grows best with a steady supply of water throughout the growing season, but can tolerate some drought.

**Landscape uses** Makes a great groundcover for dry, rocky slopes. It also looks charming as an edging for sunny beds and borders or cascading out of containers and hanging baskets.

**Cultivars** 'Cloudbeater Mixed' grows to 6 inches (15 cm) tall and has double flowers that stay open all day.

*Portulaca grandiflora*

# CASTOR BEAN

*Ricinus communis* Euphorbiaceae

Castor beans add a touch of the tropics to any garden. Stake the tall plants to keep them upright, especially in windy or exposed sites, and water them during dry spells.

**Description** This tender perennial is usually grown as a half-hardy annual. The huge, fast-growing plants produce thick, sturdy stems with large, deeply lobed, green or purplish brown leaves. Small, ½-inch (12-mm) wide, creamy-looking, petal-less flowers bloom in spiky clusters along the upper part of the stems. These summer flowers are followed by showy, spiny, reddish burs.

*Ricinus communis*

**Height and spread** Height usually to 6 feet (1.8 m) or more; spread 3–4 feet (90–120 cm).

**Best site** Full sun; average to moist, well-drained soil.

**Growing guidelines** For an early start, sow seed indoors six to eight weeks before your last frost date. Soak the large, speckled seeds in warm water overnight, then sow seed ¾ inch (18 mm) deep in individual pots (two or three seeds per pot). If all of the seeds germinate, thin to one per pot. Set plants out 12 weeks after the last frost date. You can also sow seed directly into the garden after the last frost date. Space plants or thin seedlings to stand about 3 feet (90 cm) apart. Plants may self-sow.

**Landscape uses** Grow castor beans as accents or backgrounds for beds and borders or as a temporary but fast-growing screen or hedge. Castor beans repel moles, voles and other animal pests. The seeds are poisonous if eaten, so avoid plantings around children's play areas.

**Cultivars** 'Carmencita' is a cultivar with brownish leaves; it sprouts bright red seedpods on plants that grow to 6 feet (1.8 m).

# SCARLET SAGE

*Salvia splendens* Labiatae

Compact cultivars of scarlet sage tend to flower mostly in summer; taller types generally start blooming in midsummer and last until frost. Pinch off faded spikes.

**Description** This tender perennial is grown as a half-hardy annual. Plants form clumps of upright stems with oval, deep green leaves that have pointed tips and slightly toothed edges. The stems are topped with thick spikes of colorful, petal-like bracts and 1½-inch (37-mm) long, tubular flowers. The flowers are most often red, but they are also available in white, pink and purple.

**Height and spread** Height usually 12–24 inches (30–60 cm); spread to 12 inches (30 cm).

**Best site** Full sun; average, well-drained soil.

**Growing guidelines** Widely sold as transplants in spring. If your spring has been on the cold side, wait for summer to plant, or cover on cold nights. If you really want to grow your own, sow indoors eight to ten weeks before your last frost date. Press the seed lightly into the soil and enclose the pot in a plastic bag until seedlings appear. Set plants out after the last frost date; space them 8–12 inches (20–30 cm) apart. Fertilize in summer.

**Landscape uses** If you enjoy mixing bright colors, grow scarlet sage as an edging or filler for flower beds and borders. For a somewhat more restrained effect, surround scarlet sage with leafy green herbs and ornamental grasses. The compact, uniform shape of the plants lends itself well to formal gardens.

**Cultivars** 'Bonfire' blooms with scarlet flowers on 24-inch (60-cm) tall plants from midsummer until frost. 'Laser Purple' grows to 12 inches (30 cm) tall and has deep purple flowers.

*Salvia splendens*

# CREEPING ZINNIA

*Sanvitalia procumbens* Compositae

Plant creeping zinnia where it can trail over walls, or allow it to cascade out of containers, raised beds, window boxes and hanging baskets.

**Description** Creeping zinnia is usually grown as a half-hardy annual for its colorful flowers. Plants form spreading or trailing mounds of branching stems and oval green leaves that taper to a point. The mounds are covered with many ¾-inch (18-mm) wide flowers from midsummer until frost. The blooms have raised, purple-brown centers surrounded by golden petals.

**Height and spread** Height to 6 inches (15 cm); spread to 18 inches (45 cm).

**Best site** Full sun; average, well-drained to dry soil.

**Growing guidelines** For earliest bloom, sow seed indoors six to eight weeks before last frost date. Sow in individual pots so you won't have to disturb the roots at transplanting time. Don't cover the fine seed; just press it lightly into the soil and enclose pots in a plastic bag for constant warmth and moisture until seedlings appear. Set plants out after the last frost date. You can also sow seed directly into the garden after the last frost date. Space plants or thin seedlings to stand 8–12 inches (20–30 cm) apart. Established plants are care-free and can usually withstand a touch of frost toward the end of the season.

*Sanvitalia procumbens*

**Landscape uses** Creeping zinnia makes a great groundcover in dry, sunny spots. It's also useful as an edging or filler for flower beds and borders. In containers, contrast by growing with plants of an upright habit.

**Cultivars** 'Mandarin Orange' has orange flowers on 6-inch (15-cm) tall plants.

# BLACK-EYED SUSAN VINE

*Thunbergia alata* Acanthaceae

If you plan to grow black-eyed Susan vine as a climber, install some type of support—such as plastic netting or a trellis—before planting.

*Thunbergia alata*

**Description** This tender perennial is grown as a tender annual. Plants produce twining vines with heart- to arrowhead-shaped, green leaves. Pointed buds open to rounded, flattened, 3-inch (7.5-cm) wide flowers. The orange-yellow flowers have a deep purple to black center. The white or creamy flowers have a yellow to green center. They may bloom from late summer until frost, but they usually put on their best show in late summer to early fall.

**Height and spread** Height to about 6 feet (1.8 m); ultimate height and spread depend mainly on the support the vine is growing on.

**Best site** Full sun to partial shade; average to moist, well-drained soil.

**Growing guidelines** For earliest flowers, start seed indoors six to eight weeks before your last frost date. Sow seed ¼ inch (6 mm) deep in peat pots (two or three seeds per pot); thin to leave one seedling per pot. Set plants out 12 weeks after the last frost date. You can also start plants from seed sown directly into the garden after the last frost date. Set plants or thin seedlings to stand 12 inches (30 cm) apart. Mulch plants to keep the roots cool. Water during dry spells.

**Landscape uses** Black-eyed Susan is a good fast-growing screen for shade or privacy, climbing quickly to cover fences or trellises with bright blooms from summer into fall. It also makes a unique feature in a hanging basket, where it will climb up the support wires to create a pyramid of foliage and flowers.

# MEXICAN SUNFLOWER

*Tithonia rotundifolia* Compositae

Mexican sunflowers are popular with bees and butterflies, and they make good cut flowers. Pinch off spent blooms to extend the flowering season.

*Tithonia rotundifolia*

**Other common names**
Torch flower.

**Description** Mexican sunflower is a half-hardy annual with colorful blooms. Plants produce tall, sturdy, hairy stems with velvety, lobed or broadly oval, pointed, dark green leaves. During summer, the shrubby clumps are accented with many 3-inch (7.5-cm) wide, glowing orange, daisy-like flowers.

**Height and spread** Height 4–6 feet (1.2–1.8 m); spread 18–24 inches (45–60 cm).

**Best site** Full sun; average, well-drained soil with added organic matter.

**Growing guidelines** For earliest flowers, start seed indoors six to eight weeks before your last frost date. Sow seed about ¼ inch (6 mm) deep in individual pots (two or three seeds per pot); thin to leave one seedling per pot. Set plants out after the last frost date. Plants also grow quickly and easily from seed sown directly into the garden about two weeks after the last frost date. Set plants or thin seedlings to stand 18 inches (45 cm) apart. Water gently by hand or a soaker hose during dry spells. Plants growing in exposed, windy sites may need staking.

**Landscape uses** Makes an attractive flowering screen or hedge. It also looks great as a tall accent or background plant in beds and borders.

**Cultivars** 'Torch' has orange flowers on 4–6-foot (1.2–1.8-m) tall stems. 'Yellow Torch' grows to 4 feet (1.2 m) tall and has bright yellow flowers.

# GARDEN VERBENA

*Verbena x hybrida* Verbenaceae

Grow garden verbena alone in masses, or mix it with other flowers for all-season color. Pinch off the stem tips in early summer to promote branching and more flowers.

**Description** This tender perennial is grown as a tender annual. Plants have upright or trailing stems with toothed or lobed, oval- to lance-shaped, dark green leaves. The stems are topped

*Verbena x hybrida*

with rounded clusters of bright, ½-inch (12-mm) wide flowers from early summer until frost. The flowers may be white, cream, pink, red, blue or purple; they often have a contrasting white eye.

**Height and spread** Height 8–12 inches (20–30-cm) ; spread usually to 12 inches (30 cm).

**Best site** Full sun; average, well-drained soil.

**Growing guidelines** Generally difficult to start from seed, so you'll probably have the best luck with purchased transplants. If you really want to try growing your

own, sow seed indoors eight to ten weeks before your last frost date. Plant it ⅛ inch (3 mm) deep and keep in a warm area. Seedlings may take several weeks to sprout. Set plants out 12 weeks after the last frost date, when the soil is warm; space them about 10 inches (25cm) apart.

**Landscape uses** Use the upright forms as fillers or edgings for beds and borders; include some in the cutting garden for fresh flowers. Grow the trailing types as groundcovers or in window boxes and hanging baskets. Use the bright blooms to add a little spark to pastel theme gardens of soft pinks, yellows and baby blues, or use the cultivars to add depth of color.

**Cultivars** 'Peaches 'n' Cream' has creamy to pale orange flowers on 8-inch (20-cm) tall stems.

# PANSY

*Viola x wittrockiana* Violaceae

To keep pansies happy, mulch the soil around them and water during dry spells to keep the roots moist. Pinching off spent flowers can prolong bloom; leave a few to self-sow.

**Description** These short-lived perennials are usually grown as hardy annuals or biennials. The plants form tidy clumps of oval to narrow, green leaves with rounded teeth. Flat, five-petaled flowers bloom just above the clumps, mainly in spring but also in fall. The 2–5-inch (5–12.5-cm) wide flowers bloom in a range of colors, including white, pink, red, orange, yellow, purple, blue and near black; many have contrasting faces with markings of solid shapes or stripes.

**Height and spread** Height 6–8 inches (15–20 cm); spread 8–12 inches (20–30 cm).

**Best site** Full sun to partial shade; moist, well-drained soil..

**Growing guidelines:** For bloom the same year, buy plants in early spring or start seed indoors eight to ten weeks before your last frost date. Sow seed about ⅛ inch (3 mm) deep. Set the pot in a refrigerator for 12 weeks, then move it to a bright place. Check regularly that the soil is moist. Set seedlings out 12 weeks before your last frost date; space them 6–8 inches (15–20 cm) apart. To grow pansies as biennials for earlier spring bloom, sow the seed outdoors in a nursery bed in late spring.

*Viola x wittrockiana*

**Landscape uses** Pansies are invaluable for early color in flower beds and borders; use them as fillers or as an edging. They are also cute in containers. When they start to fade, follow them with summer bloomers, such as impatiens and begonias. For the more adventurous, pansies are a colorful addition to the salad bowl and can be crystallised, like violets, to use as an edible decoration for cakes and desserts.

111

# NARROW-LEAVED ZINNIA

*Zinnia angustifolia* Compositae

Narrow-leaved zinnia is a tender annual grown for its colorful flowers. The established plants are trouble-free; they are also quite disease- and drought-resistant.

**Other common names**
Classic zinnia.

**Description** Narrow-leaved zinnia form loose mounds of slender, dark green leaves. The mounds are covered with open, daisy-like blooms to 1½ inches (37 mm) wide from midsummer through until frost. The flowers are most often a very bright orange color, with a gold stripe in the center of each petal; white- and yellow-flowered types are also available in some areas.

**Height and spread** Height 8–12 inches (20–30 cm); spread to 12 inches (30 cm).

**Best site** Full sun; average, well-drained to dry soil.

**Growing guidelines** For earliest flowers, sow seed indoors three to four weeks before your last frost date. Plant seed ¼–½ inch (6–12 mm) deep in peat pots (two or three seeds per pot). Thin seedlings to leave one per pot. Set plants out after the last frost date. It's also easy to start these fast growers from seed sown directly into the garden twelve weeks after the last frost date. Space plants to stand 10–12 inches (25–30 cm) apart. Plants are self-sowing, depending on your region and the microclimate of your yard.

*Zinnia angustifolia*

**Landscape uses** Grow in masses as a groundcover, or use it as an edging or filler for beds and borders. It also looks super in window planters and in pots on a sunny patio. Use the taller forms for fresh arrangements.

**Cultivars** 'Classic' has single, golden to orange blooms on 10–12-inch (25–30-cm) tall plants. 'Star White' has white flowers on 14-inch (35-cm) tall plants.

# COMMON ZINNIA

*Zinnia elegans* Compositae

Common zinnias are excellent for replacing early-blooming annuals and filling in gaps left by dormant spring-flowering bulbs and perennials. They are also great cut flowers.

**Description** Plants produce stiff, sturdy stems with pairs of oval to pointed, green leaves. The stems are topped with blooms from mid-summer until frost, in nearly every color (except true blue). Common zinnias come in a range of flower forms, 1–6 inches (2.5–15 cm) across. The single or double blooms may have petals that are quilled (curled), ruffled or flat.

**Height and spread** Height 6–36 inches (15–90 cm), spread usually 12–24 inches (30–60 cm).

**Best site** Full sun; average, well-drained soil with added organic matter.

**Growing guidelines** For an extra-early start, buy transplants in spring, or grow your own by sowing seed indoors three to four weeks before your last frost date. Plant seed ¼–½ inch (6–12 mm) deep in peat pots (plant two or three seeds per pot). Thin seedlings leaving one per pot. Set the plants out after the last frost date. Common zinnias also grow quickly from seed sown directly into the garden one to two weeks after the last frost date. Space plants or thin seedlings of the compact types 12 inches (30 cm) apart; leave 18–24 inches (45–60 cm) between tall cultivars. Mulch plants to keep the roots moist. Tall cultivars may need staking.

**Landscape uses** Grow them alone in masses, or mix them with other plants in flower beds, borders and cottage gardens. Use the tall types as backgrounds, the medium-sized ones as fillers, and the compact types for edgings or container plants.

*Zinnia elegans*

# PART THREE

# FLOWERING BULBS

# BULBS IN YOUR GARDEN

**B**eautiful and versatile, bulbs belong in every landscape. Many popular bulbs—including daffodils, crocus, hyacinths and tulips— are traditionally associated with spring gardens. You can celebrate surviving another long winter with colorful displays of these dependable, easy-care bulbs. Then extend the season with lovely late bloomers, such as showy crocus and hardy cyclamen. And to fill the few months that bulbs are not blooming outdoors, you can bring some kinds indoors and enjoy their flowers all winter long. With a little planning, you can have bulbs in bloom in your garden from late winter through midfall.

# BULBS FOR SPRING

Many gardeners have a special affection for spring bulbs. These early-blooming beauties signal the return of life to the garden after the rigors of a long, cold winter, adding welcome color and fragrance to any planting. Bulbs from around the world have found a home in American gardens, despite our wide diversity of climate conditions. Most of the best-loved bulbs—including daffodils and crocus—have earned their popularity because of their ability to adapt to a wide variety of growing conditions. Not all bulbs thrive in all parts of the country, but there are at least a few beautiful spring bulbs for virtually every area.

*Chinonodoxa*

### How spring bulbs grow

Spring-flowering bulbs are best adapted to temperate areas, where they can take advantage of a particular weather "window." These bulbs send up shoots early in the season—sometimes before winter has finally relinquished its icy grasp. Melting snow and ample spring rain provide a good supply of moisture as the bulbs send up their buds, hoping to attract the first bees and other insects to ensure pollination. Even though the ground is still cool, the lengthening rays of sunshine provide enough warmth to promote bloom. As summer approaches, the days get longer and the bulbs set seed and ripen their foliage, preparing to end this part of their life cycle. By the time summer arrives, the bulbs are plump with stored nutrients.

*Irises may appear before the thaw.*

**Some like it cool** An important step in the life of most spring bulbs is winter chilling. If you live in a warm climate, where winter temperatures generally stay above freezing, you may find that some spring bulbs bloom poorly or don't bloom at all in the years after planting. Hybrid tulips commonly have this problem; some daffodils and crocus also grow poorly without a chilling period. To have a great show of blooms each year, look for species and cultivars that don't need much chilling. You can also look for "precooled" bulbs, or give new bulbs an artificial cold period by storing them in the vegetable drawer of your refrigerator for six to eight weeks before planting them in early- to mid-winter.

**Little bulbs** In much of the nation, the first flowering bulbs often jump the gun and bloom in late winter. These little treasures are often called "minor" bulbs because of their small stature compared to the taller flowering bulbs such as tulips, hyacinths and daffodils. But even though they're small in size, they're big on charm and all the more welcome due to their early appearance in fields by the roadside and in the garden.

*February gold daffodils produce dainty flowers in very early spring.*

# BULBS FOR SPRING continued

**Showy spring standbys** The early-spring show of minor bulbs sets the stage for the most spectacular spring-flowering favorites, including daffodils, hyacinths, tulips and crown imperials. Let's face it—spring just wouldn't be spring without daffodils. With hundreds of species and perhaps thousands of hybrids and cultivars, the variations on the standard yellow, large-cupped daffodil are almost endless. There are types that bear a single flower on each stem and those that produce clusters of blooms. The stems themselves range in size from just a few inches (7.5–10 cm) tall to nearly 2 feet (60 cm) tall. For extra interest, consider the variety of single and double flower forms and the range of colors (including yellow, cream, white, chartreuse and bicolors). As

a plus, most daffodils have a light scent, and many have distinct, powerful fragrances. Of course, when you're thinking about fragrant spring bulbs, you can't forget the heady scent of hybrid hyacinths. The impressive flower spikes, packed with many small blooms, usually grow 6–10 inches (15–25 cm) tall. Hyacinths come in a wide range of colors, including white, blue, pink, coral and pale yellow. Double-flowered cultivars were popular in Victorian times and are enjoying a renewed wave of interest. Along with daffodils and hyacinths, tulips are a spring-garden standby. Blooming in white and nearly every shade of red, pink, orange, yellow and purple, hybrid tulips are only lacking true

*Daffodils are a spring favorite.*

blue in the color department. Their flowers come in many forms, from the classic chalice shape to petal-packed doubles, exotically "feathered" parrot types, and elegant, pointed-petal lily types.

## SPECIAL CARE FOR SPRING BULBS

Water spring bulbs just after planting and again as needed if the soil dries out in winter or spring. Scatter compost or balanced organic fertilizer over the soil when the new shoots appear in spring to provide a nutrient boost for healthy growth and good flower bud formation for next year. Most spring bulbs thrive in full or partial sun (at least six hours of sun a day). They are ideal for planting under deciduous trees, since the bulbs can bloom and ripen their foliage before the tree leaves expand fully and block the sunlight. Unless you're planning to plant replacement bulbs each year (as you may with hybrid tulips), always allow the bulb leaves to wither away naturally. If you cut off, pull off, or bundle the leaves together, the bulb won't be able to store all the energy it needs, and it may bloom poorly or even die by the next year.

Smaller-flowered and shorter tulips are also great in the garden and provide a useful addition to a cutting garden. Some tulips offer striped, mottled or variegated leaves to complement their lovely blossoms. Ask your local garden center to help you choose a range of cultivars with different bloom times and leaf patterns; you will be able to enjoy tulips throughout the entire spring season.

### CHARMING COLOR
Create a sea of spring color by planting some crocus in your lawn. Wait to mow until the crocus leaves have yellowed. The mauve of the crocus and the bright yellow of winter aconite (left) make a charming potted combination.

# BULBS FOR SUMMER

Don't think the bulb season is over when the last spring blossom fades! The tulips may be just a memory, but there are many more beautiful blossoms ahead.

*Begonias*

**Ornamental onions** While onions, garlic and leeks are staples of the vegetable garden, ornamental onions are a mainstay of the early-summer flower garden. The most impressive of the ornamental onions is giant onion. Its strong flower stems—up to 4 feet (1.2 m) tall—are topped with grapefruit-sized globes of tightly packed purple flowers in early summer.

Persian onion is slightly smaller but also quite showy, with softball-sized clusters of lavender-purple flowers on 3-foot (90-cm) tall stems. Other popular early summer ornamental onions include star of Persia, drumstick chives and lily leek. Star of Persia grows 10–24 inches (25–60 cm) tall and has cantaloupe-sized heads of starry, pale violet flowers. Drumstick chives have tight, oval-shaped, maroon-red flower heads, not much bigger than a golf ball,

*Tuberous begonias bloom in summer.*

on wiry stems from 2–4 feet (60–120 cm) tall. Lily leek offers a different look from the other ornamental onions, with small heads of yellow flowers in late spring or early summer on stems 8–14 inches (20–35 cm) tall.

**Lovely lilies** Lilies are the stars of the mid- to late-summer garden. True lilies grow from a bulb and have straight stems with many short leaves. Although their flower form resembles that of the daylily, true lilies have individual blooms that can stay open for several days, as opposed to the one-day duration of a daylily blossom. Hybrid lilies are divided into several broad groups. The three main groups are the Asiatic hybrids, trumpet lilies and oriental hybrids. Asiatic hybrids are the first to bloom, flowering from late May into July in most parts of the country. They are noted for their

*Drumstick chives are a common feature of the early summer garden.*

large, beautifully colored and shaped flowers; most are not fragrant but it is possible to find scented cultivars. July and August belong to the trumpet lilies (also known as Aurelian hybrids). They come in a more limited color range (mainly white, yellow, pink and apricot), but their huge, horn-shaped blooms bear a sweet

perfume. Fragrance is also a feature of the oriental hybrids, which bloom from midsummer into fall (depending on the cultivar). Their incredibly beautiful flowers bloom in white and shades of pink to cherry red, often with raised spots.

**Great gladioli** Gladioli are flower-garden favorites with spikes of satin-textured blooms in an almost infinite variety of colors— from pastel pink, white and yellow to rich purple, orange and magenta. Breeders have also created many bicolor types, with various degrees of petal ruffling and feathering. The showy flower spikes are super for bouquets and the blooms generally last a long time. If you plant at two-week intervals from midspring through to midsummer, you can enjoy waves of blooms throughout the growing season.

# BULBS FOR SUMMER continued

**Other super summer bulbs**
If you're looking for more bulbs to brighten up your summer garden, there are some super ones to try.

**Caladiums** The bold, beautiful leaves of caladiums are ideal for accenting the summer shade garden. The fabulous white, green or pink foliage is a real attention-getter, with prominent patterns and veining in contrasting shades of red and green.

**Cannas** Cannas produce clumps of broad, tropical-looking leaves, topped by clusters of brilliant flowers in pink, coral, red, orange, yellow and bicolors. Cannas thrive in warm weather and can reach 10 feet (3 m) tall when they

Crocus

### DELIGHTFUL DAHLIAS

Dahlias are available in many colors and flower forms. The double-flowered types may be more decorative, but for the companion gardener, the daisy-like forms are more attractive to beneficial insects. Wait until the ground has warmed and the danger of frost is long past before planting out market packs or tubers.

get plenty of water. (Dwarf types are also available.) Cannas are hardy in many parts of the south but need to be dug for indoor winter storage elsewhere.

**Dahlias** Dahlias are a signature plant of summer gardens across much of the country. These tender Mexican natives bloom best when the weather is hot and moist. They range in size from compact container plants to 5-foot (1.5-m) tall giants, with showy flowers in an amazing array of colors, sizes and forms.

**Tuberous begonias** Tuberous begonias thrive in partial shade and produce a long show of brilliant flowers during the heat of summer. Try the upright types in shady beds and patio pots; allow cascading types to spill out of hanging baskets and window boxes.

*Asiatic lilies are excellent for adding height to summer beds and borders.*

**Summer care** Some summer bulbs—including lilies and ornamental onions—can live from year to year, so you'll plant them once and enjoy their blooms for years to come. These hardy bulbs are usually planted in fall for bloom the following summer, although lilies can also adapt to early-spring planting. The key is to plant early enough so the root system can get established before warm weather promotes lush topgrowth. Other summer bloomers are classified as tender bulbs. These cold-sensitive beauties may not be able to survive the winter in your area. Unless you live in a warm climate (roughly Zone 8 and south), you'll need to plant gladioli, cannas, dahlias and other tender bulbs in spring to early summer and dig them up in the fall for winter storage indoors. Check which zone you live in on page 311.

# BULBS FOR FALL

**The end of summer doesn't spell the end of the bulb season. The fall show continues with holdovers from summer, such as dahlias, cannas, tuberous begonias and some oriental lilies. These are complemented by bulbs that wait until the return of cold weather to bloom.**

**Fall variety** The charm of fall-blooming bulbs is the grace and freshness they add to the late-season garden. They are wonderful companions for fall-flowering perennials, including asters, mums and Japanese anemone. For extra interest, plant low-growing groundcovers, such as sedums, creeping veronicas, creeping Jenny and thyme, directly over the bulbs. As the bulbs bloom, the groundcover provides a leafy backdrop that is far more pleasing than bare soil. Enjoy the variety in height, color and shape.

**Tall fall flowers** If you're looking to add some excitement to your late-season plantings, consider adding a few magic lilies or naked ladies to your flower beds. Magic lilies, also known as surprise lilies, seem to appear out of nowhere in late summer to early fall. They send up leafless, 2-foot (60-cm) tall stems topped with pale pink, lily-like flowers. The infamous naked lady has a similar habit and look but is less cold-hardy, growing best in Zones 7 to 9 (as compared to Zones 5 to 9 for magic lilies).

*Naked ladies are a good tall addition to the fall garden.*

*Italian arum has striking winter leaves, interesting spring flowers and brilliant fall berries.*

patterned with cream or white markings. The leaves emerge in fall, persist through the winter, and disappear in late spring. Italian arum also has hooded white flowers in spring, but the blooms are not nearly as spectacular as the fall berries.

*Hardy cyclamen make an unusual groundcover under trees and shrubs.*

Both plants produce leaves in spring and early summer; these leaves wither away a month or two before the flowering stems appear. Italian arum is another dramatic addition to the garden. It is especially showy in fall, when it produces round, orange berries in clusters atop thick stems up to 18 inches (45 cm) tall. The berries are complemented by arrow-shaped green leaves that are often

# BULBS FOR FALL continued

**Little late bloomers** Smaller fall-flowering bulbs are equally valuable for late-season interest in garden beds or naturalized in lawns. Naturalizing is planting bulbs in random drifts under trees, in woodlands, or in grassy areas. It's easy to do, and the results look better every year as the bulbs multiply to produce more blooms.

*Combine fall crocus with groundcovers, such as leadwort, to help support the blooms.*

**Showy crocus** Showy crocus has thin, grass-like leaves with a white center stripe which rise in spring, grow and go dormant by midsummer. The stemless flowers emerge from the soil in early- to mid-fall. The goblet-shaped, 1–2-inch (2.5–5-cm) wide blooms are usually lavender purple with violet purple veins.

**Saffron crocus** Saffron crocus blooms with its leaves, which persist through winter and die back in spring. Saffron crocus is the source for the yellow spice, which is made from the dried stigmas (female flower parts). The flowers are similar in height and color to those of showy crocus.

**Dutch crocus** Dutch crocus appears in late winter to early spring; like saffron crocus, it grows

## SPECIAL CARE FOR FALL BULBS

Once you get them in the ground, fall-flowering bulbs are easy to grow. The trick is remembering to plant them at the right time of year. Magic lilies and naked ladies are best planted in early summer, when the bulbs are dormant. Late summer or early fall, just before their bloom starts, is the best time for most other fall-flowering bulbs. Like other bulbs, fall bloomers need to ripen their leaves fully to store enough food for good flowering. Live with their leaves until they wither away—don't cut or pull them off before they turn yellow. If you naturalize fall bulbs in grassy areas, you'll also need to remember to stop mowing as soon as you see the first flower buds emerging from the soil in late summer to early fall. Thick grass may be too competitive for some bulbs, but a sparse lawn—especially under deciduous trees—is just the right environment to help bulbs take hold. Groundcovers also make great companions for naturalized bulbs.

with leaves and flowers at the same time. Goblet-shaped, stemless flowers up to 3 inches (7.5 cm) across bloom just above the leaves. The flowers are white, lavender, purple or yellow; they may be striped with contrasting colors. After bloom, the leaves continue to elongate until they ripen and die back to the ground in early summer.

**Hardy cyclamen**  A charming addition to any garden is the cyclamen. In fall, its pink flowers flutter over the soil on stems up to 6 inches (15 cm) tall. The dark green leaves mottled with frosty silver emerge soon after the blooms fade. Many gardeners prize this late show, especially since hardy cyclamens thrive in shady spots and bring a touch of spring-like beauty to wooded areas. You can combine naturalized cyclamen with other shade-loving plants.

*Showy crocus is excellent for naturalizing.*

# BULBS FOR INDOOR BLOOM

There's nothing more heartwarming to a gardener than a pot of flowering bulbs on the windowsill in the depths of winter. Happily, it's relatively easy to convince most spring bulbs to rush the season a bit. The process is called "forcing," although there's not much force involved. You simply provide a condensed version of the winter the bulbs would otherwise get when growing in the ground outdoors.

**WINTER COLOR**
Extend the gardening season through winter by growing a variety of bulbs for indoor bloom. To get a good show in a small space, you can plant many bulbs close together in one pot; it's okay if the bulbs touch.

## Choosing indoor blooms

Most spring bulbs can be forced, but some perform better in pots than others. Spring-blooming crocus, Siberian squill, glory-of-the-snow and reticulated iris are very easy to chill and bring into bloom. A few tulips that perform especially well in pots include pale orange 'Apricot Beauty', plum purple 'Atilla' and some of the small, rock garden species. Daffodils are also gratifyingly easy to force. Although the large, yellow, trumpet daffodils are traditional favorites, many gardeners also enjoy smaller, free-flowering cultivars such as 'Pipit', 'Hawera', and 'Tete-a-tete'. Hyacinths, too, usually perform well in pots; a few that are especially good include pale pink 'Lady Derby', darker pink 'Pink Pearl', deep blue 'Blue Jacket' and salmon-pink 'Gypsy Queen'. Their sweet scent is ideal for curing a case of the winter blues!

## Preparing bulbs for forcing

The best time to plant bulbs for forcing is in late fall and early winter. Set the bulbs shoulder to shoulder in clay or plastic pots in ordinary, well-drained potting soil. The bulb should just peek above the soil surface. Label the pot with the name of the bulb and the date using a waterproof pen, water it thoroughly and stash it in its winter quarters for chilling. For more ideas on bulbs that are well suited to forcing, check catalogs or garden center displays.

*Hyacinths perform well in pots indoors.*

*Paperwhite narcissus grow without soil.*

# BULBS FOR INDOOR BLOOM continued

**Giving bulbs a chance to chill** Your bulbs need a cool, dark place while they're producing roots. The ideal temperatures for forcing bulbs are between 33° and 45°F (1° and 7°C). Some people use an unheated garage or basement; others set their bulbs in a crawl space or potting shed. You may need to protect the bulbs with a heavy layer of straw, newspapers, or even old blankets to keep them from getting too cold.

*Reticulated irises may bloom in as little as eight weeks.*

If you live in a warm climate, where winter temperatures generally stay above freezing, you will need to create a superficially cold environment for the bulbs.

**Mechanical chilling** Ordinary refrigerators can work well for chilling if you only have a few pots. They're especially useful if you live in a mild climate where outdoor winter temperatures don't get cold enough for proper chilling. An old-fashioned, round-top refrigerator (which does not have a frost-free feature) is the perfect place for storing potted bulbs. Modern refrigerators tend to be rather dry, so you should enclose the potted bulbs in plastic bags to keep them from drying out too much; punch a few small holes for air with a thin metal skewer or a long, thin nail.

**Chilling outdoors** If you don't have another place to chill your bulbs, you can try the mounding technique. Simply set the bulb pots on the ground outdoors (perhaps in a corner of the vegetable garden), cover them with several inches of commercial potting soil and top the whole thing with a thick insulating layer of straw or wood chips. Do not use plastic because it will create conditions that are too damp and will not allow enough oxygen in. Keep in mind when you use mounding that this pile will provide an inviting home for mice and other vermin, which may move in and snack on your bulbs. It's also a messy and sometimes difficult job to dig your bulbs out of a snow-covered pile in the middle of winter.

**Bringing bulbs into bloom**
No matter where you chill your bulbs, check on them every few weeks to see if they need more water. At the same time, look for signs of growth. Your bulbs will signal they're ready to grow in two ways: Tiny white roots will be visible in the drainage holes of the pot, and new shoots will appear at the tops of the bulbs. Crocus and reticulated iris may be ready in as little as eight weeks, while larger bulbs can take twelve weeks or more. When the shoots are an inch or two (2.5–5 cm) tall, bring them inside to a cool, bright window. Fertilize lightly each time you water, and turn the pots regularly to keep the shoots from stretching unevenly toward the light. Keep pots away from radiators, hot-air registers and other heat sources; bulbs like it cool. Keep watering and fertilizing the bulbs until the foliage begins to wither. Transplant the bulbs to your garden at that time, or wait until fall.

**TENDING TO TULIPS**
If you plan to grow tulips indoors, look for those labeled "good for forcing." In catalogs, hybrid tulips are often listed under different divisions, based on their flower forms and times. Look at the photographs and check the descriptions to find the colors, heights and bloom times that will work best for you indoors and outdoors.

# BULBS AND COMPANIONS

**Whether you enjoy growing bulbs in formal displays or more natural-looking plantings, you can add extra interest by choosing compatible companion plants. Ideal companions will enhance the looks of the bulbs at bloom time and help to cover the ripening foliage later on.**

*Tall bulbs are complemented by smaller borders of annuals.*

**Bulbs and annuals** Showy bulbs such as tulips and hyacinths can make a dramatic feature when planted in rows or blocks. But it's even more exciting when you fill in between the bulbs with a pretty carpet of early-blooming annual flowers rather than leaving the soil bare or mulched. Good candidates for planting under bulbs include pansies, Johnny-jump-ups, English daisies and forget-me-nots. As you choose companions, look for flower colors that complement those of your bulbs. Summer-blooming annuals make great companions for bulbs in more informal plantings. As they grow, the annuals cover the bare soil and disguise the maturing bulb leaves. Self-sowing annuals are ideal for this purpose, since they will return year after year with little or no help from you. Good choices for sunny beds include California poppy, corn poppy, cornflower and love-in-a-mist. You can also use annual transplants to fill in around bulbs, tucking them in before or just after the bulb blooms fade.

**Bulbs and perennials** Tall bulbs, including lilies, ornamental onions and crown imperial usually look best near the middle or back of a bed or border. Planting them in between clumps of slightly shorter perennials makes attractive combinations, especially if the perennials bloom at the same time as the bulbs. For instance, Asiatic lilies are especially pretty with shasta daisies, coral bells and Cupid's dart at their feet. You can also combine bulbs with taller perennials, such as delphiniums, mulleins and meadow rues, for a colorful background.

### Bulbs and groundcovers

Combining colorful bulbs with groundcovers is a great way to go. The groundcover provides a pretty backdrop for the bulbs' flowers and then remains to add interest when the bulbs go dormant. Most bulbs have no trouble poking their flowers through a carpet of creeping stems and leaves. Many low-growing, spreading perennials, including thyme, sedums, creeping baby's-breath, creeping veronicas, rock soapwort and sun rose, can be used as groundcovers. In shady areas, try common periwinkle, creeping Jenny, English ivy, spotted lamium and self-heal.

### Bulbs and shrubs

Shrubs make wonderful companions for bulbs. You can create stunning garden scenes by grouping flowering shrubs and bulbs with similar bloom times and colors. Forsythia, for instance, creates a golden glow behind a mass of daffodils, while lilac beautifully echoes the colors of ornamental onions. The arching branches and fragrance of old-fashioned roses make them a classic companion for summer-blooming lilies. Viburnums, mock oranges, hydrangeas, azaleas and rhododendrons are some other wonderful flowering shrubs that look super with spring bulbs. Evergreen shrubs, such as junipers, yews and arborvitaes, complement flowering bulbs throughout the year. Some evergreens have a gold, blue or reddish cast to their foliage; keep this in mind as you combine them with bulbs so you can contrast and complement. White or pink tulips, for instance, can create a soothing scene against the blue-gray cast of a juniper.

### Bulbs and trees

Bulbs and trees can also make colorful garden groupings. Spring bulbs are especially well suited for growing under deciduous trees, since they can get the sunlight they need before the leaves shade the ground. Spring-flowering bulbs that perform well under trees include crocus, squills, snowdrops and daffodils. Summer-flowering bulbs that prefer some shade include tuberous begonias and caladiums. For fall interest, add hardy cyclamen and Italian arum.

*Tulips can accent other shrubs and trees.*

# BULBS FOR CONTAINER GARDENS

Pots filled with bright flowers add a colorful touch to decks, patios and entryways. As you plan your container plantings, don't stop with common favorites like geraniums and petunias; liven them up with some colorful bulbs! Bulbs make excellent companions for annuals in pots, since the annuals usually root in the top soil layer while the bulbs are planted much deeper. The bulbs also benefit from the covering of annuals, which shade the soil and pot to some extent, keeping the bulbs cool. Some bulbs provide beautiful blooms; others provide eye-catching foliage. And there's a bulb for almost every exposure, from bright sunshine to dappled shade.

*Spring bloomers combine well with smaller cool-season annuals.*

**Pots in season** Pots of traditional spring bulbs—including hyacinths, tulips and daffodils—are especially welcome early in the growing season. To coax them into bloom in pots, you need to give them a chilling period, as explained on page 132. These spring bloomers combine beautifully with cool-season annuals, such as pansies, common stock and English

daisy. When warm weather sets in, summer bulbs come into their glory. Asiatic lilies make a lovely show in early summer and look especially good with a cascade of annual blooms beneath them. Other great summer bulbs for containers include small gladioli, Peruvian daffodil and calla lilies. Clumps of cannas or dahlias make a dramatic impact in large pots, tubs and planters, especially if you choose unusual cultivars or grow a variety of cultivars in the one pot.

**Pots for shade** For partially shady spots, tuberous begonias are one of the most enduring and attractive bulbs for potting. They bloom over a long period, in a wide range of colors and flower forms. The cascading types look charming tumbling out of hanging baskets or over the sides of large pots. For extra excitement, grow tuberous begonias with

*Potted color (above and left) is useful in fully paved courtyards and entryways.*

shade-loving annual companions, such as coleus, fibrous begonias, browallia and wishbone flower. Caladium is another good bulb for shady pots and planters, especially when little else is in bloom. It provides substance and color with its tropical-looking, intricately veined leaves in shades of pink, rose, red, green and white.

# BULBS FOR CONTAINER GARDENS continued

**Choosing containers** For best results, choose a large pot that can hold an ample amount of potting mix. Large pots will provide plenty of rooting room for your annuals and bulbs, and they tend to dry out less quickly than small pots. For lilies, choose a pot that is at least 10 inches (25 cm) wide and deep. Smaller bulbs can grow in slightly smaller pots, but they'll also do well in large containers. Big plants such as cannas and dahlias need plenty of room; try them in large planters, hollowed logs or half-barrels.

Large planters can hold a whole garden on a deck or patio.

**Mixed plantings** First cover the bottom of the container with a well-drained commercial potting mix. You'll need to adjust the thickness of this layer to match the needs of the bulbs you're planting. Lily bulbs should sit deep enough to have 5–6 inches (12.5–15 cm) of potting mix over their tops; set smaller bulbs so they're covered with 3–4 inches (7.5–10 cm) of mix. Fill the container with potting mix to within an inch or two (2.5–5 cm) of the rim.

Plant the annual seedlings into the container as you would normally, firming them in well and watering thoroughly around the base.

**Early bulbs** For mixed plantings with warmth-loving summer bulbs—including cannas, dahlias and caladiums—you can get a head start on the season by starting the bulbs indoors. Plant them inside in 6–8-inch (15–20-cm) pots, six to eight weeks before the evening temperatures hit 50°F (10°C). Grow them under lights, in a greenhouse or on a sunny porch or windowsill while you wait for the weather to warm up. When you're ready to set them out into their permanent container, gently remove the bulbs from their pot; it isn't necessary to shake off all the soil. Plant them at the same depth they were growing. Then plant annual seedlings around the sides, being careful not to damage the bulb shoots.

## Caring for container bulbs

Through the season, keep a close eye on your containers to make sure the soil doesn't dry out completely. In hot, dry weather, you may need to water every day, especially for small containers. Fertilize several times during the summer to keep the plants growing vigorously. At the end of the season, dig out the bulbs or tubers of tender bulbs for winter storage. Shake off the soil and let the bulbs air dry for several days. Store them in labeled paper or mesh bags, or bury them in wood shavings, styrofoam packing material or peat moss to prevent the bulbs from drying out too much. Check the bulbs monthly and sprinkle them lightly with water if they look shriveled. Or simply leave the bulbs in their pot and bring the whole pot indoors for winter storage in a cool basement. Continue to check for dryness.

*Use potted bulbs to add height to areas with low-growing plants.*

# BULBS FOR CUTTING GARDENS

The qualities that make bulbs great garden plants—their spectacular, long-lasting blooms and lovely scents—make them ideal cut flowers as well. But after you've put careful thought into combining your bulbs with other plants to create pretty garden scenes, the last thing you want to do is spoil the display by cutting the bulb flowers for indoor arrangements. The answer is to plant extra bulbs in a separate area—called a cutting garden—so you can pick all the flowers you want.

*Collect cut flowers when the buds are just opening.*

## Starting a cutting garden

You can start planning your cutting garden any time of the year, although summer is usually the best time; that will give you plenty of time to prepare the soil and place your bulb orders for fall planting. Bulbs for cutting need the same conditions as those growing in ornamental gardens. A sunny area with fertile soil that is well-drained suits most bulbs. If you have extra room in your vegetable garden, that's usually an ideal site to add a few blocks or rows of flowers for cutting. Otherwise, you'll need to remove grass and weeds from your chosen site, dig the soil to loosen the top 8–10 inches (20–25 cm), and work in liberal amounts of organic matter to provide ideal rooting conditions. Plant hardy bulbs in fall and tender ones in spring after

*Small bulbs, such as grape hyacinths, can be charming for tiny bouquets.*

the soil has warmed sufficiently. During the growing season, water as needed to keep the soil evenly moist. Mulch regularly with organic matter to keep the roots cool; mulching with straw will help to keep the flowers free from dirt. Stake tall plants, such as dahlias and gladioli, to make sure that the stems grow straight.

**Gathering cut flowers** The best time to collect cut flowers is when the buds are just opening, not when they are in full bloom. If you are picking from bulbs that produce many flowers on a single stem, such as lilies or gladioli, cut them when the first few flowers at the bottom are opening. When you cut the flowers, try to do it during a cool part of the day; morning is usually best. Take a bucket of lukewarm water and a sharp pair of clippers with you. Pick flowers with as few leaves as possible, so the bulbs can store enough energy for the next bloom season. As you snip the stem from the rest of the plant, make a sloping, rather than straight, cut; this opens up a little more room for the stems to absorb water. Immediately plunge the cut flowers into the bucket, so they are in water up to the base of the flower. (If you are cutting dahlias,

*Use stakes to keep long stems straight.*

sear the bottom of the stem with the flame from a match before putting it in the water.)

# GROWING BULBS

**P**lanting bulbs for spring bloom requires some imagination on your part. After all, when you buy a six-pack of begonias, you can see just what you're getting. But when you buy bulbs, you get a bagful of promises: A bunch of brown-wrapped packets of plant energy that have the potential to transform themselves into colorful crocus or delightful daffodils. With proper planting and good care, your bulbs will be able to fulfill that potential, adding welcome color to your yard year after year. This chapter has all the information you need to grow strong, healthy bulbs and keep them vigorous for seasons to come. As long as you give them the right growing conditions, bulbs are guaranteed to bloom.

# BUYING HEALTHY BULBS

**A key part of growing bulbs successfully is starting with healthy plants. By being a smart shopper, you can get the best bulbs for your garden at the best possible price.**

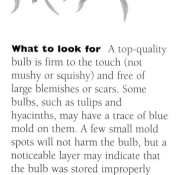

*Fritillaria imperalis*

*Bulbs come in many shapes and sizes.*

**Money well spent** With bulbs, as with most things, you get what you pay for. High-quality, full-sized bulbs command top dollar, based on the amount of time and labor it takes to produce them, but you can rely on them for spectacular results. A higher price, however, doesn't always mean that one tulip or daffodil cultivar is better than another. New cultivars tend to be much more expensive than older ones that have been around awhile. New cultivars are fun to try, but the proven performers are usually both economical and highly dependable.

**What to look for** A top-quality bulb is firm to the touch (not mushy or squishy) and free of large blemishes or scars. Some bulbs, such as tulips and hyacinths, may have a trace of blue mold on them. A few small mold spots will not harm the bulb, but a noticeable layer may indicate that the bulb was stored improperly before being offered for sale. Look for bulbs that show little or no root or shoot growth except for a pale growth bud at the top. (Lilies are an exception, since they often have fleshy roots attached.) It's wise to shop early in the season so you can get bulbs before they dry out from sitting in the store. Make sure the bulbs you buy come from cultivated stock and were not collected from the wild. If you can't tell, ask the supplier or find another source.

**Handling bulbs** You've shopped carefully to get the best bulbs. Now follow through and handle them properly when you get them home. In most cases, it's best to plant the bulbs within a few days so they'll have plenty of time to adapt to their new home and send out a good crop of roots. If you can't plant right away, store your bulbs in a cool, dark, relatively dry

*Plant bulbs in drifts or large clumps to create a dramatic display.*

place until you're ready for them. Keep them in the paper or mesh bags they came in. A refrigerator can be handy for storing spring bulbs but is too cold for summer bulbs, such as gladioli or dahlias.

Keep summer bulbs in a cool spot—such as a closet in a garage or basement—until you're ready to start them indoors or plant them outdoors after your last spring frost date.

# PLANTING BULBS

**EASY PLANTING**
It's easy to plant in a prepared bed: Just dig a hole, set in the bulbs, and cover them with the soil you remove. When you're planting in masses, it's usually easiest to dig a large planting area that can hold many bulbs at once.

The great thing about most bulbs is that they can adapt to a wide range of growing conditions. But if you really want your bulbs to thrive, it's worth putting some thought into giving them the best conditions possible. Take a little time to prepare a good growing site and plant your bulbs properly. Then you can stand back and enjoy the bounty of beautiful flowers in the years to come.

**Knowing your soil** Many bulbs can grow for years in the same place, so it's worth putting some effort into preparing an ideal planting site. How much work that will take depends on what kind of soil you have. Bulbs tend to thrive in soil that's on the loamy or sandy side, since good drainage is critical for most bulbs. Very sandy soil, however, can be too dry and infertile. Clayey soil holds a good amount of nutrients, but it can also hold too much water. Loamy soil tends to hold an adequate supply of nutrients and moisture without getting waterlogged.

**Getting the soil ready** If your soil isn't naturally loamy, you can improve its drainage and fertility by adding some organic matter

Scilla sibirica

*Get good blooms from your soil the first year by planting in clumps, not as individuals.*

before you plant your bulbs. Spread a 3-inch (7.5-cm) layer of compost or chopped leaves over the planting area, then work it into the top 10–12 inches (25–30 cm) of soil. When you're only planting small bulbs, such as crocus and grape hyacinths, you can loosen just the top 6 inches

(15 cm) of soil. Or, if you're digging individual holes, work a handful of organic matter into the soil at the base of each hole, and add another handful to the soil you use to refill the hole. As it breaks down, the organic matter will release a small but steady supply of nutrients for good bulb growth.

# PLANTING BULBS continued

### Planting in beds and borders

Once you've loosened the soil, planting is easy—just dig the hole to the proper depth, pop in the bulb and cover it with soil. The proper depth will vary, depending on what bulbs you're growing. A general rule of thumb is that the base of a bulb or corm should be planted three to four times as deep as the height of the bulb. For example, a crocus corm measuring 1-inch (2.5-cm) high should be planted 3–4 inches (7.5–10 cm) deep; a 2-inch (5-cm) high tulip bulb needs a hole 6–8 inches (15–20 cm) deep. If your soil is on the sandy side, plant a bit deeper. Set the bulb in the hole with the pointed growth bud facing upward. If you can't tell which side should be up—as often happens with small bulbs such as Grecian windflowers—set the bulb

**SMALL PLANTINGS**
When you're planting just a few bulbs for a feature in a garden bed, or in grassy areas, use a small trowel or a special bulb planter to make individual holes.

on its side or just drop it in the hole and hope for the best. Most bulbs have a strong will to grow, and they'll find a way to send up their shoots. Space the bulbs so each has ample room to grow. Generally, leave about 6 inches (15 cm) between large bulbs and 1–3 inches (2.5–7.5 cm) between small bulbs. Once you've got the spacing the way you want it, carefully replace the soil around the bulbs to refill the hole. Firm the soil by patting it with your hand, then water thoroughly.

### Small bulbs for grassy areas

When you choose to plant bulbs in a lawn or meadow, you don't have the luxury of preparing a nice, loose planting area all at once. Fortunately, the bulbs that grow well in these situations are pretty tough. The easiest bulbs to plant are the small ones, such as crocus and Siberian squill. Simply get down on your hands and knees with a narrow trowel, dandelion digger or garden knife. Insert the tool into the soil to lift up a flap of turf, or wiggle the tool back and forth to make a small hole. Insert the bulb, firm the soil and sod over it, and water thoroughly so it is soaked.

### Big bulbs for grassy areas

For planting bigger bulbs in lawns and meadows, it's often easier to use a shovel or spade to remove a larger section of turf, about 12 inches (30 cm) square in one go. Loosen the soil to the proper depth, plant the bulbs, replace the turf and water. You can also buy special bulb planting tools to make individual holes for your large bulbs. Hand-held planters look like deep cookie cutters and work pretty much the same way. They are fairly inexpensive but can be really tiring to use. A similar type of planter that's mounted on a handle is a little easier to use, since you can push the cutting edge into the ground with your foot instead of your hand. For even easier planting, try an auger attachment that connects to a regular hand-held power drill. These tools can be hard to use around rocks and tree roots, but they let you make many holes quickly.

*Plant large bulbs together in one section.*

# CARING FOR BULBS

Hardy bulbs—including daffodils, crocus and other dependable favorites—are about as close to "no work" as you can get. You just plant them once, and they come back year after year. Many will even multiply over time to produce large sweeps of blooms. But as with any other garden plants, a little extra care from you can help your bulbs grow and look better. In this section, you'll find tips for keeping your bulbs in the best condition possible, with good gardening practices such as watering, mulching, fertilizing, staking, deadheading and controlling pests and diseases.

Keep the roots moist with mulch.

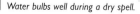

Water bulbs well during a dry spell.

**Watering well** Watering is most important when your bulbs are actively growing. This means fall and spring for fall- or spring-blooming bulbs and spring through summer for summer-blooming bulbs. During these times, most bulbs can survive a moderate drought without watering, but they may not bloom well the following year. To get your bulbs off to a good start, water them thoroughly at planting time. If there's a dry spell when your bulbs are growing, water them as you would your other garden plants to keep the soil evenly moist.

## Mulching for good health

Mulching your bulbs is one of the best ways to keep them healthy. Mulch will help to hold moisture in the soil and minimize rapid temperature changes, providing ideal rooting conditions. It shades the soil and helps to keep bulbs cool, protecting the shoots of bulbs from being lured out of the ground too early in spring. Mulch also benefits summer-flowering bulbs, such as lilies, which dislike hot, dry soil. Mulch discourages weeds from sprouting and prevents rain from splashing soil onto a bulb's leaves and flowers, keeping your bulb plants clean and discouraging disease problems.

## Choosing a mulch

There's no one ideal mulch. They each do a similar job, but look very different, so when you shop for mulches, choose the kind that looks best to you and that you can afford.

Mulches help to keep weeds down.

Depending on where you live, you may be able to find locally available materials—such as cocoa bean shells or pine needles—at good prices. Wood chips or shredded bark are available in most parts of the country. (Look for small chips, not big bark nuggets.) A mulch of pea-sized gravel can work well, too. Homemade or purchased compost can make a good mulch, either alone or as a layer under another mulch. A "living mulch" of low-growing annuals or perennials may be the best of all, since it serves the purpose of a regular mulch and provides flowers as well.

## CARING FOR BULBS continued

**EXTRA CARE**
Fertilize both spring-blooming and fall-flowering bulbs in spring. Summer-flowering bulbs usually grow best with several small applications of fertilizer in early- to mid-summer. You can also add bonemeal to the soil in fall.

**When to mulch** Mulch your bulbs after planting in fall or spring. Apply a 2-inch (5-cm) layer over the soil. Avoid putting on too much, or your bulbs may have trouble poking their shoots up through the mulch. To protect hardy bulbs (such as daffodils and crocus), add more mulch each fall to keep it at the right depth.

**Fertilizing** Most bulbs will get along just fine without a lot of extra fertilizer. Working compost or other organic matter into the soil at planting time and using it as a mulch will provide much of the nutrient supply your bulbs need. For top-notch growth, however, you can also sprinkle commercial organic fertilizer over the soil, following the package directions. Use a mix blended especially for bulbs, if you can find one; otherwise, a general garden fertilizer is acceptable. Tuberous begonias, lilies and other bulbs growing in pots benefit from weekly or bimonthly doses of liquid fertilizer. Spray the leaves or water the plants with diluted fish emulsion or compost tea (made by soaking a shovelful of finished compost in a bucket of water for about a week, then straining out the soaked compost).

**When to stake** The easiest approach to staking plants is to reduce the need for it. Whenever possible, site your bulbs on the sheltered side of hedges, fences or screens, so the plants will be protected from the wind. Also look for compact cultivars of your favorite flowers; shorter stems are less prone to damage. Of course, there are also times when you

*Individual stakes support tall stems. For a more blended look, use green stakes.*

don't want all of your bulbs to stand stiff and upright. Perhaps you enjoy a more casual look, where the bulbs are allowed to lean against and mingle with other plants. If you aren't sure which of your bulbs would benefit from staking, watch them for a year or two and see which look like they could use some help.

**Choosing stakes** There are two tricks to staking bulbs properly—the first is choosing stakes that blend into your garden. There is a good variety available in both metal and wood. Materials painted green or brown tend to be the least noticeable. Some gardeners use twiggy tree or shrub prunings for plant supports. These brushy stakes are plentiful and free, and they are nearly invisible in the garden when the plants grow up through them. Select supports that are about three-quarters of the

potential height, allowing another 6 inches (15 cm) for the part of the stake that will be under the ground. Top-heavy plants, such as lilies, need stakes that are about the same height as the mature height of the plant.

**Placing stakes** The second trick is putting the stakes in early, as soon as the bulb shoots are visible. Place the stake behind the plant so the support is less visible. Insert each stake a few inches away from the shoot to avoid stabbing the bulb. Push the stake at least 6 inches (15 cm) into the soil to steady it. As the bulb shoot grows, attach it to the stake with a flexible tie, such as green or brown yarn or string. Tie a knot to the stake, loop the yarn or string around the stem, and then tie it back to the stake. Never choke a stem by tying a knot directly around it. Start tying near the base of the stem; add

# CARING FOR BULBS continued

another tie every 6–8 inches (15–20 cm) as the stem grows.

**Deadheading and disbudding**
To gardeners, deadheading means removing faded flowers and developing seedpods from plants. Some gardeners routinely deadhead large bulbs, such as daffodils, hyacinths and tulips. They claim that this prevents the bulbs from expending energy on seed production, directing all their energy to ripening their leaves and replenishing their food reserves. However, many bulbs grow just fine year after year if allowed to set seed; in fact, they may even reseed and form large sweeps of bloom. To form a larger bloom on individual plants, some gardeners use disbudding, which involves removing the side buds of a plant to leave one or two main buds on

*When you want the biggest dahlia flowers, remove the side buds.*

each stem. Whether or not to deadhead or disbud is really a matter of personal choice.

**How to deadhead** If you do choose to deadhead your bulbs, pinch off the developing seedpod with your fingernails, or cut it

off with clippers. For a neater appearance, you can instead cut the seedpod and the stem beneath it down to the top stem leaves (if there are any) or to the ground. On lilies, remove only the top part of the stem that holds the seedpods; don't cut off any leaves.

**Under attack** Most bulbs suffer from few pests and diseases. Those pests and diseases that do attack are usually the same as those you find on your other garden plants. Some of the most common problems include aphids, whiteflies, Japanese beetles, spider mites, slugs and snails, thrips, cutworms, Botrytis blight and powdery mildew. Deer, rabbits, mice and other animal pests can also plague bulb gardeners.

*Good air circulation can prevent powdery mildew.*

### Controlling pests and diseases

You can try to discourage pests by planting daffodil bulbs, which are poisonous and usually avoided by animals. Some say that the strong odor of crown imperial bulbs and plants repels voles, mice and squirrels. Pet dogs and cats can be useful for discouraging local wildlife, but they may cause damage, too. It is possible to take preventive measures when planting where mice, voles, shrews and squirrels are especially troublesome. Although it takes some doing, you can fashion bulb crates—sort of like lobster traps—out of sturdy wire mesh. Choose a mesh that has a grid size of about 1 inch (2.5 cm). Small animals can sneak through larger mesh, while your bulb shoots may not be able to poke through smaller mesh. Dig a hole large enough to hold the crate, so the top is just below the soil surface. Place the crate in the hole and backfill with some of the soil you removed. Plant your bulbs in the crate, then fill the rest of the cage with soil and close the lid. Use the remaining soil to cover the lid and fill in around the rest of the cage.

*Foil animal pests by planting bulbs in buried wire crates.*

FLOWERING BULBS

# A GUIDE
## TO BULBS

Like the guide to annuals, this guide to bulbs provides you with information about some of the many flowering bulbs that are available to you. Each entry has a color photograph, a description of the plant, details on the conditions that best suit the plant and suggestions on how to use the plant in your landscape. Not all the entries included in this guide are common or popular; some are unusual, and worth trying because they will offer added interest to your garden in spring, and sometimes throughout the year.

# GRECIAN WINDFLOWER

*Anemone blanda* Ranunculaceae

Grecian windflowers bloom in mid- to late-spring in most areas; in warm Southern gardens, they may appear in late winter or early spring. They thrive in sun or light shade.

**Description** Grows from knobbly tubers to produce carpets of deeply lobed, toothed, sage green leaves. Daisy-like blue, pink, mauve or white spring flowers up to 2 inches (5 cm) across bloom just above the ferny leaves.

**Height and spread** Height of leaves and flowers to 6 inches (15 cm); spread is 4–6 inches (10–15 cm), depending on the dryness of the soil.

**Best site and climate** Full sun to partial shade (ideally under deciduous trees and shrubs); average to moist, well-drained soil. Zones 5–8.

**Growing guidelines** Buy and plant the tubers in late spring through early fall. Soak them overnight before planting, and set them in individual holes or larger planting areas dug about 2 inches (5 cm) deep. It can be hard to tell which side is up. If you can see a shallow depression on one side, plant with that side up; otherwise, plant the tubers on their sides or just drop them into the hole. Space the tubers 4–6 inches (10–15 cm) apart. Grecian windflowers propagate themselves by spreading and self-sowing.

**Landscape uses** Naturalize masses of Grecian windflowers under trees for sheets of spring color. The results will look better and better each year as the bulbs multiply to produce more blooms. They combine well with daffodils and with shade-loving annuals. Try them in well-drained pots and window boxes, too.

**Cultivars** 'White Splendor' has large, white-petaled, yellow-centered flowers. 'Blue Star' produces deep blue flowers.

*Anemone blanda*

# ITALIAN ARUM

*Arum italicum* Aracae

By late summer, the spring flowers of Italian arum mature into columns of reddish orange berries. These colorful spikes add interest until the new leaves appear in fall.

**Description** Italian arum grows from tubers. It blooms in mid- to late-spring and has a greenish white, hood-like spathe sheltering a narrow column known as the spadix. These unusual flowers are interesting, but the plant is mainly grown for its arrowhead-shaped, semiglossy, dark green leaves that are marked with creamy white lines. The leaves emerge in fall and last through winter and spring. They die off in summer, becoming curled and brown just as the flowers transform into clumps of berries.

**Height and spread** Height 12–18 inches (30–45 cm); spread to 12 inches (30 cm).

**Best site and climate** Partial shade; average, well-drained soil with organic matter. Zones 6–10.

**Growing guidelines** Plant in late summer or early fall. Set the tubers into individual holes or larger planting areas dug 2–3 inches (5–7.5 cm) deep. Space the tubers 8–12 inches (20–30 cm) apart. Keep the soil moist during leaf growth and flowering. For propagation, divide in early fall; otherwise, allow plants to form handsome clumps.

**Landscape uses** With its striking winter leaves, interesting spring flowers and showy fall fruit,

*Arum italicum*

Italian arum adds spectacular multiseason interest in any garden. It also looks marvelous in masses along streams and in woodland gardens, when planted under trees to emerge through beds of English ivy and common periwinkle. For a dramatic display in late summer, combine it with magic lilies and naked ladies. For an extra-pretty picture in late winter, combine it with hellebores and snowdrops.

# COMMON CAMASS

*Camassia quamash* Liliaceae

In full sun, steady soil moisture is critical for success with common camass; in lightly shaded spots, the bulbs can withstand drier conditions.

**Other common names**
Quamash, wild hyacinth.

**Description** In spring, common camass produces grassy clumps of long, narrow, gray-green leaves. By late spring, these clumps have sent up leafless stems topped with dense, spiky, flower clusters. These spikes are made up of many 1–2-inch (2.5–5-cm) wide, star-shaped flowers in white or pale to deep blue. Usually by mid- to late-summer, the leaves have completely died off.

**Height and spread** Height usually 24–30 inches (60–75 cm); spread to 12 inches (30 cm).

**Best site and climate** Full sun to partial shade; moist but not waterlogged soil. Zones 4–8.

**Growing guidelines** The bulbs usually aren't available for sale at garden centers, so you'll probably have to buy them from a mail-order source. Plant the bulbs as soon as they arrive in fall. Set them in individual holes or in larger planting areas dug about 4 inches (10 cm) deep. Space the bulbs 8–10 inches (20–25 cm) apart. Cut down faded flower stems after bloom. Divide in late summer if needed for propagation; otherwise, leave bulbs undisturbed to form showy clumps.

*Camassia quamash*

**Landscape uses** Common camass is a natural choice for planting in low spots or along streams and ponds. It grows well in moist meadow and bog gardens and is a good companion to other moisture-loving shrubs and perennials. After watering, use organic mulch on the soil around the plants; it will help to maintain even moisture levels when conditions are dry.

# CANNA

### Canna x generalis  Cannaceae

Cannas are drought-tolerant, but they grow even better with mulch and watering during dry spells. Pinch off spent flowers to prolong bloom.

**Description**  Cannas are classified as tender bulbs because they are sensitive to cold and may not survive harsh winters. They grow from thick rhizomes. They produce tall, sturdy stems with large, oval, green or reddish purple leaves from spring until frost. The stems are topped with showy clusters of broad-petaled flowers up to 5 inches (12.5 cm) across from mid- through late-summer. The flowers bloom in shades of pink, red, orange and yellow, as well as bicolors.

**Height and spread**  Height 2–6 feet (60–180 cm) or more; spread 12–24 inches (30–60 cm).

**Best site and climate**  Full sun to partial shade; average to moist, well-drained soil with added organic matter. Usually hardy in Zones 7–10; elsewhere, grown as annuals or stored indoors during the winter months.

**Growing guidelines**  For the earliest show, start rhizomes indoors in pots about a month before your last frost date. Set out started plants two to three weeks after the last frost date. Or plant rhizomes directly into the garden around that time, setting them 3–4 inches (7.5–10 cm) deep and 12–18 inches (30–45 cm) apart. North of Zone 7 (and in Zone 7, if you want to ensure survival), dig the rhizomes before or just after the first frost and store them indoors for winter. In warm areas, divide the rhizomes every three to four years in spring.

**Landscape uses**  Grow them alone in masses, or plant them with annuals and perennials in beds and borders. Cannas also grow well in containers.

*Canna x generalis*

161

# DUTCH CROCUS

*Crocus vernus* Iridaceae

Dutch crocus are a welcome sight after a long, cold winter. After bloom, the leaves continue to elongate until they ripen and die back to the ground in early summer.

**Description** Dutch crocus grow from small corms. They appear in late winter to early spring, with leaves and flowers at the same time. The grass-like leaves are thin and green with a white center stripe. Goblet-shaped, stemless flowers up to 3 inches (7.5 cm) across bloom just above the leaves. The flowers are white, lavender, purple or yellow; they may be striped with contrasting colors. Most have tall, yellow stamens that reach the top of the petals.

**Height and spread** Height of leaves to 8 inches (20 cm); flowers usually to 4 inches (10 cm) tall. Spread 1–3 inches (2.5–7.5 cm).

**Best site and climate** Full sun to partial shade (under deciduous trees and shrubs or in lawns); average, well-drained soil. Zones 3–8.

*Crocus vernus*

**Growing guidelines** Plant the corms in fall. Set them pointed side up in individual holes, or in larger planting areas, plant a few in holes that are at least 2–4 inches (5–10 cm) deep. Space the corms 2 inches (5 cm) apart. Dutch crocus usually return year after year and spread to form showy clumps. Interplanting crocus corms with daffodil bulbs (which are toxic if eaten) may help discourage damage from mice.

**Landscape uses** Include Dutch crocus in garden beds and borders for early color. Grow them in containers for outdoor spring bloom or for winter forcing indoors. They are excellent for naturalizing in lawn areas and meadows. Remember, if you choose an area that needs mowing, you will have to wait until late spring, which is when the leaves have turned yellow.

# Hardy Cyclamen

*Cyclamen hederifolium* Primulaceae

Hardy cyclamen grow well under shrubs and trees even in dry summer shade—and are attractive through most of the year. Top-dress with a thin layer of compost in late summer.

**Description** Hardy cyclamen grow from smooth tubers. They bloom in early fall, with leafless flower stalks topped with pink or white flowers. The 1-inch (2.5 cm) long, goblet-shaped, nodding flowers have upward-pointing petals. Heart-shaped, green leaves marked with silver emerge shortly after the blooms finish. The leaves die back by midsummer.

**Height and spread** Height and spread of flowers and foliage 4–6 inches (10–15 cm).

**Best site and climate** Partial shade; average, well-drained soil. Zones 5–9.

**Growing guidelines** Many commercial cyclamen sources sell wild-collected tubers. Avoid supporting this irresponsible practice: Buy nursery-propagated tubers or start your own from

*Cyclamen hederifolium*

seed. Soak the seed overnight, then sow it ¼ inch (6 mm) deep in a pot. Enclose the pot in a plastic bag, then set it in a dark place. Check every month for signs of sprouting; this can take from just a few weeks to a few years to occur. Set the plants into the garden in spring or summer. Or plant dormant tubers in a shallow amount of soil in summer, making sure the smooth, unmarked side is on the bottom. The top of the tuber should be about 1 inch (2.5 cm) below the soil surface. Space hardy cyclamen 6 inches (15 cm) apart.

**Landscape uses** Hardy cyclamen look good in shady spots with ferns and hellebores. They make an unusual groundcover under trees and shrubs, with the handsome leaves providing interest and color to the garden after the blooms have died off.

# CHECKERED LILY

*Fritillaria meleagris* Liliaceae

The nodding flowers of checkered lilies add a charming touch to spring gardens. Naturalize them in wild areas, or plant them in clumps in beds and borders.

**Other common names**
Guinea-hen flower, snake's head lily, snake's head fritillan.

**Description** Checkered lily grows from small bulbs. Slender, arching stems with narrow, gray-green leaves rise in early spring. By midspring, broad, nodding, bell-like blooms dangle from the ends of the slim stems. The 1–2-inch (2.5–5-cm) long flowers range in color from white through to deep purple; many are marked with a checkered pattern, similar to the pattern on a snake's skin or a guinea-hen's feathers. Checkered lilies die back to the ground by midsummer.

**Height and spread** Height to 12 inches (30 cm); spread 2–4 inches (5–10 cm).

**Best site and climate** Partial shade; average, well-drained soil. Zones 3–8.

**Growing guidelines** Plant in early fall, as soon as the bulbs are available. Dig the holes or planting areas 2–3 inches (5–7.5 cm) deep. Space bulbs 4–6 inches (10–15 cm) apart. Leave established clumps undisturbed to form large sweeps of spring color. Checkered lilies can tolerate some dryness, but generally need consistent, even moisture in order to thrive.

*Fritillaria meleagris*

**Landscape uses** Checkered lilies do well when naturalized in masses. Or grow them in beds and borders under deciduous trees; these small bulbs combine beautifully with all kinds of ferns and hellebores.

**Cultivars** 'Alba' is a checkered lily with white flowers.

# COMMON SNOWDROP

*Galanthus nivalis* Amaryllidaceae

Common snowdrops are among the earliest flowers to bloom in the spring garden. Established bulbs are trouble-free; they will spread and reseed freely.

**Description**  Common snowdrops grow from small bulbs. Each bulb produces two or three flat, narrow, green leaves and an upright to arching green flower stem in midwinter through to early spring. Dainty, nodding flowers to 1 inch (2.5 cm) long bloom at the tips of the stems in late winter or early spring. The single or double flowers are white; each of the shorter, inner petals has a green tip. The plants will die back to the ground by early summer.

**Height and spread**  Height of flowers and foliage to about 6 inches (15 cm); spread 2–3 inches (5–7.5 cm).

**Best site and climate**  Full sun to partial shade; average to moist, well-drained soil with added organic matter. Zones 3–9.

**Growing guidelines**  Plant bulbs in fall. Set them in individual holes or larger planting areas dug 3–4 inches (7.5–10 cm) deep. Space bulbs 3–4 inches (7.5–10 cm) apart.

**Landscape uses**  Common snowdrop looks lovely when grown in clumps with other early flowers, such as snow crocus and Christmas rose. It also looks pretty naturalized in lawns, or as groundcover under deciduous

*Galanthus nivalis*

trees and shrubs. (If you grow it in lawns, you'll have to wait until the leaves have turned yellow or brown to mow.) Combine it with annuals and perennials that also produce white blooms to create an elegant garden.

**Cultivars**  'Flore Pleno' has double flowers.

# Hyacinth

*Hyacinthus orientalis* Liliaceae

After the first year, hyacinth bloom spikes tend to be smaller; in some cases, they may not flower at all. Plant new bulbs every year or two to ensure a good display.

**Description** Hyacinths grow from plump bulbs. Sturdy shoots with wide, strap-shaped, green leaves and upright flower stalks emerge in early spring. By midspring, each stalk is topped with a dense spike of starry, 1-inch (2.5-cm) wide, powerfully fragrant flowers. The single or double flowers bloom in a wide range of colors, including white, pink, red, orange, yellow, blue and purple. The flowers have a powerful, sweet fragrance. Hyacinths go dormant in early summer.

**Height and spread** Height 8–12 inches (20–30 cm); spread to 4 inches (15 cm).

**Best site and climate** Full sun or under deciduous trees; average, well-drained soil with added organic matter. Zones 4–8.

*Hyacinthus orientalis*

**Growing guidelines** Plant bulbs in mid-fall. Set them in individual holes or larger planting areas dug 5–6 inches (12.5–15 cm) deep. Space the bulbs 6–10 inches (15–20 cm) apart. Double-flowered types may need staking because they are heavy and tend to droop, especially in rain and wind. Remove spent flower stalks. For propagation, dig up and divide crowded clumps as the leaves die.

**Landscape uses** Hyacinths contribute spring color and fragrance to flower beds and borders. Combine them with primroses and pansies for extra cheer. Try them in containers for spring bloom outdoors or winter forcing indoors.

**Cultivars** 'Carnegie' has white flowers. 'Delft Blue' produces pale blue blooms.

# RETICULATED IRIS

*Iris reticulata* Iridaceae

Reticulated irises return year after year to grace your garden with their delicate spring flowers. Tuck them into beds, borders and rock gardens; they look great in pots too.

**Description** Reticulated irises grow from small bulbs. The dainty blue, purple or white, early spring flowers have three upright petals (known as standards) and three outward-arching petals (known as falls). The falls have gold and/or white markings. The grass-like, dark green leaves are short at bloom time but elongate after the flowers fade; they ripen, turn a yellow-brown and die back to the ground by early summer.

*Iris reticulata*

**Height and spread** Height of flowers is about 4–6 inches (10–15 cm); leaves grow to about 12 inches (30 cm) tall. The plants spread to 2 inches (5 cm).

**Best site and climate** Full sun or partial shade under deciduous trees; grows best in sandy to average, well-drained soil. Zones 5–9.

**Growing guidelines** Plant the bulbs in fall. Set them in individual holes or larger planting areas dug 3–4 inches (7.5–10 cm) deep. For propagation, lift and divide clumps after the leaves turn yellow. Reticulated irises are easy to chill.

**Landscape uses** The delicate, lightly fragrant blooms are beautiful in spring beds and borders. For extra depth of color, combine them with Grecian windflowers and early crocus. Reticulated irises also grow well in pots for spring bloom outdoors or winter forcing indoors.

**Cultivars** 'Cantab' is pale blue with orange-marked falls. 'Clairette' has sky blue standards and deep blue falls marked with white. 'Harmony' is medium blue with gold markings. 'Natascha' has white flowers with yellow-striped falls.

# MAGIC LILY

*Lycoris squamigera* Amaryllidaceae

Magic lily bulbs produce leaves in spring and leafless flower stalks in late summer. Some gardeners like to combine them with bushy plants to hide the bare stems.

**Description** Slender, greenish brown, leafless stems rise from the ground in late summer to early fall. They are topped with loose clusters of funnel-shaped, rosy pink flowers up to 4 inches (10 cm) long. The broad, strap-shaped, green leaves usually begin to emerge several weeks after the blooms fade. The foliage elongates in spring and dies back to the ground in summer, one to two months before new blooms appear.

**Height and spread** Height of flowers to 24 inches (60 cm); leaves to 12 inches (30 cm). Spread to 6 inches (15 cm).

**Best site and climate** Full sun to partial shade; average, well-drained soil that's dry in summer. Zones 5–9.

**Growing guidelines** Plant magic lily bulbs as soon as they are available in midsummer. Set in individual holes or larger planting areas dug 4–5 inches (10–12.5 cm) deep. Space bulbs about 8 inches (20 cm) apart. Water thoroughly during dry spells in fall and spring. Protect the leaves over winter with a loose mulch, such as evergreen branches, pine needles or straw. For propagation, divide bulbs in early- to mid-summer, as soon as the leaves have died; otherwise, leave the bulbs undisturbed to form large clumps.

**Landscape uses** Magic lilies grow best when naturalized on slopes, in groundcovers, around rock beds and in areas where they generally won't be disturbed.

*Lycoris squamigera*

# GRAPE HYACINTH

*Muscari armeniacum* Liliaceae

Once planted, grape hyacinths are trouble-free. They naturalize well under trees and shrubs, and they look quite attractive combined with groundcovers.

**Description** Grape hyacinths grow from small bulbs. The narrow, grass-like, green leaves appear in fall and elongate through the spring. The clumps are accented by short, leafless stems topped with dense spikes of grape-like blooms in early spring. The individual purple-blue, white-rimmed flowers are only ¼ inch (6 mm) wide. The leaves turn yellow and die back to the ground by early summer.

**Height and spread** Height of flowers and foliage 6–8 inches (15–20 cm); spread 3–4 inches (7.5–10 cm).

**Best site and climate** Full sun to partial shade (under deciduous trees and shrubs); average, well-drained soil. Zones 4–8.

**Growing guidelines** Plant grape hyacinth bulbs in early- to mid-fall, as soon as they become available in the garden centers. Set them in individual holes or larger planting areas dug 2–3 inches (5–7.5 cm) deep. Space the bulbs about 4 inches (10 cm) apart. For propagation, divide just after the leaves die back in early summer. Otherwise, leave the bulbs undisturbed to form sweeps of spring color.

*Muscari armeniacum*

**Landscape uses** Scatter the bulbs liberally throughout flower beds and borders. Mix grape hyacinths with primroses, pansies, daffodils and tulips for an unforgettable spring show. You can also grow them in containers for outdoor bloom in spring or indoor forcing in winter. The sweet scent is mild enough for small spaces.

# TULIPS

*Tulipa* hybrids Liliaceae

Hybrid tulips often bloom poorly after the first year.
For a great show each year, pull them out after bloom and
replace them with summer annuals; plant new tulips in fall.

**Description** Tulips grow from plump, pointed bulbs. The bulbs produce broad, dusty-green leaves that are sometimes striped with maroon in early- to mid-spring. The slender, upright, usually unbranched flower stems are topped with showy single or double flowers up to 4 inches (10 cm) across. They bloom in practically every color, including white and near black; some also have stripes. By midsummer, leaves gradually turn yellow and die back to the ground.

**Height and spread** Height from 6–30 inches (15–90 cm), depending on the cultivar; spread 6–10 inches (15–25 cm).

**Best site and climate** Full sun to partial shade; average, well-drained soil. Usually best in Zones 3–8; in Zones 9 and 10, treat hybrid tulips as annuals and plant precooled bulbs in late fall.

**Growing guidelines** Plant bulbs in mid- to late fall. Set them in individual holes or larger planting areas dug 4–6 inches (10–15 cm) deep. (If possible, planting 8 inches [20 cm] deep is even better, since it can discourage bulbs from splitting and in turn promote better flowering in following years.) Space bulbs about 6 inches (15 cm) apart. Pinch off the developing seedpods after flowering, and allow the leaves to yellow before removing them. Or treat the hybrids like annuals and pull them out after their blooming season finishes.

**Landscape uses** The stately, colorful flowers of tulips are an indispensable part of the spring garden. In beds and borders, grow them with daffodils, pansies, primroses, bleeding hearts, grape

*Tulipa* hybrids

hyacinths and forget-me-not flowers; for fresh arrangements, pick them when the flowers are fully colored but in bud. Keep them in a vase away from direct sunlight. You can grow tulips in containers and force them for winter bloom indoors.

**Cultivars** In catalogs, hybrid tulips are often listed under different divisions, based on their flower forms and bloom times. Look at the photographs and check the descriptions to find the colors, heights and bloom times that will work best in your garden. 'Angelique' has ruffled, petal-packed, double, pale pink flowers on 16-inch (40-cm) tall stems. 'Apricot Beauty' has beautiful peach-colored blooms on 14-inch (35-cm) tall stems. 'Ballade' grows to 24 inches (60 cm) tall and has reddish purple, white-edged, pointed petals that arch outward.

'Maureen' reaches 30 inches (90 cm) tall and has white flowers. 'Mrs. J. T. Scheepers' has sunny yellow blooms on 30-inch (90-cm) tall stems. 'Negrita' grows to 16 inches (40 cm) tall and has light to deep purple flowers. 'Queen of the Night' has dark maroon-black blooms on 24-inch (60-cm) tall stems. 'Red Emperor' grows to 18 inches (45 cm) tall and has large, scarlet flowers with wide petals. 'Red Riding Hood' has red flowers with black centers and purple-striped leaves on 8-inch (20-cm) tall stems.

# PART FOUR

# FLOWERING PERENNIALS

174

# PERENNIALS
## IN YOUR
## GARDEN

From matched pairs of planted urns and formal herb gardens to casual meadow and cottage gardens, the possibilities for enjoying perennials in your landscape are endless. You might design a geometric garden with a color-theme perennial border or plant a meadow garden with perennials that will attract butterflies. Colorful, fragrant and flavorful herbs are equally at home in formal or more casual settings, either alone or mixed with traditional perennials in a bed or border. Growing perennials in pots is a great way to create movable, easily changed displays to perk up an otherwise plain patio or front porch.

# PERENNIAL COLOR

You can design beautiful gardens around a theme as simple as a single color. This may sound plain, but it's anything but that—color-theme gardens are attractive and dramatic additions to any landscape. Even if the flowers you choose are all in the same color group, the many different shades and tints create a mosaic of changing colors throughout the season.

**PERFECT MATCH**
Maroons, mauves and blues go well together.

**Single color theme** Start planning a perennial color-theme garden by picking the color you want to work with. Try a monochrome (based on one flower color) border if you have a favorite color or love collecting flowers of a particular color. Or make a small monochromatic section part of a long mixed-color border, perhaps using silver foliage to separate it from flowers of other colors. If you have a couple of unconnected small beds, you might want to try a different color in each. Or choose a single color for the whole garden in each season: perhaps pink for spring, white for summer and yellow for fall, or whatever colors appeal to you.

**Two-color theme** Another option to consider is a two-color border. Blue and white are a classic combination. Or perhaps pinks and yellows are more to your liking. Yellow or chartreuse with maroon or burgundy is a popular color combination. The key to creating a beautiful and effective two-color garden is to pick the colors that you like and those that blend well with your house. White flowers, for instance, can look dirty against cream-colored siding, while bright pinks can clash unmercifully with rusty orange brick. If white suits your home, it is often a good choice in a two-color garden; it will highlight pastels and won't clash with bright colors. Remember, too, that striking foliage can provide green for your two-color scheme; green goes particularly well with pastels and white.

**Experimenting in containers**

If you're not sure how certain colors will look in a given setting,

---

## GOOD CHOICES

### BEAUTIFUL BLUE GARDENS
Blue is a popular color theme for perennial plantings. Many beloved summer-blooming perennials have blue flowers, including delphiniums, Siberian iris, bellflowers and pincushion flower.

### WONDERFUL WHITE GARDENS
Elegant white theme gardens offer perhaps the widest range of flower choice. All-white designs are sometimes called "moon gardens" because the flowers almost glow under the light of a full moon.

### ROUSING REDS, ORANGES AND YELLOWS
Hot-color borders are exciting and vibrant. Yellow gardens have a cheerful look and are easy to arrange without fear of clashing colors. Reds and oranges make the loudest statements of the color themes, but red flowers also have the greatest potential to clash with each other. Before planting a whole border of these bright colors, try a small bed first to see if you like the effect. Plants with delicate foliage and inconspicuous flowers make a good backdrop for hot colors.

---

try growing the plants there in a container for a year. If the colors look good to you, go ahead and plan a full-scale garden; if they don't fit the bill, move the pot elsewhere and try a different combination in that spot next year. You'll save yourself a lot of time and money this way and you'll be more confident about the results.

*Experiment with pots.*

# PERENNIALS FOR BUTTERFLIES

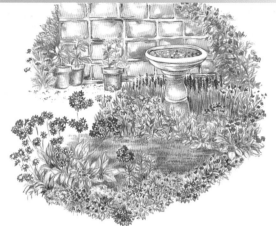

To have a great butterfly garden, you must get used to a few holes in the leaves of your perennials. You need to let the caterpillars feed in order to keep the adult butterflies around. Adult butterflies that are ready to lay eggs are attracted by the plants that will feed their developing larvae. Some adults also feed on flower nectar. Plants that have clusters of short, tubular, brightly colored flowers are especially popular.

**Arranging your butterfly plantings** Grow some of the many wildflowers that double as garden perennials, such as asters and coneflowers. Scatter these plants throughout your landscape or put several of them together in a special butterfly garden. Large splashes of color are easier for butterflies to find than a single plant, so group several plants of the same color together.

**Make a spot for sunbathing** Along with growing their favorite food and nectar plants, you can take a number of steps to encourage butterflies to stay in your yard. Butterflies like sun and dislike wind, so plant flowers in sunny spots where fences, walls or shrubs act as windbreaks. Set flat stones in a sheltered, sunny spot for butterflies to bask on.

**Just add water** Butterflies are attracted to shallow puddles and muddy soil. Dig a small, shallow hole, line it with plastic and cover it with sandy soil and gravel to form a butterfly-luring water source. Or plant a shallow, plastic basin into the ground, cover it with soil and grow butterfly-attracting perennials around it. If small children will be in your garden, make sure you create the watering hole away from areas they can access.

**Diversify your yard** Adding diversity to your landscape means creating different mini-environments as well as increasing the number of different plants. Edge habitats—where woods meet lawn or meadow and lawn meet garden or shrub plantings—provide great environments for butterflies. If you can, allow a corner of your yard to go wild; a tangle of bush provides

---

### BEST BETS FOR BUTTERFLIES

Here are some beautiful perennials that are especially popular with butterflies.

- ✿ Fern-leaved yarrow
- ✿ New England aster
- ✿ Blue false indigo
- ✿ Red valerian
- ✿ Cheddar pinks
- ✿ Spotted Joe-Pye weed
- ✿ White snakeroot
- ✿ Garden lupine
- ✿ Orange coneflower
- ✿ Pincushion flower
- ✿ Butterfly weed
- ✿ Astilbe
- ✿ Boltonia
- ✿ Shasta daisy
- ✿ Purple coneflower
- ✿ Daisy fleabane
- ✿ Blanket flowers
- ✿ Bee balm
- ✿ Garden phlox
- ✿ Showy stonecrop

---

protection from predators. Most butterflies have very specific tastes, so increase the variety of plants to provide a smorgasbord of food and nectar sources and attract many different species from early spring through fall.

**Avoid using pesticides** One of the most important steps in developing a butterfly haven is creating a safe, pesticide-free habitat. Even organically acceptable

pesticides such as rotenone and pyrethrin kill butterflies and their larvae. BT, a biological control used against many garden pests, is also fatal to the larvae of desirable butterflies. Use safer techniques such as water sprays and handpicking to remove pests from plants. If you don't want butterfly larvae to munch on your vegetable garden, protect crops with floating row covers.

*Stonecrop is a haven for butterflies.*

# FLOWERING HERBS

Versatile, colorful and flavorful, herbs have a place in any flower garden. Mix them with other perennials in beds and borders or group them together in a formal herb garden. Either way, you can enjoy their delightful scents and colors in crafts and in the kitchen as well as in the garden.

**VISUAL DELIGHTS**
Herbs look wonderful any way you use them— grouped into a special herb garden or mixed with perennials and bulbs.

**Using herbs around your yard** Deciding which herbs you'll grow and where you'll grow them is basically no different than choosing other perennials for your garden. You either need to make a list of the herbs that you want to grow and then find a place for them or pick a site and look for herbs that will thrive there.

**Creating a formal herb garden** Some gardeners like to group a collection of herbs into a special herb garden. This makes it easier to find the ones you want so you can enjoy their various scents or harvest them for cooking or crafts. Plan your herb garden as a regular perennial bed or border or give it a more formal look with paths, edgings and separate growing beds. A basic herb garden could consist of several square

*Chives produce graceful pink or lavender to purple globular blossoms.*

raised beds edged with wooden sides and separated by paths. For even more formality, you could lay out the garden beds in geometric shapes, wheel spokes or intricate knots. The key to having a beautiful and productive flowering herb garden is using herbs that are adapted to your climate.

**Adding herbs to other plantings** If you don't have room for a separate herb garden, tuck your favorite flowering herbs into other perennial beds and borders. A number of herbs are also well suited to container gardening, so you can move them around to add fragrance and color wherever you need it.

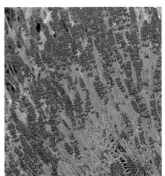

*Lavender is valued in crafts for its blooms and its fragrance.*

## FLOWERING PERENNIAL HERBS

If you want to get the most enjoyment possible from your yard, why not grow perennials that are useful as well as attractive. Listed below are some popular perennial herbs, with notes on their ornamental features and other uses. You'll find herbs to be among the least demanding plants to grow.

Fern-leafed yarrow: showy yellow flowers; crafts

Feverfew: small white, daisy-like flowers; crafts

Hyssop: blue flowers; culinary, tea

Lavender: scented gray leaves and purple flowers; crafts, culinary

Lemon balm: white flowers; tea

Bee balm: showy red flowers; crafts, tea

Catmint: blue flowers; crafts

Garden sage: blue flowers; culinary, tea

# PERENNIAL COTTAGE GARDENS

The ultimate in informality, cottage gardens display a glorious riot of colors, textures, heights and fragrances. Cottage gardens defy many gardening "rules": Plants are packed closely together, ignoring standard spacing; colors aren't organized into large drifts; tall plants pop up in front of shorter ones; flowers are allowed to flop over and grow through each other to create a delightful, casual mixture.

**Choosing a site** Locate cottage gardens next to the house, especially by a door. Climbing roses or honeysuckles look great trained over a door or archway. If your front or side yard is small, you may want to devote the whole space to the garden. In this case, a gravel, brick, stone or even cement path is essential; make it wide (at least 3 feet [90 cm]) to allow room for plants to spill out onto it.

**EDIBLE SURPRISES**

Accent your cottage garden with dwarf fruit trees and tuck in some other edibles for surprise: try colorful lettuces, curly parsley, red-stemmed 'Ruby' chard and maroon-podded 'Burgundy' okra.

**Picking the plants** To create a pleasing jumble rather than a chaotic mess, combine a variety of different flower shapes and sizes. Thinking of flowers in terms of their visual impact will help you get the right balance. "Feature" flowers are the ones that first catch your eye; they have strong shapes—like spiky lupines and massive peonies—or bright colors. "Filler" flowers tend to be smaller and less obvious than the feature plants. Baby's-breath is a classic filler flower. "Edgers" are low plants used in the fronts of beds or spilling over onto paths; think of thymes and catmint. As you choose plants for the garden, include some that have scented foliage or flowers; fragrance is a traditional part of the cottage garden. It's also important to choose flowers that bloom at different times for a continuous display.

Perennials aren't the only plants you can grow in your cottage garden: Annuals,

*Garden lupine is a classic cottage garden flower.*

## COTTAGE GARDEN FAVORITES

**Feature Flowers**
✿ Hollyhock
✿ Peach-leaved bellflower
✿ Belladonna delphinium
✿ Gas plant
✿ Bearded iris
✿ Siberian iris
✿ Garden lupine
✿ Common garden peony
✿ Oriental poppy
✿ Garden phlox
✿ Nettle-leaved mullein

**Edging Plants**
✿ Purple rock cress
✿ Basket-of-gold
✿ Dalmatian bellflower
✿ Snow-in-summer

✿ Cheddar pinks
✿ Cushion spurge
✿ Coral bells
✿ Catmint
✿ English primrose
✿ Bethlehem sage

**Filler Flowers**
✿ Lady's mantle
✿ Hybrid columbine
✿ New England aster
✿ Masterwort
✿ Knapweed
✿ Red valerian
✿ Shasta daisy
✿ Thread-leaved coreopsis
✿ Blood-red cranesbill
✿ Baby's-breath
✿ Rose campion

herbs, shrubs, vines, bulbs and even vegetables all can have a place in your cottage garden, too. Old-fashioned roses, either shrub types or climbers, are a classic ingredient and an important source of fragrant flowers.

*Let plants spill over the path for that casual, unorganized look.*

# FRAGRANT PERENNIALS

Perennials with fragrant flowers have a place in any landscape. Who could resist resting on a cozy garden bench near a patch of peonies in full, fragrant bloom? In beds, borders, cottage gardens and foundation plantings, mixing in some scented perennials will add an extra special touch to your yard.

### SPARKLING WITH SCENT

Cultivate lily-of-the-valley in a shady, sloped area of your yard to turn an otherwise dull spot into a fragrant, eye-catching feature. It combines well with shasta daisies.

### Siting the scent

Traditionally, scented flowers were grown close to the house so their fragrance could be appreciated through open doors and windows. They're equally nice near outdoor eating areas, patios and porches—any place where people linger. Raised planters are great for short, fragrant flowers so you don't have to get down on your hands and knees to enjoy the scents. Many fragrant flowers are also beautiful, so you can enjoy the double pleasure of looking at them and sniffing them as you walk around or work in the yard. Cutting these flowers for arrangements brings this pleasure indoors.

### Choosing fragrant perennials

The real key to having a scented garden that you enjoy is smelling plants before you buy them.

## POPULAR PERENNIALS FOR FRAGRANCE

✿ Red valerian (especially the white flowers)
✿ Lily-of-the-valley
✿ Cheddar pinks
✿ Daylilies (mainly the yellow flowers)
✿ Hyacinth
✿ Bearded iris
✿ Lavender
✿ Lilies
✿ Daffodils
✿ Common garden peony
✿ Garden phlox
✿ Fragrant Solomon's seal

*Peonies are a popular fragrant flower.*

### VARIETY OF SCENTS

Bearded irises are cottage garden favorites. They bloom in a rainbow of colors and many have a lovely scent. If fragrance is important to you, sniff the blooms before you buy; the scents can vary a great deal. If you're concerned about confusing scents, plant bearded irises with ornamental grasses.

The fragrance that a friend raves about may be undetectable or even unpleasant to you. Visit nurseries or public gardens when the plants you want are blooming and sniff the flowers or foliage to see what you think. Different cultivars of the same plant may vary widely in their scents, so smell them all before you choose. Just as a bed of many different flower colors can look jumbled, a mixture of many strong fragrances can be distracting or even downright repulsive. As you plan your garden, try to arrange it with just one or two scented plants in bloom at any given time. That way, you can enjoy different fragrances all through the season without being overwhelmed by too many at once. Remember to include a few plants with fragrant foliage; herbs especially fall into this category. You'll need to touch the leaves to release the scent.

# PERENNIALS IN CONTAINERS

No matter what size or style of garden you have, growing perennials in pots can greatly expand your planting options. Try a few container perennials and discover how fun, practical and versatile these movable gardens can be.

The range of pots gives you design options.

**USING WICKER**

Plastic pots are great if your summers tend to be hot and dry, since you'll have to water less often; unfortunately though, they are often unattractive. If you want to leave your plant in a plastic container, put it into a decorative basket. Remove to water.

**Solving challenges with containers** With a little creativity, you'll find many different ways to use containers to solve problem spots. If you can't kneel or if you garden from a wheelchair, you can grow plants at a convenient height in raised planters. If your soil is too hard or rocky to dig, grow flowers in half-barrel planters instead of in the ground. If you've got a shady spot that's crying out for color, use potted perennials to create a rotating display: As flowers fade, move the shady pot to a sunnier spot and replace with one that's robust from sunshine. Or tuck a few pots into a dull planting to add quick color. If space is really limited, create your own garden paradise on a rooftop, porch or window box.

### Playing with combinations

Don't limit your container gardens to just practical uses. Growing perennials in pots is a great way to experiment with different flower combinations before you commit to putting them in the ground. If you don't like a combination, just separate the pots and group them with other possibilities. Containers can also make great garden accents. Choose bold, sculptural perennials such as Adam's needle for formal designs; mix lots of different colors and cascading plants for a cottage look.

### Choosing a container

Pot possibilities are endless. You may buy commercially made plastic or clay containers or make your own out of old barrels, washtubs or even buckets. Be creative; almost anything you can put drainage holes in—from clay drainage tiles to old leather work boots—can be pressed into service. Solid-sided containers, such as plastic pots, hold water longer than porous clay but if you live in a wet climate or if you tend to overwater, porous containers are probably best. Plastic pots are lighter, making them easier to move, but they are more prone to blowing over. Clay pots are heavy and less likely to blow over, but they often crack when they do tip. In windy areas or for tall plants, place rocks in the bottom of any pot to increase stability. Empty clay pots or bring them indoors before freezing weather; wet soil expands as it freezes and will crack the pot. Dark pots heat up in bright sun and dry out quickly; avoid black plastic pots for container gardens that are growing in full sun.

### Picking plants for containers

Just about any perennial will grow well in a pot, as long as you give it the growing conditions and routine care that it needs. Plant several perennials in one pot or group several in individual containers. Include plants with attractive foliage—such as spotted lamium, heart-leaved bergenia and ornamental grasses—to extend the period of interest. Hardy bulbs add spring color to all containers.

# GROWING PERENNIALS

C areful planning and plant selection will take you a long way toward a great-looking landscape. The next step is to follow through with good soil preparation and after-care to get those plants off and growing. Making a place for your perennials takes more care than that required for a plot of vegetables or annuals. Perennials will grow in the same spot for years, so you won't have the chance to correct any soil problems once you plant. If the soil conditions are not right, your perennials will be weak, less attractive and more prone to pest and disease problems. But when you choose plants that are naturally adapted to your soil's characteristics, you're providing the right conditions for vigorous growth.

# SELECTING AND BUYING PERENNIALS

Starting with healthy plants is a key step in having a naturally healthy garden. As you shop by mail and at a variety of garden centers, nurseries and farms, you will find that there are several ways to sell the same plant—in a container, bareroot or field-dug. Here are some specifications that will let you evaluate how to use your plant budget most wisely.

**SYMPTOMS OF ILL-HEALTH**
Before you buy, look at the leaves. Off-color leaves may indicate nutrient deficiencies or pest problems.

**SYMPTOMS OF HEALTH**
Healthy plants have strong, evenly colored leaves. Check leaf undersides to make sure no pests are lurking.

**Container-grown perennials**
Perennials are most commonly sold in containers. Container-grown perennials are convenient and easy to handle. You can keep the pots in a well-lit location until you are ready to plant. Then you can slide the root ball out and plant it in the garden with minimal disturbance. However, there is a catch. Horticultural researchers are finding that roots tend to stay in the light, fluffy "soil" of synthetic mixes, rather than branching out into the surrounding garden soil. But you can avoid this problem by loosening roots on the outside of the ball and spreading them out into the soil as you plant.

**Bareroot perennials** You will come across many species of dormant bareroot plants for sale early in the growing season. In late

summer or early fall, you can also find bareroot items such as bearded irises, common bleeding heart, peonies and oriental poppies. You may choose to buy bareroot plants to save money—they are usually less expensive than large container-grown plants—or you may receive them unexpectedly. Mail-order companies often send plants bareroot to save on space and shipping. These plants look more dead than alive but, fortunately, in this case looks are deceiving. If you keep the roots moist and cool and plant them quickly and properly, most plants will recover and thrive. When the plants arrive, tend to them promptly. Open the box to let some air in. Your plants' roots should be wrapped in a protective medium like shredded newspaper, excelsior or sphagnum moss. Keep this medium moist but not soggy. When it's time to plant,

soak the roots in a bucket of lukewarm water for a few hours, then plant. If you can't plant right away, keep the roots moist and store them, in their original package, in a cool location for a day or two. If you need to wait longer than that to plant, pot up the roots or set them into a nursery bed until you are ready.

**Field-dug perennials** You may be able to find a farmer, hobbyist plant breeder, plant collector or nursery owner who will sell you mature plants dug from the field. If you handle the root ball carefully, you can move field-dug perennials much later into the summer than bareroot plants because the roots are protected by soil. Set the root ball, surrounded by soil, in a firm wooden flat or sturdy bucket. Cover it with a moist towel, damp peat moss or compost to keep the roots and soil

*Find out the origins of your perennial so you can nourish it properly.*

moist. Replant it as soon as you get home. Be on the lookout for weed shoots emerging through or near the base of the plant.

# SELECTING AND BUYING PERENNIALS continued

### THOROUGH INSPECTION

Don't be afraid to have a good look at every aspect of the plant you are about to buy. Root-bound plants are a common problem in nurseries. Gently slide the plant from its pot to check its base; avoid plants with massed or circling roots, as shown below.

### Healthy plant checklist

Before you pull out your wallet to buy a new perennial, follow this checklist to make sure you verify the plant's quality:

1. Look to see if the plant is tagged with its botanical and cultivar name. If not or if it's labeled only by common name or color, chances are that it's not an improved type and you may not want it.

2. Test for root-bound plants, which may have been sitting around for a long time in a small pot. Give the plant a soft tug from the top and see if the root ball pops out of the pot readily. If the roots are packed into a solid mass or are circling around the inside of the pot, the plants are root-bound and may be slow to adapt to garden conditions.

3. Look at the roots. Firm, white roots are a sign of good health. If you can't pull the plant out of its pot to see the roots, check where the shoots emerge from the soil. Emerging stems should not be brown, soft, blemished or wilted; these are symptoms of rots and other diseases.

4. Give the same thorough inspection to the stems and foliage. Look for signs of diseases such as brown or black leaf spots, white powdery mildew or tiny orange spots of rust. You don't want to bring these problems home.

5. Check the color of the foliage. If it is a deep and uniform color, the plant is most likely healthy and well fed.

6. Be on the lookout for weed shoots emerging through or near the crown (base) of the perennial. Although the weed leaves may have been clipped off in a presale grooming, grasses and perennial weeds will reemerge and can invade your newly planted garden.

7. Last, check for insect pests. Look beneath the leaves, along the stems, in shoot tips and on flower buds for soft-bodied aphids, cottony mealybugs and hard-shelled scale insects. Spider mites, another common pest, will make leaves stippled or turn them yellow or bronze. If pests are on one plant, they may be on every plant in that greenhouse or garden center. Consider shopping elsewhere.

# PREPARING FOR PLANTING

**Healthy landscapes start with healthy soil. The effort you put into working the soil and preparing a good planting site will be more than repaid by the strong, vigorous growth of your perennials.**

**When to start** Prepare planting areas at least a month before you plant to give soil time to settle. Start in the fall for spring planting or in spring for fall planting. Start digging when the soil is moist, but not wet. Digging dry soil requires extra effort; working soil that's soggy can turn it into rock-like lumps. After two or three days without rain, dig up a shovelful in a couple of spots and test for moisture by squeezing a handful of soil. If the soil oozes through your fingers or forms a sticky lump, it's too wet; wait a few days and repeat the test before digging.

*The success of your garden depends on its environment.*

**What to do** First lay out the area you want to dig. Use stakes and string for marking the straight sides; lay out curves with a rope or garden hose. Step back and double check your layout from several viewpoints, including indoors. Next, remove existing grass and weeds. Slice off manageable pieces of sod by cutting small squares, then sliding your spade just under the roots. Toss the sod into the compost pile or use it to repair bare spots in your lawn. Now loosen the soil over the entire planting area. Dig down as far as your spade or shovel will reach and turn over this top layer of the soil or use a rotary tiller. For even better results, double dig.

**Adding fertilizer** Once your soil is loose, mix in fertilizer to feed the plants and organic matter

*Double-digging thoroughly loosens soil.*

to condition the soil. Any balanced organic fertilizer will do. Scatter the fertilizer over the planting area at the application rate listed on the label. Now spread organic matter about 4 inches (10 cm) deep over the entire area (you'll need about 2 cubic yards [1.5 cu m] for every 50 square feet [4.5 sq m]). If your soil feels as loose as sand (indicating drainage that's too fast) or if puddles always remain after a rain (indicating poor drainage), add more organic matter. Compost is the best source of organic matter. Leaves are excellent, too; run the lawn mower over piles to chop them first or mix them with grass clippings. Sawdust and straw are good if you also add a source of nitrogen (in the form of manure or bloodmeal) to help them decompose. Manure alone is fine but can contain many weed seeds. Whatever material you choose, mix it well into the top 8 inches (20 cm) of soil. After digging it in, water the area thoroughly. Let the soil sit for a month before planting to give the organic matter time to break down (unless you used well-decomposed compost, in which case you could plant right away). The levels of the bed will change: Rake just before planting.

### DOUBLE-DIGGING FOR DEEP ROOTING

The idea behind double-digging is to improve the soil to two spade depths. The well-prepared soil encourages deeper rooting, so perennials are more drought-tolerant. Double-digging takes some time and lots of energy, but you'll know it's worth the effort when you see the results: strong, healthy, free-blooming plants. To deeply loosen the soil, dig a trench along the long side of your bed, dumping soil on a plastic tarp or in a cart. Use a garden fork to loosen the soil at the bottom of the trench to a depth of 8–10 inches (20–25 cm), working in organic matter, like compost. Dig another trench alongside the first, turning each shovelful into the first trench. Work organic matter into the newly moved top layer and into the newly exposed bottom layer of the second section. Repeat the process across your bed, filling the final trench with the soil you removed from the first trench. Rake smooth.

# PLANTING PERENNIALS

**Once the site is prepared and your perennials are by your side, you are ready to turn your dream garden into reality.**

**MULCHING FOR MOISTURE**
Mulch bareroot and container-grown perennials after planting to keep the soil moist and to promote root growth. Plant when rainfall is abundant or water regularly at soil level rather from above to keep soil evenly wetted.

**When to plant** Your perennials will grow best if you wait for an overcast afternoon to plant. If you must plant on a sunny day, leave the perennials in the shade while you dig all of the holes. Space the holes according to the spacings you worked out on your planting plan.

**Planting container-grown perennials** Container-grown perennials are easy to plant; just follow these simple steps:

1. Dig a hole as deep as the soil level in the pot.
2. Gently remove the plant from its pot. To do this, place one hand over the soil, with the plant stems between your fingers. Invert the pot so it's resting on this hand, then use the other hand to pull off the pot. Don't yank; if the pot refuses to come off, cut it off to avoid damaging roots.
3. If you find a mass of crowded roots, gently loosen them with your fingers. If the roots have formed a tight mat, take a sharp knife and cut a slit ¼ inch (6 mm) deep from top to bottom in three or four places. This encourages the production of new roots that will grow into the surrounding soil.
4. Set the plant in the hole and backfill with the soil you took out until the soil level is even with the rest of the bed. Be sure you don't pile extra soil around the base of the stems (the crown).
5. Water thoroughly and mulch, leaving a zone about

2 inches (5 cm) around the crown free of mulch. If it's sunny out, shade the plants by inverting paper grocery bags over them as soon as they're in the ground. (Weight down the edges of the bags with rocks to keep them from blowing away.) Remove the bags after two days. Water if needed to keep the soil moist.

**How to plant bareroot perennials** Bareroot perennials aren't difficult to plant, but they need a little extra care to get settled.

1. Remove any packing material and prune off any damaged or broken roots. Cover the rest with room-temperature water for an hour or two before planting to make sure the roots are moist. (Bareroot perennials won't last more than two weeks without being planted. If you have to wait longer, pot the plants temporarily in a good growing medium).

2. Check to see whether roots grow from one large central root (a taproot) or as a mass of many smaller fibrous roots. Taprooted plants need a narrow, deep hole, while fibrous-rooted plants need a wide, shallow hole. Dig the hole accordingly.

3. If you're planting a taprooted species, hold the crown (which is where the stems meet the roots) even with the soil surface and backfill with the soil you removed.

4. If you're planting a fibrous-rooted perennial, form a mound of soil in the center of the hole, then gently spread the roots out over the mound. Check that the crown is even with the soil surface; if not, add or take away some of the soil in the mound. Once the

level is correct, fill in the soil.

5. Gently tamp down the soil around the base of the plant with your hand or foot. Water the soil thoroughly and spread mulch, leaving a zone about 2 inches (5 cm) around the crown free of mulch.

*Get your flowers off to the best start by planting in moderate temperatures.*

# CARING FOR YOUR PERENNIALS

Taking regular walks through your perennial landscape is a great way to enjoy your flowers and appreciate the progress you've made. And by checking the condition of your plants as you stroll through the garden, you'll be helping to keep it healthy.

To keep flowers fresh as you cut them, put them in a bucket of cool water.

**Weeding** Weeding isn't just for looks. Underground, weeds compete with your perennials for water and nutrients; aboveground, they compete for space and light. If left to rampage, weeds could smother or strangle your plants in as little as a year or two. Weeding is easiest and most enjoyable if you do it regularly; you'll find young weeds easier to pull and you'll catch them before they go to seed. Weeding a day or two after good

rain makes the job even simpler, since the weeds' roots will come out of the soft soil more easily. If you weed thoroughly before planting and use a mulch, your weeding chores should be fairly minimal. Eventually, a bed that is weeded regularly produces fewer and fewer weeds.

**Watering** Except for drought-tolerant types, most perennials need about 1 inch (25 mm) of rainfall a week during the growing season. This general guideline is handy to keep in mind, but it's not infallible; it's really best to see how much water is available to the roots of your plants. To check the moisture of the soil around your plants, pull aside the mulch and dig a small hole with a trowel. If the top 1–2 inches (2.5–5 cm) is dry, it's time to water. Avoid using

*Use garden shears to deadhead.*

**Pinching and pruning** Judicious pruning keeps perennials looking their best. Remove flowers after they've faded, a process called deadheading. Doing this will keep plants from putting all their energy into producing seeds and will prevent unwanted seedlings from popping up all over. If plants like phlox and bee balm tend to get gray patches on their leaves (a sign of powdery mildew), thin the clumps in spring by cutting out the weakest stems; by improving air circulation, you'll discourage mildew. Leggy, late-blooming perennials benefit from pinching back; these include daisy-like plants—asters, boltonia and chrysanthemums—as well as obedient plant, garden phlox and turtleheads. In late spring, prune out the growing tips with your fingers (literally pinch them off). You'll be rewarded with more flower stems and shorter plants that are less likely to need staking.

sprinklers; they waste water and encourage disease by wetting plant leaves. Instead, use a soaker hose or a drip irrigation system to water the roots in your garden beds; water container plantings by hand. Watering the soil thoroughly encourages roots to grow deep, so they'll be better able to withstand dry spells. Each time you irrigate, make sure the water has moistened the top 4–6 inches (10–15 cm) of soil before you stop.

*Whenever possible, avoid overhead watering. It wastes water and can encourage the spread of diseases.*

## CARING FOR YOUR PERENNIALS continued

**Staking** If you grow only short perennials or if you don't mind your flowers sprawling or leaning on each other, you won't have to worry about staking. But anyone who has seen peonies flattened by rain or has watched a perfect giant delphinium toppled in a strong wind knows that a few minutes spent placing a few stakes is time well spent. Slender green bamboo or plastic stakes will blend in well behind tall flower stalks. It's best to put the stakes out in early spring as new growth begins. Push each stake as deeply into the ground as you can so it won't fall over. As the flower stalk grows, secure it to the stake with string. Green yarn or twine is less conspicuous than white string; loop it around the stem once before tying it loosely to the stake.

Peonies, asters, lupines and other bushy, multistemmed plants with many or large flowers are better supported by a wire ring or linking metal stakes. Buy commercial wire stakes or make your own from wire coat hangers.

Stake tall plants like delphiniums.

Install the rings or stakes as soon as leaves emerge, being careful to push the legs into the soil outside of the crown. Baby's-breath, many hardy geraniums and other light but floppy perennials don't need the rigid support of a wire ring. Instead, try a small dead branch with several branchlets as a support. Or set three small sticks or stakes in a 4-inch (10-cm) triangle around the stem, then surround the plant and stakes with string. As the plant grows, it will cover the support. Be aware that a plant that seems to need staking may be in need of special attention. Weak stems may indicate that a plant has been overwatered or is in soil that is not balanced in nutrients. It could also mean that the plant needs dividing or transplanting.

*Fall leaves are an effective and natural-looking mulch, especially in woodland gardens.*

spring. Most of the garden won't look as tidy if not cut back, but it will get through the winter just as well. Standing stems actually help hold lightweight mulches in place through winter storms. Focus your cleanup time on any plants that showed signs of disease, pest infestation or general ill health this year or in previous years; fall cleanup reduces the chance of future recurrence.

**Fall cleanup** The last outdoor maintenance task of the season is preparing your perennials for winter. Give beds a thorough watering before the ground freezes. Remove dead foliage and cut dead stems back to the ground. Compost garden debris, unless it's diseased or full of seeds; then bury or dispose of it. If fall is always a busy time for you and you never quite finish your garden cleanup, don't worry. Some plants, such as ornamental grasses and plants with interesting seedpods (including astilbes and blue false indigo), are beautiful well into winter. You can leave these standing until early

*Preparing your perennials for winter is the last outdoor task.*

# CARING FOR YOUR PERENNIALS continued

**Spring workout** In spring, get into the garden early (when the soil dries out and no longer squishes underfoot) to cut

*The right nutrients in the right balance will ensure a good spring growth.*

remaining stems back before new spring growth starts. Otherwise, it will become a much more complicated and time-consuming task as you try to trim out the old growth without damaging the new shoots. If you've had problems in the past with certain perennials (such as mulleins) reseeding too prolifically, also cut off those seed heads in the fall.

**Compost and fertilizer** In mid- to late spring, spread about 1 inch (2.5 cm) of compost over the bed; this will provide most of the nutrients your perennials need to thrive. For perennials that benefit from extra nutrients, including delphiniums, peonies and phlox, scatter some balanced organic fertilizer around the base of the plant (following the label

directions), and scratch it into the soil. It's important to feed in the spring rather than in the fall so your plants will use the nutrients for flowers instead of making lots

*Mulches come in a variety of colors.*

of new growth right before frost. After adding compost and any fertilizer, replace the old mulch. If the garden bed you're working on is an old, established bed, you can use compost as your mulch.

**Mulching** A couple of inches of mulch greatly reduces your weeding and watering, shields your soil from hard rains and protects your plants from frost heaving. Organic mulches are best because they add organic matter to the soil as they break down, helping to keep the soil healthy. Plants generally thrive with mulch over their roots because it keeps them cool and moist. (Don't pile mulch around the bases of plants stems, though; mulch can hold too much moisture around the stems and encourage disease problems.) Aged bark chips make great mulch for perennial plantings. (Let freshly chipped material sit for a year and

Kitchen scraps are great in compost.

turn the pile every month or two before putting it on the garden.) Shredded leaves and compost are also good. Grass clippings are okay too, if you're sure they came from a lawn that wasn't treated with herbicides. Pine needles look great but make the soil more acid, so use them only around plants that prefer acid soil, such as ferns, lilies and woodland wildflowers. Avoid mulching with peat moss or fresh

sawdust; both form crusts that shed water rather than soaking it up. If you know weeds will be a problem, lay sheets of newspaper beneath the mulch. After the first hard frost, give your beds a generous layer of mulch to protect plants from frost heaving and dramatic temperature changes. Use about 1 inch (2.5 cm) of heavy materials, like bark chips, or about 3 inches (7.5 cm) of light mulches, such as pine needles or chopped leaves. In particularly cold or exposed sites without dependable snow cover, also add an extra cover of light branches (those from pine or fir work well), pine needles or (after the holidays) boughs from a discarded Christmas tree. Remove any covering and pull the mulch back from around the base of the plants in early spring to let the soil warm up. Add more mulch as needed over the summer to keep it the right depth.

# A BRIEFING ON BUGS

**"A stitch in time saves nine" is an old saying that's particularly appropriate where perennial gardening is concerned. Spotting developing problems early and dealing with them as soon as they appear simplifies pest and disease control dramatically.**

*Handpicking is effective for slow-moving pests like snails.*

*Slugs are a particular problem after heavy rains.*

### Discovering the problem

Insect damage on your perennials can vary widely, depending on the pest causing the problem. If you figure out which bug is at the source of the damage, you'll be able to choose the best control. If you use a commercial organic spray, always read the label first. Labels list important information on proper storage, target pests and effective application. Even organic sprays and dusts can irritate skin or lungs, so wear gloves and protective clothing to be on the safe side.

### Distorted or discolored leaves

Small green, black or pink insects called aphids cluster on young leaves and growing tips and may cause leaves to pucker or buds to drop. Tiny, light-colored specks on the tops of leaves and often bits of webbing on the undersides and stems are signs of spider mites. Stunted growth and streaked or withered flowers (especially on gladiolus, chrysanthemums and daisies) are signs of thrips, small silvery pests that are usually too tiny to see. If clouds of white specks fly up from disturbed foliage, your plants have whiteflies. If you suspect any of these problems, cut off and destroy severely infested shoots. For less-serious infestations, try dislodging the pests with a strong spray of water. If several days of such treatment isn't enough, spray with insecticidal soap; buy a commercial product or make your own by

Grapefruit rinds are great slug traps.

mixing 1 to 3 teaspoons of liquid dish soap (not laundry or dishwasher detergent) in 1 gallon (4 L) of water. Repeat every two or three days for two weeks until insects disappear.

**Holes in leaves**  When large holes appear in leaves, look for beetles or caterpillars. Handpicking pests and dropping them into a jar of soapy water controls most infestations. In extreme cases, spray or dust caterpillar-infested plants with BT (Bacillus thuringiensis), rotenone or pyrethrin. In humid climates, slugs and snails chew leaves and flowers in the dark of the night. They leave unmistakable evidence: a shiny trail. Both are easy to trap under boards or grapefruit halves or in shallow dishes of beer. Lift boards and fruit traps daily and dispose of the pests; empty beer traps as they get full.

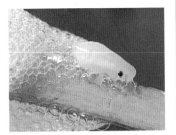

Spittlebugs suck the sap from plants, causing distinctly stunted growth.

**Tunnels in leaves**  Leafminers disfigure the leaves of columbines, chrysanthemums, delphiniums and other perennials with tan tunnels or splotches. Immediately remove and destroy infected leaves. If leafminers are a problem in your garden, remove garden debris in the fall (don't wait until spring); lightly scratch the soil around plants in fall and spring to expose overwintering pupae.

# A DIGEST OF DISEASES

**The best defense against diseases is strong, vigorous plants. Building healthy soil, keeping the garden clean and planting disease-resistant species and cultivars will go a long way toward keeping your perennials problem-free.**

*Rusts produce orange or yellowish spots on leaves and stems.*

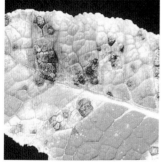

**STOPPING THE SPREAD**
Leaf spots can be caused by either fungi or bacteria. Removing affected foliage may stop the spread of disease.

**Stunted growth or discolored foliage** Diseases usually appear on particular species while ignoring others. If several types of plants growing together have similar symptoms, suspect a nutrient deficiency, not a disease. Pale or yellowing leaves may indicate a lack of nitrogen or iron. Dark leaves with purple or red near the veins may lack phosphorus. Mottled leaves may need magnesium. Distorted growth and the death of young leaves and buds may indicate various micronutrient deficiencies. The best approach to handling suspected nutrient deficiencies is to take a soil test so you'll know what's missing and what you need to add. Sometimes it's just a matter of adjusting the soil pH, so the nutrients that are already in your soil can become available to your perennials. For a quick but short-term solution, spray the leaves of plants with fish emulsion or liquid seaweed available from most garden centers. Working compost into the soil before planting and using it as a mulch should keep your soil well stocked with a balanced supply of nutrients.

**White spots on leaves** In humid areas, powdery mildew is a common but not-too-serious disease. This fungus looks like grayish white powder dusted on leaves, especially on phlox and bee balm. Leaves may drop, but plants rarely die. In late spring, cut out weaker stems in dense clumps of phlox or bee balm to improve air circulation. Keep infections from spreading by picking off or picking up dropped, infected leaves. Treat the remaining foliage with baking soda spray (1 teaspoon in 1 quart [1 L] of water with a few drops of liquid dish soap), fungicidal soap or sulfur. When you're shopping for new plants, look for and ask for resistant cultivars.

**Spots on leaves** Rusts are named for the distinct orange color of their raised or powdery spots on leaves. These fungi appear most often on hollyhocks but may infect irises, pinks and other perennials. Pick off and destroy infected leaves; treat remaining foliage with sulfur dust or fungicidal soap. Other spots on leaves may be caused by several different factors, including fungi and bacteria. Pick off infected leaves and treat the rest with baking soda spray or fungicidal soap. If symptoms reappear, insect pests may be at fault.

**Damaged or dead** When shoots or plants suddenly droop and die, suspect a blight or wilt. A common culprit is Botrytis blight, a disease caused by several species of fungi. It is also known as gray mold because it produces a brownish gray mold that usually

*Downy mildew produces white spots on the undersides of leaves.*

appears while plant parts wither, blacken and rot. It can afflict peonies and bulbs, especially after long spells of damp weather or in soil that isn't well drained. The blight produces microscopic spores which are carried to other plants by the wind. The best solution is to remove and destroy infected parts, and move unaffected plants to a spot with better air circulation and drainage.

# PLANNING FOR LOW MAINTENANCE

With today's busy lifestyles, it is hard for many gardeners to find the time they need to keep their yard looking great all year long. The key to landscaping for low maintenance is identifying your most bothersome gardening tasks. Which chores take the most time? Which do you like least?

**Edging** If you hate edging flower beds and digging out the grass that invades from the lawn, install edging strips. Make sure the strips are level with or slightly below the top of the grass blades so you can mow over them.

**Hand trimming** Reduce hand trimming around tree trunks, fences, posts and bird baths by replacing the grass there with hostas, daylilies or other groundcovers.

**Mowing** You can reduce the area of your lawn in favor of perennial flowers, shrubs or groundcovers. If the site is sunny, convert part or all of it into a wildflower meadow; you'll reduce mowing chores to once or twice a year. Landscape shady areas where grass grows poorly with shade-tolerant groundcovers or woodland plants; convert high-traffic areas into shady patios that are connected by paved or mulched pathways. In small yards, urban areas and dry climates, consider eliminating the lawn altogether. Perennials look great next to paving stones, bricks, cement pavers or gravel.

*Reticulated iris are easy to maintain.*

## DEPENDABLE, EASY-CARE PERENNIALS

Here's a list of some of the most trouble-free flowering perennials you can grow. All of the plants below thrive in sun and average, well-drained soil with little fuss.

- ✿ Fern-leaved yarrow
- ✿ Lady's-mantle
- ✿ Japanese anemone
- ✿ Common thrift
- ✿ Butterfly weed
- ✿ New England aster
- ✿ Blue false indigo
- ✿ Boltonia
- ✿ Red valerian
- ✿ Shasta daisy

- ✿ Thread-leaved coreopsis
- ✿ Purple coneflower
- ✿ Globe thistle
- ✿ Blanket flower
- ✿ Blood-red cranesbill
- ✿ Daylilies
- ✿ Siberian iris
- ✿ Spike gayfeather
- ✿ Lilies

- ✿ Daffodils
- ✿ Catmint
- ✿ Common garden peony
- ✿ Obedient plant
- ✿ Balloon flower
- ✿ Orange coneflower
- ✿ Sedums
- ✿ Violet sage
- ✿ Spike speedwell
- ✿ Adam's needle

to keep the soil moist. If you must water, consider laying soaker hoses or drip irrigation systems; then you'll only have to hook up the hose or turn on the system when you need to water, instead of watering by hand.

**Weeding** Minimizing weeding starts at planting time. First, don't skimp on site preparation. Every weed you remove before you start means a whole bucketful of weeds you won't have to remove later. After planting, apply and maintain a good mulch cover. Check the mulch depth three or four times a year and add more if needed. Get in the habit of pulling weeds as soon as you see them. Carry a basket, bag or bucket with you every time you walk around the yard to collect pulled weeds.

**Watering** Planning a water-wise garden will cut down on your watering chores. Look in fields, roadsides and abandoned lots for plants that thrive in your area without extra water. The mulch that you use on finished plantings to keep weeds down will also help

*Make mowing easier by using edgings or pathways to prevent sprawling.*

# HANDLING HILLSIDES

With a little imagination, you can transform a sloping site from a maintenance headache to an eye-catching landscape asset. Hillsides are awkward to mow and weed, so the best strategy is to cover them with plants that take care of themselves. Or, if you're willing to invest some time and money, you can build retaining walls or terraced beds that will safely and attractively support a wide range of beautiful perennials.

**WALL PLANTING**
When planting walls and terraces, remember that they dry out more quickly than regular in-ground beds, so you should look for plants that can take dry conditions.

**Sunny slopes** One good option for sunny slopes is planting a mixture of sun-loving groundcovers, taller spreading perennials (such as daylilies) and spreading shrubs, such as creeping juniper. Or, if you like a casual look and you're willing to mow the slope once a year, consider turning it into a wildflower meadow. Building a rock garden is another great solution for a sunny, well-drained slope. Place large rocks at irregular intervals throughout the area. Bury each so that over half is underground to keep it from rolling or washing away. Large, secure stones will give you a steady foothold so you can get into the garden for occasional weeding. Between the stones, plant sprawling, sun-loving perennials, such as wall rock cress, snow-in-summer and basket-of-gold with

*Plant low-growing perennials along walls.*

small hardy bulbs, such as crocus and reticulated iris.

**Shady slopes** On shady slopes, spreading species and cultivars of hostas make great groundcovers, alone or combined with other perennials. Other good companions include lily-of-the-valley, pachysandra and common periwinkle. For extra interest, add spring-flowering bulbs to get early color from groundcover plantings.

If the slope is shaded by deciduous trees, create a woodland garden by combining groundcovers such as ajuga and European wild ginger with early-blooming wildflowers. Creeping phlox, wild bleeding heart and Allegheny foamflower are a few species that will bloom in spring before the trees leaf out fully and shade the area.

**Terraces for trouble-free slopes** Constructing permanent terraces requires more time, effort and money up front, but the terraces last for years and dramatically increase the variety of perennials you can grow. Low retaining walls (up to 2 feet [60 cm] high) are reasonably easy to construct from flat stones or lumber. Consult a professional landscaper or builder for any wall that must be taller than 2 feet (60 cm): Large retaining walls must be well anchored and

properly designed to keep them from washing out, cracking or tumbling down after a few years. Fill finished terraces with good topsoil. After the soil settles for a few weeks, add a bit more if needed to level the top of the beds; then you'll be ready to plant your perennials.

### GREAT GROUNDCOVERS FOR SLOPES

Here are some tough and trouble-free perennials that adapt well to life on a sloping site.

**Groundcovers for sun**
- ✿ Snow-in-summer
- ✿ Moss phlox
- ✿ Lamb's-ears
- ✿ Cheddar pinks
- ✿ Two-row sedum

**Groundcovers for shade**
- ✿ Ajuga
- ✿ Red epimedium
- ✿ Sweet woodruff
- ✿ Hostas, spreading types
- ✿ European wild ginger
- ✿ Spotted lamium
- ✿ Allegheny foamflower

# SUCCEEDING IN SHADE

Shady nooks provide a cool, peaceful refuge for plants and people who can't take the hot summer sun. They may not glow with the vibrant colors of poppies and peonies, but they offer many wonderful possibilities to the open-minded gardener who wants to experiment with subtle shades and textures. Success in shady sites, as in any kind of garden, depends on careful planning and on choosing plants that grow happily in such conditions.

**ROOT CARE**
If planting under trees, you'll need to dig and enrich individual planting pockets close to the tree trunk; dumping organic matter over the top of the roots will hurt the tree.

**Picking your plants** The two main factors that determine which plants can grow well in your shade garden are how much light the garden gets and how much water is available. Sites that get a few hours of direct sun or a full day of filtered light can support a wider range of plants than a spot that's in deep shade all day. Gardens under deciduous trees may get lots of sun until early summer, when the developing tree leaves begin to block the light. Shady gardens can also vary widely in the amount of moisture that's available. Plants that grow well in moist woodland soils usually aren't happy in the dry shade under roof overhangs or shallow-rooted trees such as maples and beeches. In moist shade, you may need to seek out slug- and snail-resistant plants. Spring tends to be the primary bloom season in a perennial shade garden, but you'll look at the plants all season long, so choose ones that also look good when they're not flowering. Include perennials that have showy, colored leaves, such as blue-leaved hostas, silver-dotted Bethlehem sage, maroon-leaved 'Palace Purple' heuchera and golden-leaved lamium.

## Planning and planting tips

Take advantage of several strategies for succeeding in shade. First, direct traffic away from shallow-rooted trees and areas you wish to keep as deep shade so you can replace scraggly lawn with groundcovers. Use stepping stones or heavily mulched paths to guide visitors around planted areas. Second, enrich the soil with lots of organic matter. A good supply of organic matter may mean the difference between death and survival in shade, especially dry shade. After planting, water thoroughly and apply a layer of mulch. In dry shade, water

*Ajuga and hostas are dependable perennials for easy-care shaded gardens.*

regularly until plants are established and plan on watering even mature plants during dry spells. If slugs and snails become a problem, you may want to remove some or all of the mulch; despite all of its benefits, mulch also provides a dark, moist shelter for these troublesome pests.

## SUPER PERENNIALS FOR SHADE

Here's a list of just some of the great-looking, easy-to-grow perennials that will thrive in a shady garden.

✿ *Actea pachypoda* (white baneberry)
✿ *Ajuga reptans* (ajuga)
✿ *Aquilegia canadensis* (wild columbine)
✿ *Arisaema triphyllum* (Jack-in-the-pulpit)
✿ *Asarum europaeum* (European wild ginger)
✿ *Astilbe x arendsii* (astilbe)
✿ *Bergenia spp.* (bergenias)
✿ *Brunnera macrophylla* (Siberian bugloss)
✿ *Cimicifuga racemosa* (black snakeroot)
✿ *Dicentra eximia* (fringed bleeding heart)
✿ *Epimedium x rubrum* (red epimedium)
✿ *Helleborus orientalis* (Lenten rose)
✿ *Hosta hybrids* (hostas)
✿ *Iris cristata* (crested iris)
✿ *Lamium maculatum* (spotted lamium)
✿ *Polygonatum odoratum* (fragrant Solomon's seal)
✿ *Pulmonaria saccharata* (Bethlehem sage)
✿ *Smilacina racemosa* (Solomon's plume)
✿ *Tiarella cordifolia* (Allegheny foamflower)
✿ *Uvularia grandiflora* (great merrybells)

# TURNING BOGS INTO BEDS

**Don't let a wet yard or soggy spot deter you from gardening: Even a year-round spring or bog can be attractively landscaped with beautiful, easy-care perennials.**

**Options for organized plantings** If your problem site is under water most of the year, go with the flow—leave it as a wetland or convert it into a small pond and plant perennials to cascade over its edges. Some of our most beautiful native plants, including cardinal flower, queen-of-the-prairie, white or pink turtleheads and some ferns, prefer to grow where their feet are wet. They look equally good in perennial beds and wild settings. For a more traditional flower bed, or a border where the soil is moist rather then soggy, raise the level of the soil in the planting area at least 4 inches (10 cm).

*A bog garden is a great site for many kinds of irises. The flowers are beautiful in early summer and the spiky leaves look great all season.*

## PERENNIALS THAT LIKE WET FEET

Here are some super perennials that will thrive in a spot with consistently moist soil.

- ✿ *Arisaema triphyllum* (Jack-in-the-pulpit)
- ✿ *Aruncus dioicus* (goat's beard)
- ✿ *Asarum europaeum* (European wild ginger)
- ✿ *Astrantia major* (masterwort)
- ✿ *Brunnera macrophylla* (Siberian bugloss)
- ✿ *Chelone glabra* (white turtlehead)
- ✿ *Eupatorium maculatum* (spotted Joe-Pye weed)
- ✿ *Filipendula rubra* (queen-of-the-prairie)
- ✿ *Galium odoratum* (sweet woodruff)
- ✿ *Iris sibirica* (Siberian iris)
- ✿ *Ligularia dentata* (big-leaved ligularia)
- ✿ *Lobelia cardinalis* (cardinal flower)
- ✿ *Lysimachia punctata* (yellow loosestrife)
- ✿ *Monarda didyma* (bee balm)
- ✿ *Physostegia virginiana* (obedient plant)
- ✿ *Polygonum affine* (Himalayan fleeceflower)
- ✿ *Primula denticulata* (drumstick primrose)
- ✿ *Smilacina racemosa* (Solomon's plume)
- ✿ *Tradescantia x andersoniana* (common spiderwort)
- ✿ *Trollius x cultorum* (hybrid globeflower)

**Natural solutions for soggy sites** If you enjoy the informal feel of naturalistic landscaping, wet spots are a perfect place to let your imagination go. Healthy wetlands also serve important ecological roles by purifying groundwater, replenishing the water table and supporting a wide variety of plants and wildlife. A mixed planting of colorful, moisture-loving perennials can provide season-long interest in a wet spot. You don't need to carefully plan out different heights, textures and colors (like a cottage garden), just set plants out in random order. Great blue lobelia, swamp milkweed, marsh marigold, yellow flag and blue flag are a few colorful perennials that grow happily in constantly soggy soil. Angelica is a native perennial herb that forms lush, leafy clumps and tall flower clusters in wet soil. Native cattails thrive in standing water, but they may choke out everything else (which isn't a problem if you like them). Royal ferns and beech ferns are also great additions for foliage interest.

*Spring-blooming marsh marigolds are a natural choice for planting near ponds.*

# GROWING A WATER-WISE LANDSCAPE

If you live where rainfall is scant or undependable or if your soil is so sandy that water runs right through, it makes sense to plan your landscape accordingly. Choosing drought-adapted plants and using water-wise gardening techniques will save you more than just water—it can save you time and money too!

Terrace plantings need tough, drought-tolerant plants.

**Keeping water in** Good soil care is a key step in keeping moisture where plant roots can get it. Loose, crumbly soil can easily soak up rainfall that would just run off compacted beds. Digging the soil thoroughly at planting time and keeping it loose by not walking on the beds will keep the soil in good shape. Adding organic matter to your soil at planting time is another way to trap moisture. Organic matter, such as mulch and compost, is a natural sponge, soaking up water when it's available and releasing it later on to plant roots. Regrading areas of your yard may help to keep rainfall from running off into the street or at least to slow down the water so it has more chance to soak in. Building terraces is also a great way to slow or stop runoff on sloping sites.

*Replace lawn with drought-tolerant plants.*

### TOUGH PERENNIALS FOR HOT, DRY SITES

These plants don't mind heat and are happiest in soils that are very well drained and even sandy. Once established, they withstand extended dry spells.

- ✿ *Achillea filipendulina* (fern-leaved yarrow)
- ✿ *Artemisia absinthium* (common wormwood)
- ✿ *Asclepias tuberosa* (butterfly weed)
- ✿ *Aurinia saxatilis* (basket-of-gold)
- ✿ *Baptisia australis* (blue false indigo)
- ✿ *Catananche caerulea* (Cupid's dart)
- ✿ *Centranthus ruber* (red valerian)
- ✿ *Cerastium tomentosum* (snow-in-summer)
- ✿ *Coreopsis verticillata* (thread-leaved coreopsis)
- ✿ *Dianthus gratianopolitanus* (cheddar pinks)
- ✿ *Echinacea purpurea* (purple coneflower)
- ✿ *Echinops ritro* (globe thistle)
- ✿ *Eryngium amethystinum* (amethyst sea holly)
- ✿ *Euphorbia epithymoides* (cushion spurge)
- ✿ *Gaillardia* x *grandiflora* (blanket flower)
- ✿ *Allium giganteum* (giant onion)
- ✿ *Helianthus* x *multiflorus* (perennial sunflower)
- ✿ *Oenothera tetragona* (common sundrops)
- ✿ *Perovskia atriplicifolia* (Russian sage)
- ✿ *Rudbeckia fulgida* (orange coneflower)
- ✿ *Salvia officinalis* (garden sage)
- ✿ *Sedum spectabile* (showy stonecrop)
- ✿ *Sedum spurium* (two-row sedum)
- ✿ *Salvia* x *superba* (violet sage)
- ✿ *Stachys byzantina* (lamb's-ears)
- ✿ *Yucca filamentosa* (Adam's needle)

### Reducing overall water needs

Choose plants that are suited to your climate and to the microclimate of your yard. Lush lawns just aren't compatible with arid climates. Prairie and meadow gardens are naturally adapted to drier conditions; once established, they don't need watering and need mowing only once a year. Next, group your plants according to their water requirements. Locate thirsty plants closest to the house or water faucet, where you can reach them easily. Landscape outlying areas with species that need little if any supplemental water. Leave a little extra space between all plants so their roots can reach farther for water without competing. (Mulch the bare soil between plants.) You can also block or moderate drying winds with a hedge. And if you must water, do it early or late in the day.

# A GUIDE
## TO
# PERENNIALS

Like the guide to annuals, each entry in this guide to perennials has a color photograph and essential information that will make your garden planning easier. You'll find details on flower color, flowering time and height and spread. You'll learn about the cultivation requirements, including when to divide or thin plants, whether they need staking and when to fertilize. And there is information on how and when to propagate, so you'll have lots of perennials to fill your garden and share with your friends.

## AZURE MONKSHOOD

*Aconitum carmichaelii* Ranunculaceae

Azure monkshood is a graceful plant with lush, three-lobed, dissected leaves, sturdy stems and hooded flowers. All parts of the plant are poisonous when ingested.

**Flower color** Deep blue hooded flowers in dense spikes.

**Flowering time** Late summer and fall.

*Aconitum carmichaelii*

**Height and spread** 2–3 feet (60–90 cm) tall; 2 feet (60 cm) wide. Open and somewhat vase-shaped, especially in shade.

**Temperature requirements** Zones 3–7. Prefers climates with cool summer nights and warm days with low humidity.

**Position** Fertile, humus-rich, moist but well-drained soil. Full sun to light shade; afternoon shade in warmer zones.

**Cultivation** Dislikes disturbance once established. Space 2–3 feet (60–90 cm) apart with the crowns just below the surface. Take care not to damage the brittle roots. Divide if plants become overcrowded.

**Propagation** Divide crowns in fall or early spring. Replant strong, healthy divisions into moist soil that has been enriched with organic matter. Water regularly at soil level.

**Pest and disease prevention** Crowns will rot if soil is wet and temperatures are hot. Site plants properly to avoid problems.

**Landscape uses** Plant azure monkshood near the middle or rear of borders with other fall-blooming perennials and ornamental grasses, or in groups with fruiting shrubs like the Viburnum species.

**Cultivars** 'Barker's Variety' has large, deep blue flowers.

## COMMON BUGLEWEED
*Ajuga reptans* Labiatae

Common bugleweed is a low, rosette-forming groundcover that spreads by creeping, aboveground stems to form broad, dense mats. The spoon-shaped leaves are evergreen in mild climates.

**Flower color** Tiered whorls of small, intense blue flowers on stalks 6–10 inches (15–25 cm) long.

**Flowering time** Late spring and early summer.

**Height and spread** 4–10 inches (10–25 cm) tall; 8–10 inches (20–25 cm) wide. Clumps may spread to several feet across from a single plant.

**Temperature requirements** Zones 3–9. Tolerates heat, humidity and cold.

**Position** Average to humus-rich, moist but well-drained soil. Will not tolerate extended drought or excessive moisture. Full sun to light shade.

**Cultivation** Plant in spring or fall. Spreads rapidly to form a dense weed-proof groundcover and may be somewhat invasive, especially in lawns.

**Propagation** Propagate by division anytime during the growing season or from seed sown in spring.

**Pest and disease prevention** Provide good drainage and air circulation to prevent crown rot, which causes patches to wither.

*Ajuga reptans*

**Landscape uses** Use as a groundcover under trees and shrubs or for edging beds. Also useful in rock garden and foundation plantings.

**Cultivars** 'Atropurpurea' has bronze-purple leaves. 'Burgundy Glow' has white, pink and green foliage. 'Catlin's Giant' has large bronze leaves. 'Silver Beauty' has silvery to gray-green leaves with white edges.

# STAR OF PERSIA
*Allium christophii* Liliaceae

Star of Persia produces straplike blue-green leaves that arch outward from the bulbs. Starry flowers radiate from stout stalks.

**Flower color** Metallic, lilac-pink, spidery flowers are carried in lacy clusters on 10-inch (25-cm) globose heads.

**Flowering time** Midsummer.

*Allium christophii*

**Height and spread** 1–1½ feet (30–45 cm) tall; 1 foot (30 cm) wide.

**Temperature requirements** Zones 4–8.

**Position** Humus-rich, well-drained soil. Full sun.

**Cultivation** New bulbs planted in fall multiply slowly to form spectacular flowering clumps. Plants go dormant after flowering.

**Propagation** Divide in mid- to late summer as plants go dormant. Sow ripe seed outdoors in summer or fall.

**Pest and disease prevention** No serious pests or diseases. Mulch with organic matter to keep the soil evenly moist.

**Landscape uses** Plant bulbs at the front of borders where their stalks will explode into bloom above mounding plants like cranesbills. Combine this tall plant with shrubs and overplant with a groundcover. Star of Persia is related to edible species of onions and may smell faintly of onion or garlic when cut.

**Other species** *A. giganteum,* giant onion, grows 3–5 feet (90–150 cm) tall, with 5-inch (12.5-cm) rounded heads of deep purple flowers. Zones 4–8. *A. sphaerocephalum,* drumstick chives, has slender 1½–3-foot (45–90-cm) stems crowned by tight heads of small, red-violet flowers. Zones 4–9.

# PERUVIAN LILY
*Alstroemeria aurantiaca* Amaryllidaceae

Peruvian lilies have tall, leafy stems crowned by clusters of flaring, trumpet-shaped flowers. The gray-green leaves are narrow and pointed. Plants grow from thick, fibrous roots.

*Alstroemeria aurantiaca*

**Flower color** Showy orange or yellow flowers with brownish purple flares on the upper petals.

**Flowering time** Throughout summer.

**Height and spread** 2–3 feet (60–90 cm) tall; 2 feet (60 cm) wide.

**Temperature requirements** Zones 7–10.

**Position** Evenly moist but well-drained, humus-rich soil. Full sun to partial shade; fine near fences, under deciduous trees. Protect from strong winds.

**Cultivation** Plant dormant roots in early spring or fall. Growth begins early in the season and plants may be damaged by late frost. Mulch with organic matter in fall to avoid frost heaving. Achieves best performance after the third year.

**Propagation** Divide clumps in early spring or fall. Take care not to damage the brittle roots. Sow fresh seed indoors after four to six weeks of cold (35°–40°F [4°–5°C]), moist stratification. To stratify, mix seed with damp peat moss or seed-starting medium in a plastic bag and close with a twist-tie. Place the bag in the refrigerator for the appropriate time period, then sow the mixture as you would other seed.

**Pest and disease prevention** No serious pests or diseases.

**Landscape uses** Plant Peruvian lilies in beds and borders with perennials, in partial shade with ferns or in containers. A fence or larger, light bush is a good backdrop. Excellent for cutting.

# JACK-IN-THE-PULPIT

*Arisaema triphyllum* Araceae

Jack-in-the-pulpits are spring wildflowers. The unusual flower hides beneath single or paired leaves, each with three broad leaflets. Plants grow from a button-like tuber.

**Flower color** Jack-in-the-pulpit produces a fleshy spike called a spadix which lies with an outer, leafy spathe that wraps over the spadix like a hood. Above the spadix and spathe are green leafy flowers striped with yellow or purple. The spadix ripens to a cluster of glossy red berries in late summer to early fall.

**Flowering time** Spring.

**Height and spread** 1–3 feet (30–90 cm) tall; 1–1½ feet (30–45 cm) wide.

**Temperature requirements** Zones 3–9.

**Position** Best in evenly moist, humus-rich soil. Thrives in partial to full shade. Will tolerate constantly moist soil but will wither in soggy conditions.

**Cultivation** Clumps grow slowly from offsets or seed. Plant tubers 4 inches (10 cm) apart.

**Propagation** To grow from seed, remove the pulp from the ripe berries and store through winter. Sow the seed outdoors in spring or fall. Seedlings develop slowly and may take several years to bloom. It is easiest to propagate Jack-in-the-pulpit by division from natural offsets in spring.

*Arisaema triphyllum*

**Pest and disease prevention** No serious pests or diseases.

**Landscape uses** The real feature of this plant is its striking greenery; plant among low wildflowers for an eye-catching vertical accent. Combine with fringed bleeding heart, bloodroot, hostas and ferns. Plant under shrubs or flowering trees.

# THRIFT

*Armeria maritima* Plumbaginaceae

Thrift forms dense tufts of grasslike, gray-green evergreen leaves. The taller bloom stalks arise from the centers of the tightly packed rosettes.

**Flower color** Small pink flowers crowded into rounded 1-inch (2.5-cm) heads.

**Flowering time** Late spring and summer.

**Height and spread**
10–14 inches (25–35 cm) tall; 8–10 inches (20–25 cm) wide.

**Temperature requirements**
Zones 4–8.

**Position** Average to humus-rich, moist but well-drained soil. Thrives in full sun. Prefers cool nights and bloom seasons with medium to low-level humidity.

**Cultivation** Drought-tolerant once established; will grow in rock crevices where water is scarce. Tolerates air- and soilborne salt; perfect for seaside gardens.

**Propagation** Divide clumps in early spring or fall. Sow seed indoors in winter on a warm (70°F [21°C]) seedbed.

**Pest and disease prevention**
No serious pests or diseases.

**Landscape uses** Plant in rock and wall gardens or along paths.

**Other common names**
Sea pink.

**Cultivars** 'Alba' has white flowers on 5-inch (12.5-cm) tall stems. 'Dusseldorf Pride' has wine red flowers on 6–8-inch (15–20-cm) tall stems. 'Robusta' has 3-inch (7.5-cm) pink flower heads on 12–15-inch (30–37.5-cm) tall stems. 'Vindictive' is only 6 inches (15 cm) tall with bright, rose-pink flowers.

*Armeria maritima*

# BLACKBERRY LILY

*Belamcanda chinensis* Iridaceae

Blackberry lilies produce showy, curved fans of foliage that resemble irises. Branched clumps grow from creeping rhizomes and may produce dozens of orange flowers.

**Flower color** Six-petaled 2-inch (5-cm) orange flowers are speckled with red. Inflated seed capsules split in fall to expose the berry-like clusters of black seeds that give the plant its common name.

*Belamcanda chinensis*

**Flowering time** Mid- to late summer.

**Height and spread** 2–4 feet (60–120 cm) tall; 1–2 feet (30–60 cm) wide.

**Temperature requirements** Zones 4–10. May need winter protection in colder areas of Zone 4. Place a frame around the plants and cover with light outdoor fabric or loosely woven hesian.

**Position** Average to humus-rich, well-drained soil. Full sun to light shade. Depending on conditions, afternoon shade may prolong the life of individual flowers.

**Cultivation** Plants spread by creeping rhizomes to form dense clumps. Divide as necessary to control spread. Self-sown seedlings often appear.

**Propagation** Divide in late summer or sow fresh seed outdoors in spring. Takes longer to flower from seed; may not bloom until the second year.

**Pest and disease prevention** No serious pests or diseases.

**Landscape uses** Plant with garden phlox, daylilies and other plants with large flowers that contrast with blackberry lily's small starry flowers. Excellent in fresh arrangements.

**Other species** The closely related *B. flabellata* grows 1–2 feet (30–60 cm) tall and has yellow flowers.

# HEART-LEAVED BERGENIA
*Bergenia cordifolia* Saxifragaceae

Heart-leaved bergenias are handsome plants with broad, oval, leathery evergreen foliage. The leaves emerge in a whorl from a stout, creeping rhizome.

**Flower color**  Nodding pink or rose flowers are carried above the foliage on thick, branched stems.

**Flowering time**  Late winter and early spring.

**Height and spread**
12–14 inches (30–35 cm) tall; 12 inches (30 cm) wide.

**Temperature requirements**
Zones 3–9. Foliage benefits from winter protection where snowfall is not consistent.

**Position**  Prefers moist, humus-rich soil. Thrives in full sun to partial shade. Provide afternoon shade in warmer zones to protect leaves from burning.

**Cultivation**  These long-lived perennials creep slowly from branching rhizomes. As clumps age, they become bare in the center. Lift plants in spring and remove old portions of the rhizome with a sharp knife. Replant into soil that has been enriched with organic matter. Protect with a winter mulch of evergreen boughs or marsh hay.

**Propagation**  Bergenias are best divided in spring. Sow ripe seed indoors on a warm (70°F [21°C]) seedbed. Leave seed uncovered.

*Bergenia cordifolia*

**Pest and disease prevention**
These plants are particularly attractive to slugs. Exclude these pests with barrier strips of wood ashes, diatomaceous earth or sand; or bait them with shallow pans of beer set flush with the soil surface.

**Landscape uses**  Use as accents at the base of rock walls or along a garden path. Plant under shrubs for a glossy, deep green groundcover.

227

# MARSH MARIGOLD

*Caltha palustris* Ranunculaceae

Marsh marigolds grow in moist soil and shallow wetlands. They produce yellow spring flowers over mounds of rounded leaves from a thick crown with fleshy white roots.

**Flower color** Butter yellow 1½-inch (3.5-cm) flowers have five shiny petals and are carried in open clusters.

**Flowering time** Early to mid-spring.

**Height and spread** 1–2 feet (30–60 cm) tall; up to 2 feet (60 cm) wide.

**Temperature requirements** Zones 2–8.

**Position** Wet, humus-rich or loamy soil. Full sun to partial shade. Grows even when covered with 1–4 inches (2.5–10 cm) of water. Once flowering is complete, moisture is less critical, though soil must not be allowed to dry out.

**Cultivation** Divide overgrown plants a month after flowering, when dormant.

**Propagation** Divide in summer. Sow fresh seed outdoors immediately upon ripening; plants will not germinate until the following spring.

**Pest and disease prevention** No serious pests or diseases.

**Landscape uses** Marsh marigold is perfect for water

*Caltha palustris*

gardens or along the low banks of streams and the edges of ponds. Plant with primroses, irises and ferns in natural and created bog gardens or in any low, wet spots in your yard.

**Other common names** Cowslip.

**Cultivars** 'Flore Pleno' ('Multiplex') has fully double flowers that last for a week or more.

# CLUSTERED BELLFLOWER

*Campanula glomerata* Campanulaceae

Clustered bellflower is a robust plant with erect, leafy, flowering stems and hairy oval leaves. Plants grow from slow-creeping rhizomes with fibrous roots.

**Flower color** Purple to blue-violet flowers are carried in tiered clusters at the nodes of the flowering stem.

**Flowering time** Late spring or early summer.

**Height and spread** 1–3 feet (30–90 cm) tall; 1 foot (30 cm) wide.

**Temperature requirements** Zones 3–8.

**Position** Evenly moist, humus-rich soil. Full sun to partial shade; grow under deciduous trees. Tolerates alkaline soil.

**Cultivation** Cut back flowering stems after blossoms fade. The striking summer foliage makes an attractive groundcover. Dividing the overgrown clumps will keep the plants vigorous.

**Propagation** Divide in fall or early spring. Sow seed indoors; leave seed uncovered as light promotes germination. Self-sown seedlings will appear. Take cuttings after flowering.

**Pest and disease prevention** Exclude slugs with barrier strips of diatomaceous earth, wood ashes or sand; bait them with shallow pans of beer set flush with the soil.

**Landscape uses** Plant in borders with Siberian iris and leopard's bane or in shaded gardens with ferns. In informal woodland gardens, combine with yellow foxglove.

**Cultivars** 'Crown of Snow' has large clusters of white flowers. 'Joan Elliot' is a delicate, floriferous selection with deep blue-violet flowers. 'Superba' grows 2½ feet (75 cm) tall with violet flowers.

*Campanula glomerata*

# KNAPWEED

*Centaurea dealbata* Compositae

Knapweeds have lobed leaves with woolly divisions. The leaves clothe thick, weakly upright stems over fibrous-rooted crowns. Use the blooms as fresh cut flowers or for drying.

**Flower color** Fringed pink flowers have broad white centers. They resemble bachelor's buttons and are borne one to a stem.

**Flowering time** Late spring and early summer.

**Height and spread** 1½–2½ feet (45–75 cm) tall; 1½ feet (45 cm) wide.

**Temperature requirements** Zones 3–7.

**Position** Prefers moist but well-drained, humus-rich soil. Thrives in full sun and will not tolerate shade.

**Cultivation** Remove flower heads as they fade to promote growth of the whole plant and rebloom of the flowers. Cut plants back to remove floppy stems when flower production wanes. Divide clumps

*Centaurea dealbata*

every two to three years to keep plants vigorous.

**Propagation** Divide in spring or fall. Sow seed outdoors in fall or indoors in late winter.

**Pest and disease prevention** No serious pests or diseases.

**Landscape uses** Combine knapweeds with ornamental grasses, coneflowers and yarrows in informal cottage gardens and meadow plantings.

**Other common names** Persian cornflower.

**Cultivars** 'Steenbergii' is a long-flowering, compact selection with rose pink flowers. 'John Coutts', a selection of the related *C. hypoleuca*, has rosy pink to purple flowers on 2-foot (60-cm) tall stems.

# RED VALERIAN
*Centranthus ruber* Valerianaceae

Red valerian is an upright perennial with opposite, gray-green oval leaves and white, pink or red flowers on branching stems. Plants grow from a fibrous-rooted crown.

**Flower color** Small flowers are carried in domed, branched clusters. Colors range from white to pink, rose or coral red.

**Flowering time**
Spring and summer.

**Height and spread** 1–3 feet (30–90 cm) tall; 2 feet (60 cm) wide.

**Temperature requirements**
Zones 4–8. Plants perform best in areas of low summer rainfall.

**Position** Average, sandy or loamy, neutral or alkaline soil. Full sun. Grows readily in rock crevices where soil is limited. Red valerian can survive for a period of up to four weeks without watering.

**Cultivation** Plants may become floppy after blooming; stake if necessary. Shear the whole plant back to promote compact growth and reblooming.

*Centranthus ruber*

**Propagation** Sow seed outdoors in summer. Plants often self-sow prolifically. To reproduce plants of a specific color, remove basal shoots and treat them as cuttings.

**Pest and disease prevention**
No serious pests or diseases.

**Landscape uses** Perfect for wall and rock gardens. The striking coral red flowers combine well with the neutral colors of stone or with creamy yellow flowers.

**Other common names**
Jupiter's beard.

**Varieties** *C. ruber* 'Albus' has white flowers; 'Atrococcineus' has deep red flowers; 'Roseus' has deep rose flowers.

# PINK TURTLEHEAD

*Chelone lyonii* Scrophulariaceae

Pink turtleheads are bushy perennials with tall, leafy stems from a stout, fibrous-rooted crown. The large leaves are broadly ovate with toothed margins.

**Flower color** Rose pink inflated, tubular flowers resemble the head of a turtle with jaws open.

**Flowering time** Late summer into fall.

**Height and spread** 1–3 feet (30–90 cm) tall; 1–2 feet (30–60 cm) wide.

**Temperature requirements** Zones 3–8; generally intolerant of excessive heat.

**Position** Evenly moist, humus-rich soil. Thrives in full sun to partial shade. Tolerates drier soil once established.

**Cultivation** Divide the crowns to reduce large, woody clumps in aged plants.

**Propagation** Divide in spring or after flowering. Take stem cuttings in early summer; remove any flower buds. Sow seed outdoors in fall or indoors in late winter after stratification. To stratify, mix seed with moist peat moss or seed-starting medium in a plastic bag. Close the bag with a twist-tie and refrigerate for four to six weeks. Then sow the mixture as you would normal seed.

**Pest and disease prevention** No serious pests or diseases.

*Chelone lyonii*

**Landscape uses** Combine with asters, phlox and goldenrods for late summer color. Use in bog gardens and around the edges of ponds and marshes.

**Other species** *C. glabra*, white turtlehead, has narrow leaves and white flowers. Zones 3–8. *C. obliqua*, rose turtlehead, is similar to *C. lyonii* but flowers later and is less cold hardy. Zones 5–9.

# GARDEN MUM

*Chrysanthemum* x *morifolium* Compositae

Hardy garden mums have stout stems clothed in lobed leaves. They grow from creeping stems with tangled fibrous roots. Most garden mums bloom in late summer and fall.

**Flower color** Garden mums bloom in a wide variety of colors from white to pale pink, rose, burgundy, red, golden brown, gold, yellow and cream. Flower shapes range from button-like heads to pom-poms. Sizes range from 1–6 inches (2.5–15 cm).

**Flowering time** Late summer through fall.

**Height and spread** 1½–5 feet (45–150 cm) tall; 1–3 feet (30–90 cm) wide.

**Temperature requirements** Garden mums vary in their hardiness. Greenhouse crops are less hardy than those selected for extreme cold tolerance. Zones 3–9.

**Position** Light, humus-rich, well-drained soil. Full sun to light shade.

**Cultivation** Tend to sprawl in summer. Pinch the stems in May or June to promote compact growth. Stop pinching altogether by July 1 or you'll sacrifice bloom.

**Propagation** Divide in spring. Tip cuttings taken in late spring or early summer root quickly.

**Pest and disease prevention** Aphids may attack the young shoots and will deform growth and decrease vigor if not controlled. Spider mites may cause stippling and leaf curl. Spray with insecticidal soap or a botanical insecticide such as pyrethrin.

**Landscape uses** The bright colors of garden mums are a familiar sight in late summer. Use them to breathe new life into tired annual displays or combine them with asters, goldenrods and anemones for a showy fall display.

*Chrysanthemum* x *morifolium*

# THREAD-LEAVED COREOPSIS

*Coreopsis verticillata* Compositae

Thread-leaved coreopsis is an airy, rounded plant with thread-like, three-lobed leaves and bright yellow summer flowers. Plants grow from a fibrous-rooted crown.

**Flower color** The 1–2-inch (2.5–5-cm) starry flowers are butter to golden yellow.

**Flowering time** Throughout summer.

*Coreopsis verticillata*

**Height and spread** 1–3 feet (30–90 cm) tall; 2–3 feet (60–90 cm) wide.

**Temperature requirements** Zones 3–9.

**Position** Average to rich, moist but well-drained soil. Thrives in full sun or light shade; drought-tolerant once established.

**Cultivation** Thread-leaved coreopsis is an easy-care perennial that demands little attention once established. Plants will eventually die out at the center. As this starts to happen, divide old clumps and replant in enriched soil.

**Propagation** Divide in spring or fall. Stem cuttings are best taken in early summer.

**Pest and disease prevention** No serious pests or diseases.

**Landscape uses** Perfect for the front of borders and low garden beds in combination with cranesbills, yarrows, daylilies and coneflowers. Grow them with ornamental grasses or use a mass planting with shrubs; they will tolerate the shade.

**Cultivars** 'Golden Showers' grows 2 feet (60 cm) tall with golden yellow flowers.
'Moonbeam' is a spreading plant from 1–2 feet (30–60 cm) wide with pale yellow flowers from early summer through fall.
'Zagreb' is a compact, 8–18-inch (20–45 cm) selection similar to 'Golden Showers'.

# CROCOSMIA

*Crocosmia x crocosmiiflora* Iridaceae

Crocosmia is a brightly colored perennial with vivid red or orange summer flowers and fans of sword-like leaves resembling gladiolus. They grow from button-like corms.

**Flower color** Tubular orange or red flowers are carried on erect, sparsely branched, zigzag stems.

**Flowering time** Summer and early fall; varies with individual cultivars.

**Height and spread** 2–3 feet (60–90 cm) tall; 1–2 feet (30–60 cm) wide.

**Temperature requirements** Zones 6–9. In colder zones, lift corms in fall and store in a cool, dry place.

**Position** Moist, humus-rich soil. Full sun.

**Cultivation** Crocosmias spread to form broad clumps of tightly packed foliage fans. Remove the spent stalks after flowering. Divide overgrown clumps in spring. If you

*Crocosmia x crocosmiiflora*

store corms over winter, replant them when temperatures moderate.

**Propagation** Remove corms from the outside of the clump in spring.

**Pest and disease prevention** Spider mites and thrips cause white or brown stippling or streaks on the leaves. Spray with insecticidal soap or with a botanical insecticide such as pyrethrin. Cut badly damaged plants to the ground and destroy the infested portions.

**Landscape uses** Plant with summer perennials like phlox, daylilies and poppies. Use large clumps as accents along walls or with shrubs.

**Cultivars** 'Citronella' has orange-yellow flowers. 'Solfatare' has golden yellow flowers.

# COMMON BLEEDING HEART

*Dicentra spectabilis* Fumariaceae

Common bleeding hearts are beloved, old-fashioned perennials with strings of hearts held above deeply divided blue-green foliage. Plants grow from thick, fleshy roots.

**Flower color** Bright pink heart-shaped flowers consist of two reflexed lobes with a central column that resembles a dangling drop of blood.

**Flowering time** Early spring to early summer.

**Height and spread** 1–2½ feet (30–75 cm) tall; 2–3 feet (60–90 cm) wide.

**Temperature requirements** Zones 2–9. Extremely tolerant of heat and cold. Mulch in winter in colder zones to keep some of the moisture in the soil and to maintain nutrient levels.

**Position** Evenly moist, humus-rich soil. Partial shade; tolerates full sun in cooler zones.

**Cultivation** Common bleeding hearts will bloom for four to six weeks in spring. In warm climates or if the soil is dry, the plants will go dormant after blooming. Top-dress with well-rotted manure in early spring for soil fertility.

**Propagation** Divide clumps in fall, as they go dormant or if they lose vigor. Replant into soil that has been enriched with organic matter. Sow fresh seed outdoors in early- to mid-summer. Take root cuttings in late summer.

*Dicentra spectabilis*

**Pest and disease prevention** No serious pests or diseases.

**Landscape uses** Plant common bleeding hearts with spring bulbs, primroses and wildflowers for a striking spring display. In warm zones combine them with hostas or groundcovers that will fill the void left by the declining foliage. Plant in front of rounded shrubs for contrast.

# GAS PLANT

*Dictamnus albus* Rutaceae

Gas plant forms shrub-like clumps of stout stems with deep green, pinnately lobed leaves and erect flower spikes. Plants grow from thick, woody crowns with fibrous roots.

**Flower color** The 1-inch (2.5-cm), showy white flowers have five starry petals and ten long, curled, protruding stamens (male reproductive structures).

**Flowering time** Late spring or early summer.

**Height and spread** 1–4 feet (30–120 cm) tall; 1–3 feet (30–90 cm) wide.

**Temperature requirements** Zones 3–8.

**Position** Well-drained, average to humus-rich soil. Full sun to light shade.

**Cultivation** Gas plants are long-lived perennials that are slow to establish and resent disturbance once planted.

**Propagation** Sow fresh seed outdoors in late summer. Seedlings appear the next season but grow slowly. Transplant young plants to their permanent position after three years of growth.

**Pest and disease prevention** No serious pests. Avoid soggy soils, which will encourage root rot. Dispose of infected plants.

**Landscape uses** Combine gas plants with other perennials that

*Dictamnus albus*

need good drainage, such as oriental poppy, yarrows and sundrops. Grows well under the shade of feathery bushes. Established plants are trouble-free.

**Other common names** Dittany.

**Cultivars** 'Purpureus' has dark-veined mauve-purple flowers. 'Rubra' has red-pink flowers.

237

# PURPLE CONEFLOWER

*Echinacea purpurea* Compositae

Purple coneflowers are showy summer daisies with sparse, oval or broadly lance-shaped leaves on stout, hairy stems. Plants grow from thick, deep taproots.

**Flower color** Red-violet to rose pink flowers have broad, drooping rays (petal-like structures) surrounding raised, bristly cones.

**Flowering time** Mid- to late summer.

**Height and spread** 2–4 feet (60–120 cm) tall; 1–2 feet (30–60 cm) wide.

**Temperature requirements** Zones 3–8. Extremely heat-tolerant.

**Position** Average to humus-rich, moist but well-drained soil. Tolerates full sun. Drought-tolerant once established.

**Cultivation** Purple coneflowers increase from basal buds to form broad, long-lived clumps. Division is seldom necessary and is not generally recommended.

**Propagation** Sow seed outdoors in fall or indoors after stratification. To stratify, mix seed with moist peat moss or seed-starting medium in a plastic bag. Close the bag with a twist-tie and place it in the refrigerator for four to six weeks. Sow the mixture as you would normal seed. Take root cuttings in fall.

**Pest and disease prevention** No serious pests or diseases.

*Echinacea purpurea*

**Landscape uses** Plant in formal perennial gardens or meadow and prairie gardens. The flowers combine well with most perennials and ornamental grasses.

**Cultivars** 'Alba' has creamy white flowers.
'Bright Star' has flat rose pink flowers.
'Magnus' has huge, flat rose-purple flowers.

## GLOBE THISTLE
*Echinops ritro* Compositae

Globe thistles are stout, coarse perennials with spiky round flower heads, erect stems and spiny, lobed leaves. They grow from thick, deep-branched taproots.

**Flower color** Globe thistle has small, spiked, steel-blue flowers packed into 1–2-inch (2.5–5-cm) spherical heads.

**Flowering time** Midsummer.

**Height and spread** 2–4 feet (60–120 cm) tall; 2–3 feet (60–90 cm) wide.

**Temperature requirements** Zones 3–8. Heat-tolerant.

**Position** Prefers average to humus-rich, well-drained soil. Tolerates full sun. Good drainage is essential, especially in winter when water may build up.

**Cultivation** Globe thistles are tough, long-lived perennials. They are drought-tolerant once established and thrive for many years without staking or division.

**Propagation** Remove sideshoots from the main clump without disturbing the crown in fall or late winter. Take root cuttings in spring or fall.

**Pest and disease prevention** No serious pests. Plant in well-drained soil to avoid root rot.

**Landscape uses** Combine showy globe thistles with other drought-tolerant perennials like

*Echinops ritro*

Russian sages, sedums, catmints and oriental poppies. Position them near the middle or rear of borders where their height will provide contrast. The flowers are perfect for cutting fresh or for drying and will retain their color.

**Other species** 'Taplow Blue' has 2-inch (5-cm) blue heads. 'Veitch's Blue' is darker with sturdier stems.

# DAISY FLEABANE

*Erigeron speciosus* Compositae

Daisy fleabane forms leafy clumps of hairy, lance-shaped leaves that spring from fibrous-rooted crowns. The colorful flowers bloom in summer.

**Flower color** The 1½-inch (3.5-cm) aster-like flowers have white, pink, rose or purple rays surrounding bright yellow centers.

**Flowering time** Early to midsummer; occasional rebloom.

**Height and spread** 1½–2½ feet (45–75 cm) tall; 1–2 feet (30–60 cm) wide.

**Temperature requirements** Zones 2–9. Tolerant of heat and cold.

**Position** Moist but well-drained, average to humus-rich soil. Full sun to light shade.

**Cultivation** Fleabanes are long-lived perennials that benefit from division every two to three years.

**Propagation** Divide in fall. Take cuttings in spring before the flower buds form. Sow seed outdoors in

*Erigeron speciosus*

fall or indoors in spring using an enriched soil mix.

**Pest and disease prevention** No serious pests or diseases.

**Landscape uses** Plant at the front of beds and borders with summer-blooming perennials like cranesbills, cinquefoils, evening primroses and phlox. Daisy fleabanes make long-lasting cut flowers and they retain their color well as dried flowers. Hang in bunches upside down to dry.

**Hybrids** Many hybrid cultivars originate from crosses with *E. speciosus.*
'Azure Fairy' has semi-double, lavender-blue flowers.
'Darkest of All' has violet-blue flowers.
'Foerster's Darling' has reddish pink flowers.
'Prosperity' has pale lilac flowers.

# AMETHYST SEA HOLLY

*Eryngium amethystinum* Umbelliferae

Amethyst sea holly is an architectural plant with stiff flowering stems and mostly basal, pinnately divided leaves. Plants grow from thick taproots.

**Flower color** Small, steel blue globose flower heads are surrounded by thin, spiny bracts.

**Flowering time** Summer.

*Eryngium amethystinum*

**Height and spread** 1–1½ feet (30–45 cm) tall; 1–2 feet (30–60 cm) wide.

**Temperature requirements** Zone 2–8. Heat- and cold-tolerant.

**Position** Average, well-drained soil. Full sun. Extremely drought-tolerant once established.

**Cultivation** Set plants out in their permanent location while they are young. Older plants resent disturbance. Division is seldom necessary.

**Propagation** Sow fresh seed outdoors in fall or indoors after stratification. To stratify, mix seed with moist peat moss or seed-starting medium in a plastic bag. Close the bag with a twist-tie and place it in the refrigerator for four to six weeks. Then sow mixture as you would normal seed. Division may not work as well as with most perennials because amethyst sea holly is so sensitive.

**Pest and disease prevention** No serious pests or diseases.

**Landscape uses** Plant in the middle of borders with asters, goldenrods, phlox and ornamental grasses.

**Other species** *E. alpinum,* alpine sea holly, is similar but has larger, showier flowers and lobed leaves. Zones 3–8.
*E.* x *zabelii,* zabel eryngo, is a showy hybrid with large blue-violet flowers. Zones 4–8.

# BLANKET FLOWER

*Gaillardia x grandiflora* Compositae

The showy hybrid blanket flower blooms throughout the summer on loose stems with hairy, lobed leaves. Plants grow from fibrous-rooted crowns and may be short-lived.

*Gaillardia x grandiflora*

**Flower color** Ragged yellow-and-orange daisy-like flowers have single or double rows of toothed petal-like rays surrounding a raised yellow center.

**Flowering time** Throughout summer.

**Height and spread** 2–3 feet (60–90 cm) tall; 2 feet (60 cm) wide.

**Temperature requirements** Zones 4–9.

**Position** Average to poor, well-drained soil. Tolerates full sun. Rich, moist soil causes plants to overgrow and flop.

**Cultivation** Blanket flowers are drought-tolerant and thrive in seaside conditions. Divide every few years to keep them vigorous.

**Propagation** Divide in early spring. Sow seed outdoors in fall or indoors in spring after stratification. To stratify, mix seed with moist peat moss or seed-starting medium in a plastic bag. Close the bag with a twist-tie and place it in the refrigerator for four to six weeks. Then sow the mixture as you would normal seed in enriched soil.

**Pest and disease prevention** No serious pests or diseases.

**Landscape uses** Choose blanket flowers for rock gardens, borders or seaside gardens.

**Cultivars** 'Baby Cole' is a dwarf 8-inch (20-cm) selection with orange-centered yellow flowers. 'Bremen' has copper red flowers tipped in yellow. 'Burgundy' has deep red flowers. 'Goblin' is 1 foot (30 cm) tall with red-and-yellow flowers.

# WHITE GAURA

*Gaura lindheimeri* Onagraceae

White gaura is a shrubby perennial with airy flower clusters on wiry stems and small, hairy leaves. This dependable, long-blooming plant grows from a thick, deep taproot.

*Gaura lindheimeri*

**Flower color** White gaura has unusual white flowers that are tinged with pink. They have four triangular petals, long curled stamens (male reproductive structures) protruding from the flower and dance in slender spikes above the foliage.

**Flowering time** Throughout summer.

**Height and spread** 3–4 feet (90–120 cm) tall; 3 feet (90 cm) wide.

**Temperature requirements** Zones 5–9. Extremely heat- and drought-tolerant.

**Position** Moist, well-drained, average to rich soil. Full sun.

**Cultivation** White gaura is an easy-care perennial that thrives for years with little attention. Plants bloom nonstop all summer despite high heat and intense humidity. Deadhead the blossoms to promote healthy rebloom and remove old bloom stalks to make way for the new ones.

**Propagation** Sow seed outdoors in spring or fall. Self-sown seedlings are likely to appear.

**Pest and disease prevention** No serious pests or diseases.

**Landscape uses** White gaura is a lovely addition to formal and informal gardens alike. The flower clusters look like a swirl of dancing butterflies. Combine them with low-mounding perennials like verbenas, cranesbills and sedums. In late summer they are a beautiful contrast with tawny ornamental grasses. They are an excellent cut flower for use as a feature in a fresh arrangement.

# BABY'S-BREATH

*Gypsophila paniculata* Caryophyllaceae

Baby's-breath is an old-fashioned perennial with airy flower clusters and sparse, smooth blue-green foliage. The stems and basal leaves grow from a thick, deep taproot.

**Flower color** Small, single or double white flowers are carried in large domed clusters.

**Flowering time** Throughout summer.

*Gypsophila paniculata*

**Height and spread** 3–4 feet (90–120 cm) tall; 2–3 feet (60–90 cm) wide.

**Temperature requirements** Zones 3–9. Heat- and cold-tolerant.

**Position** Near neutral to alkaline, moist, humus-rich soil. Full sun to light shade.

**Cultivation** Set out in spring and do not disturb the crowns once plants are established. Good drainage is essential for longevity. Some double-flowered cultivars are grafted onto seed-grown, single rootstocks. Plant them with the crowns below the surface to encourage stems to form their own roots. Tall cultivars may have weaker stems and need staking.

**Propagation** Take cuttings in summer. Sow seed outdoors in spring or fall, or indoors in spring.

**Pest and disease prevention** No serious pests or diseases.

**Landscape uses** Use the airy sprays to hide the yellowing foliage of bulbs and perennials such as oriental poppy that go dormant in summer. Combine them with bold and spiky perennials for dramatic effect.

**Cultivars** 'Bristol Fairy' has double flowers on compact 2-foot (60-cm) plants. 'Perfecta' has large double flowers. 'Pink Fairy' has double pink flowers.

# Common Sneezeweed

*Helenium autumnale* Compositae

Common sneezeweed is a showy, late-season perennial with tall, leafy stems that spring from a fibrous-rooted crown. The hairy, lance-shaped leaves are edged with a few large teeth.

*Helenium autumnale*

**Flower color** The 2-inch (5-cm), yellow, daisy-like flowers have broad, petal-like rays.

**Flowering time** Late summer and fall.

**Height and spread** 3–5 feet (90–150 cm) tall; 2–3 feet (60–90 cm) wide.

**Temperature requirements** Zones 3–8.

**Position** Prefers evenly moist, humus-rich soil. Thrives in full sun or light shade. Plants tolerate wet soil.

**Cultivation** Either stake it or pinch the stem tips in early summer to promote compact growth. Divide the clumps every three to four years to keep them growing vigorously.

**Propagation** Divide in spring or fall. Take stem cuttings in early summer. Sow seed of the species outdoors in spring or fall.

**Pest and disease prevention** No serious pests or diseases.

**Landscape uses** Common sneezeweeds offer late-season color. Combine them with asters, goldenrods and garden phlox.

**Other common names** Helen's flower.

**Cultivars** 'Butterpat' has bright yellow flowers on 3–4-foot (90–120 cm)-stems. 'Crimson Beauty' has mahogany flowers. 'Riverton Beauty' has golden yellow flowers with bronze-red centers.

# CHRISTMAS ROSE

*Helleborus niger* Ranunculaceae

Christmas roses are winter or early-spring perennials with deeply lobed, leathery leaves growing from a stout crown with fleshy roots. The flowers open white and turn pink with age.

**Flower color** White flowers have five petal-like sepals surrounded by green leafy bracts.

**Flowering time** Early winter through spring.

*Helleborus niger*

**Height and spread** 1–1½ feet (30–45 cm) tall; 1–2 feet (30–60 cm) wide.

**Temperature requirements** Zones 3–8.

**Position** Prefers evenly moist, humus-rich soil. Thrives in light to partial shade. Established plants tolerate dry soil and will do well in deep shade.

**Cultivation** In spring, remove any damaged leaves. Christmas rose takes two to three years to become established and resents disturbance. Divide rarely and only to propagate.

**Propagation** Lift clumps after flowering in spring and separate the crowns. Replant the divisions immediately. Self-sown seedlings often appear. Sow seed outdoors in spring or early summer.

**Pest and disease prevention** No serious pests or diseases.

**Landscape uses** Combine with early spring bulbs, wildflowers and ferns. The lovely foliage is attractive all season. The inconspicuous flower will not clash with many plants.

**Other species**
*H. argutifolius*, Corsican hellebore, has three-lobed leaves and green flowers. Zones 6 (with winter protection)–8.
*H. orientalis*, lenten rose, is similar to *H. niger* but has broader leaflets and pink, red or white flowers borne in loose clusters. Zones 4–9.

# DAYLILY

*Hemerocallis* hybrids  Liliaceae

Daylily hybrids are among the most popular perennials. Although each flower only lasts one day, a profusion of new buds keeps the plants in bloom for a month or more.

**Flower color**  Flowers vary in color and form. Wild species are mostly orange or yellow with wide petals and thin, petal-like sepals. Hybrids come in many colors.

**Flowering time**  Late spring through summer.

**Height and spread**  1–5 feet (30–150 cm) tall; 2–3 feet (60–90 cm) wide. There are miniature and standard sizes as well as extremely tall kinds.

**Temperature requirements**  Zones 3–9 for most hybrids.

**Position**  Prefers evenly moist, average to humus-rich soil. Thrives in full sun to light shade. Most of the modern hybrids need at least eight hours of direct sunlight to flower well. Some of the older selections and the species will bloom in partial shade.

*Hemerocallis* hybrid

**Cultivation**  Daylilies are long-lived, easy-care perennials. Plant container-grown or bareroot plants in spring or fall. Plants take a year to become established. and then spread quickly to form dense clumps. Most hybrids and species can remain in place for many years without disturbance. Some hybrids have so many bloom stalks that the flowers crowd together and lose their beauty. Divide these plants every three years. Deadhead the plants regularly to keep them looking their best.

**Propagation**  Hybrids must be propagated by division only in fall or spring. Seed-grown plants will be variable and are often inferior to the parent plant.

**Pest and disease prevention** Aphids and thrips may attack the foliage and flower buds. Wash aphids off with a stream of water; spray thrips with insecticidal soap.

# HOSTA

*Hosta* hybrids  Liliaceae

Hostas are indispensable foliage plants for shaded gardens. Their thick, pleated or puckered leaves grow from stout crowns with thick fleshy roots.

*Hosta* hybrids

**Flower color**  Lavender, purple or white flowers are carried in slender spikes. Individual flowers have three petals and three petal-like sepals.

**Flowering time**  Summer or fall depending on hybrid and origin.

**Height and spread**
6 inches–3 feet (15–90 cm) tall; 6 inches–5 feet (15–150 cm) wide.

**Temperature requirements**
Zones 3–8. Some selections are probably hardy to Zone 2.

**Position**  Evenly moist, humus-rich soil. Light to full shade.

Adaptable to both dry and wet soil conditions. Filtered sun encourages the best leaf color in the gold- and blue-leaved forms. All hostas need protection from hot afternoon sun, especially in warm zones. Variegated and yellow-leaved cultivars are particularly susceptible to burning.

**Cultivation**  Hostas take several years to reach mature form and size, especially the large-leaved cultivars. Allow ample room when planting to accommodate their ultimate size. New shoots are slow to emerge in spring, so take care not to damage them during spring cleanup. Plant small bulbs such as snowdrops (*Galanthus spp.*) and squills (*Scilla spp.*) around the clumps to mark their location.

**Propagation**  Divide in late summer.

**Pest and disease prevention**
Set shallow pans of beer flush with the soil surface to drown slugs and snails or exclude them with a barrier of diatomaceous earth, wood ashes or sand around each plant.

# PERENNIAL CANDYTUFT

*Iberis sempervirens* Cruciferae

Perennial candytuft is a floriferous, semiwoody subshrub with persistent stems tightly clothed in narrow deep green leaves. Plants grow from fibrous-rooted crowns.

*Iberis sempervirens*

**Flower color** The tight, rounded clusters consist of many ¼-inch (6-mm), four-petaled flowers.

**Flowering time** Early spring.

**Height and spread**
6–12 inches (15–30 cm) tall; 12–24 inches (30–60 cm) wide.

**Temperature requirements**
Zones 3–9.

**Position** Average to humus-rich, well-drained soil. Full sun to light shade.

**Cultivation** Space plants 1–1½ feet (30–45 cm) apart in informal plantings or 6 inches (15 cm) apart if edging a planting. Shear after flowering to promote compact growth. Mulch plants in Zones 3 and 4 to protect stems from winter damage.

**Propagation** Layer or take cuttings in early summer. Sow seed outdoors in spring or fall.

**Pest and disease prevention** No serious pests or diseases.

**Landscape uses** Use perennial candytuft to edge formal plantings, walks or walls. Plant it in rock gardens or in combination with spring bulbs and early-blooming perennials. Try them with bleeding hearts, basket-of-gold, rock cresses and columbines.

**Cultivars** 'Autumn Snow' has large, white flowers and reblooms in fall.
'Pygmaea' is a low-spreading selection.
'Snowflake' has large, white flower clusters on 8–10-inch (20–25-cm) stems.

# COMMON TORCH LILY

*Kniphofia uvaria* Liliaceae

Common torch lily is a commanding perennial with tufts of narrow evergreen leaves from a fleshy rooted crown. The flower spikes add a dramatic accent to summer gardens.

*Kniphofia uvaria*

**Flower color** Long slender spikes consist of tightly packed, tubular flowers. The lowest on the spike are yellow-white; the upper ones are red.

**Flowering time** Late spring and summer.

**Height and spread** 3–5 feet (90–150 cm) tall; 2–4 feet (60–120 cm) wide.

**Temperature requirements** Zones 5–9.

**Position** Average to humus-rich, well-drained soil. Full sun. Established plants are quite drought-tolerant.

**Cultivation** Set out 2–2½ feet (60–75 cm) apart. Leave established plants undisturbed. Will increase to form clumps.

**Propagation** Remove a few crowns from the edges of clumps in fall. Sow seed indoors in winter after stratification. To stratify, mix seed with moist peat moss or seed-starting medium in a plastic bag. Close the bag with a twist-tie and place it in the refrigerator for four to six weeks. Then sow the mixture as you would normal seed, using enriched soil.

**Pest and disease prevention** Provide excellent drainage to avoid crown rot.

**Landscape uses** The bold, vertical form of common torch lilies adds excitement to perennial borders and rock gardens. Combine with ornamental grasses, wormwoods, sundrops and other summer perennials.

**Other common names** Red-hot poker.

# LAVENDER

*Lavandula angustifolia* Labiatae

Lavender is a small, rounded shrub beloved for its herbal and ornamental qualities. The fragrant gray-green leaves clothe soft hairy stems topped with spikes of purple-blue flowers.

**Flower color** The ½-inch (1-cm) purple-blue flowers are carried in tight, narrow clusters.

**Flowering time** Early to late summer.

**Height and spread** 2–3 feet (60–90 cm) tall; 2–3 feet (60–90 cm) wide.

**Temperature requirements** Zones 5–8.

**Position** Average to humus-rich, well-drained soil. Thrives in full sun to light shade. Neutral or slightly alkaline soil is best. Extremely drought-tolerant.

**Cultivation** Shoots may be partially killed in winter. Prune out any dead wood and reshape the shrubs in spring. Shear plants every few years to encourage fresh new growth and to promote bloom.

**Propagation** Layer or take tip cuttings in summer. Place cuttings in a well-drained medium; transplant them as soon as they root to avoid rot.

**Pest and disease prevention** No serious pests or diseases.

**Landscape uses** Plant lavender in ornamental and herb gardens. Use as an edging plant or to configure knot gardens. In borders combine them with other plants that need excellent drainage such as yarrows and sundrops.

**Cultivars** 'Dwarf Blue' has dark blue flowers on 1-foot (30-cm) plants. 'Hidcote' grows 1½ feet (45 cm) tall with purple-blue flowers. 'Jean Davis' has pale pink flowers. 'Munstead' has lavender flowers on 1½-foot (45-cm) plants.

*Lavandula angustifolia*

# SEA LAVENDER

*Limonium latifolium* Plumbaginaceae

Sea lavender has airy clusters of pink flowers above showy rosettes of spatula-shaped to narrowly oval shiny green leaves. Plants grow from stout, woody crowns.

**Flower color**  Tiny pink flowers are carried in broad, domed clusters.

**Flowering time**  Summer.

**Height and spread**  2–2½ feet (60–75 cm) tall; 2–2½ feet (60–75 cm) wide.

**Temperature requirements** Zones 3–9.

**Position**  Prefers average to humus-rich, moist but well-drained soil. Thrives in full sun. Extremely drought-tolerant. Grows in alkaline or saline soil.

*Limonium latifolium*

**Cultivation**  Sea lavender takes time to establish and is sensitive to disturbances; best untouched after planting.

**Propagation**  Remove small crowns from the main clump in fall. Sow seed outdoors in fall. Seedlings are slow-growing.

**Pest and disease prevention** Plant on a well-drained site; subject to crown rot in wet soil.

**Landscape uses**  Plant in borders or seaside gardens. Combine the airy flowers with irises, phlox, yarrows, asters and ornamental grasses in a cottage garden. Create a delicate, fine-textured edging to a narrow pathway or around a patio using sea lavender, amethyst sea holly, baby's breath and coral bells. It can also be used in a mass planting.

**Other common names**  Statice.

**Cultivars**  'Violetta' has dark purple-blue flowers.

# CARDINAL FLOWER

*Lobelia cardinalis* Campanulaceae

Cardinal flowers have fiery colored flower spikes on leafy stems and grow from a fibrous-rooted crown. The lance-shaped leaves may be fresh green or red-bronze.

*Lobelia cardinalis*

**Flower color** Brilliant scarlet tubular flowers have three lower and two upper petals that look like delicate birds in flight.

**Flowering time** Late summer to fall.

**Height and spread** 2–4 feet (60–120 cm) tall; 1–2 feet (30–60 cm) wide.

**Temperature requirements** Zones 2–9.

**Position** Prefers evenly moist, humus-rich soil. Thrives in full sun to partial shade.

**Cultivation** Cardinal flowers are shallow-rooted and subject to frost heaving. Where winters are cold, mulch plants to protect the crowns. In warmer zones winter mulch may rot the crowns. Replant in spring if frost has lifted them. Plants may be short-lived, but self-sown seedlings are numerous; cut back regularly.

**Propagation** Divide the plants in late fall or spring. Sow seed uncovered outdoors in fall or spring, or indoors in late winter. The seedlings grow quickly and will bloom the first year from seed; they may die quickly also.

**Pest and disease prevention** No serious pests or diseases.

**Landscape uses** Cardinal flowers need even moisture so they are commonly used around pools, along streams or in informal plantings. Combine them with irises, hostas and ferns.

**Cultivars** 'Royal Robe' has ruby red flowers.

# PLUME POPPY

*Macleaya cordata* Papaveraceae

The imposing plume poppy is tree-like in stature, with lobed leaves clothing erect stems. Plants grow from stout, creeping roots that can quickly become invasive.

*Macleaya cordata*

**Flower color** The 12-inch (30-cm) plumes consist of small cream-colored flowers that give way to showy, flat, rose-colored seed pods.

**Flowering time** Summer.

**Height and spread** 6–10 feet (1.8–3 m) tall; 4–8 feet (1.2–2.4 m) wide.

**Temperature requirements** Zones 3–8.

**Position** Moist, average to humus-rich soil. Full sun to partial shade. Stems are not as sturdy on shade-grown plants.

**Cultivation** Established clumps of plume poppy can double in size each season. Control is inevitably necessary to avert a total takeover. Chop off the creeping roots with a spade as soon as you see new stems emerging.

**Propagation** Remove new offsets in spring or fall or take root cuttings in winter.

**Pest and disease prevention** No serious pests or diseases.

**Landscape uses** Place plume poppies at the rear of borders where there is ample room for them to grow. A mature clump is a lovely site. Plant them as accents along stairs or fences or use them like shrubs as a focal point. Plume poppy will provide blossoms even in withering heat, which makes it a very useful garden addition.

# VIRGINIA BLUEBELLS

*Mertensia virginica* Boraginaceae

Virginia bluebells are lovely spring wildflowers with graceful flowers on arching stems clothed with thin blue-green leaves. Plants grow from thick roots and go dormant after flowering.

*Mertensia virginica*

**Flower color** Nodding sky blue bells open from pink buds.

**Flowering time** Spring.

**Height and spread** 1–2 feet (30–60 cm) tall; 1–2 feet (30–60 cm) wide.

**Temperature requirements** Zones 3–9.

**Position** Prefers consistently moist, well-drained, humus-rich soil; water at soil level for best results. Thrives in full sun but will tolerate shade.

**Cultivation** Virginia bluebells emerge early in spring and go dormant soon after flowering. Sun is essential to bloom but plants are shade-tolerant once dormant. Place where you will not dig into them by accident.

**Propagation** Divide large clumps after flowering or in fall; leave at least one bud per division. Self-sown seedlings are usually abundant. They will bloom the second or third year.

**Pest and disease prevention** No serious pests or diseases.

**Landscape uses** Plant Virginia bluebells along a woodland path with spring bulbs such as daffodils and squills, as well as wildflowers like spring beauty and bloodroot. For interest, interplant clumps with foliage plants such as ferns and hostas; this will also fill the gaps left by dormant plants.

# OZARK SUNDROPS

*Oenothera macrocarpon* Onagraceae

Ozark sundrops are showy perennials with yellow flowers and narrow pale green leaves on sprawling stems. Plants grow from a deep taproot and spread by creeping stems.

**Flower color** Bright lemon yellow flowers are saucer-shaped and 3–4 inches (7.5–10 cm) wide.

**Flowering time** Late spring and early summer, sporadically throughout the season.

**Height and spread**
6–12 inches (15–30 cm) tall;
12–36 inches (30–90 cm) wide.

**Temperature requirements**
Zones 4–8.

**Position** Average to humus-rich, well-drained soil. Full sun. Established plants are extremely drought- and heat-tolerant.

**Cultivation** Plants form large clumps with age so space at least 30 inches (75 cm) apart. Stems root as they spread.

*Oenothera macrocarpon*

**Propagation** Divide rosettes in early spring. Take stem cuttings in early summer. Sow seed outdoors in fall or indoors in early spring in enriched, moist soil or a commercial potting mix.

**Pest and disease prevention**
No serious pests or diseases.

**Landscape uses** Use Ozark sundrops at the front of borders with phlox, cranesbills, catmints, yarrows and other early-season perennials. Performs well in rock gardens and meadow plantings. Can be planted in pots for outdoor use on sunny patios.

**Other common names**
Missouri primrose. Formerly known as *O. missouriensis*.

**Cultivars** 'Greencourt Lemon' has 2-inch (5-cm) soft, sulfur yellow flowers.

# COMMON GARDEN PEONY

*Paeonia lactiflora*  Ranunculaceae

Common garden peonies are shrub-like, with sturdy stalks clothed in compound, shiny green leaves. Plants grow from thick, fleshy roots and may live for 100 years.

**Flower color**  Ranges in color from white, cream and yellow to pink, rose, burgundy and scarlet. Flowers may be single, semidouble or double.

**Flowering time**  Common garden peonies are classified by their bloom time; early May (April in the South) blooming; mid-May blooming; and late May (early June in the North) blooming.

**Height and spread**  1½–3 feet (45–90 cm) tall; 3–4 feet (90–120 cm) wide.

**Temperature requirements**  Zones 2–8. Extremely cold-tolerant. Winter temperatures in the deep south are not cool enough to initiate flowering.

**Position**  Moist, humus-rich soil. Full sun to light shade.

*Paeonia lactiflora*

**Cultivation**  Plant container-grown peonies in spring or fall. Plant bareroot plants in September and October. Dig a hole 8–10 inches (20–25 cm) deep in well-prepared soil. Place the "eyes" (buds) 1–1½ inches (2.5–3 cm) below the soil surface. Space plants 3–4 feet (90–120 cm) apart to allow for spreading.

**Propagation**  Divide in fall.

**Pest and disease prevention**  Spray or dust foliage with an organically acceptable fungicide such as sulfur to discourage the fungal disease Botrytis.

**Landscape uses**  Combine the deep red new shoots of common peony with early spring bulbs like snowdrops and squills. Spring and early-summer perennials such as irises, foxgloves and columbines are excellent companions.

# COMMON BEARDTONGUE

*Penstemon barbatus* Scrophulariaceae

Common beardtongue is a showy plant with erect flower spikes clothed in shiny, broadly lance-shaped leaves. Flowering stems and basal foliage rosettes grow from fibrous-rooted crowns.

**Flower color** The 1–1½-inch (2.5–3.5-cm) irregular, tubular, pink flowers have two upper and three lower lips.

**Flowering time** Late spring to early summer.

**Height and spread** 1½–3 feet (45–90 cm) tall; 1–2 feet (30–60 cm) wide.

**Temperature requirements** Zones 3–8.

**Position** Average to humus-rich, well-drained soil. Full sun to light shade. Good drainage is essential for success.

**Cultivation** Plants form dense clumps with maturity and benefit from division every four to six years. More frequent division is required when plants are growing in rich soil.

**Propagation** Divide in spring. Sow seed outdoors in fall or indoors in winter after stratification. To stratify, mix seed with moist peat moss or seed-starting medium in a plastic bag. Close the bag with a twist-tie and place it in the refrigerator for four to six weeks. Then sow the mixture as you would normal seed. Seedlings may bloom the first year.

*Penstemon barbatus*

**Pest and disease prevention** No serious pests or diseases.

**Landscape uses** Plant beardtongues in formal borders, informal gardens and rock gardens. Combine their spiky flowers with rounded plants like cranesbills, yarrows and coral bells.

**Cultivars** 'Bashful' has salmon-pink flowers.

# RUSSIAN SAGE

*Perovskia atriplicifolia* Labiatae

Russian sage is a shrubby, branching summer-blooming perennial with erect stems clothed in gray-green deeply lobed leaves. Plants grow from fibrous-rooted crowns.

**Flower color** Small, irregularly shaped blue flowers are carried in slender 12–15-inch (30–37.5-cm) wiry sprays.

**Flowering time** Mid- to late summer.

**Height and spread** 3–5 feet (90–150 cm) tall; 3–5 feet (90–150 cm) wide.

**Temperature requirements** Zones 4–9.

**Position** Prefers average to rich, well-drained soil. Thrives in full sun. Good drainage in the soil is essential for success.

**Cultivation** The stems of Russian sage become woody with age. After hard frost, cut the stems back to 1 foot (30 cm). In cooler zones plants die back to the soil line but resprout from the roots. Division is seldom necessary.

**Propagation** Take stem cuttings in early summer.

**Pest and disease prevention** No serious pests or diseases.

**Landscape uses** Plant toward the middle or back of borders where the airy gray flower buds and soft-blue flowers mix well with yellow, pink, deep blue and

*Perovskia atriplicifolia*

purple flowers. Combine with yarrows, gayfeathers, balloon flower, sedum, phlox and ornamental grasses. Use in color-theme gardens with white or with other pastels.

**Cultivars** 'Blue Spire' has violet-blue flowers on strong upright stems.
'Longin' has stout stems and grows 3–4 feet (90–120 cm) tall.

# OBEDIENT PLANT
*Physostegia virginiana* Labiatae

Fast-spreading obedient plant is named for the tendency of its flowers to remain in any position when shifted in their four-ranked clusters. Plants grow from creeping stems.

**Flower color** The tubular, fleshy, bilobed flowers are rose pink to lilac-pink.

**Flowering time** Late summer.

*Physostegia virginiana*

**Height and spread** 3–4 feet (90–120 cm) tall; 2–4 feet (60–120 cm) wide.

**Temperature requirements** Zones 3–9.

**Position** Prefers moist, average to humus-rich soil. Full sun to light shade. Grows well in moist to wet soil.

**Cultivation** Wild forms of obedient plant tend to flop in rich soil. In formal gardens, stake the plants or choose a compact cultivar. It is important to divide the plants every two to four years to control their spread.

**Propagation** Divide in spring. Take stem cuttings in early summer.

**Pest and disease prevention** No serious pests or diseases.

**Landscape uses** Use cultivars of obedient plant in formal gardens with asters, goldenrods, garden phlox, boltonia and ornamental grasses. The wild form is lovely in informal plantings.

**Other common names** False dragonhead.

**Cultivars** 'Pink Bouquet' has bright pink flowers on 3–4-foot (90–120-cm) stems. 'Summer Snow' has white flowers on compact, 3-foot (90-cm) stems. 'Variegata' has leaves edged in creamy white and pale pink flowers. 'Vivid' has vibrant rose pink flowers.

# Balloon Flower

*Platycodon grandiflorus* Campanulaceae

Balloon flowers are showy summer-blooming plants with saucer-shaped flowers on succulent stems clothed in toothed, triangular leaves. Plants grow from thick, fleshy roots.

**Flower color** The rich blue flowers have five, pointed petals that open from inflated buds that resemble balloons.

**Flowering time** Summer.

**Height and spread** 2–3 feet (60–90 cm) tall; 1–2 feet (30-60 cm) wide.

**Temperature requirements** Zones 3–8.

**Position** Prefers well-drained, average to humus-rich soil. Thrives in full sun to light shade. Once established, the plants are drought-tolerant.

**Cultivation** New shoots are slow to emerge in spring. Take care not to damage them by mistake. Remove spent flowers to encourage more bloom. Established clumps seldom need division unless to propagate.

**Propagation** Lift and divide clumps in spring or early fall; dig deeply to avoid root damage. Take basal cuttings of nonflowering shoots in summer, preferably with a piece of root attached. Sow seed outdoors in fall. Self-sown seedlings may appear.

**Pest and disease prevention** No serious pests or diseases.

**Landscape uses** Plant with summer perennials like yellow yarrow, sage, bee balm and phlox.

**Cultivars** *F. apoyama* has blue-violet flowers on 6-inch (15-cm) plants.
'Double Blue' has double flowers on 2-foot (60-cm) plants.
'Shell Pink' has pale pink flowers on 2-foot (60-cm) plants.

*Platycodon grandiflorus*

# SNAKEWEED

*Polygonum bistorta* Polygonaceae

Snakeweed is a vigorous perennial with upright flower spikes and pointed, broadly lance-shaped leaves with prominent central veins. The plants grow from creeping stems.

**Flower color** Small pink flowers are tightly packed into erect spikes.

**Flowering time** Early summer.

**Height and spread**
1½–2½ feet (45–75 cm) tall; 1–3 feet (30–90 cm) wide.

**Temperature requirements**
Zones 3–8.

**Position** Constantly moist, humus-rich soil. Full sun to partial shade. Plants tolerate wet soil.

**Cultivation** Plants spread rapidly to form wide clumps. Frequent

*Polygonum bistorta*

removal of some plants is necessary to keep them from taking over.

**Propagation** Divide in fall or spring. Sow seed outdoors in fall.

**Pest and disease prevention** No serious pests or diseases.

**Landscape uses** Snakeweed is a showy, fast-spreading groundcover. Combine it with irises, astilbes, hostas, ferns and ornamental grasses. Cut back regularly to contain its growth.

**Other common names** Bistort.

**Cultivars** 'Superbum' has thick, showy flower spikes.

**Other species** *P. affine*, Himalayan fleeceflower, grows 6–10 inches (15–25 cm) tall. Plants grow from creeping roots to form wide patches of lance-shaped leaves. The narrow spikes of pink flowers open in summer. 'Border Jewel' has rose pink flowers. 'Dimity' has light pink flowers. Zones 3–7.

# POLYANTHUS PRIMROSE

*Primula x polyantha*  Primulaceae

Polyanthus primroses are hybrids with large, showy flowers in a rainbow of colors. The broad, crinkled leaves rise directly from stout crowns with thick, fibrous roots.

**Flower color**  Flat, five-petaled flowers vary in color from white, cream and yellow to pink, rose, red and purple. Many bicolored and eyed forms are available.

*Primula x polyantha*

**Flowering time**  Spring and early summer.

**Height and spread**
8–12 inches (20–30 cm) tall; 12 inches (30 cm) wide.

**Temperature requirements**
Zones 3–8.

**Position**  Evenly moist, humus-rich soil. Light to partial shade. Plants can tolerate dryness in the summer if they go dormant.

**Cultivation**  In cooler zones mulch plants to avoid frost heaving and crown damage. Divide overgrown clumps after flowering and replant into soil that has been enriched with organic matter.

**Propagation**  Divide in fall to increase your stock. Species are easy to grow from fresh seed sown in early spring.

**Pest and disease prevention**
No serious pests or diseases.

**Landscape uses**  Plant drifts of primroses with spring bulbs like daffodils, tulips and Spanish bluebells. Combine them with early-blooming perennials like hellebores, lungworts, forget-me-nots and cranesbills. Wildflowers and ferns are good companions.

**Cultivars**  Many hybrids and strains are available. 'Barnhaven Hybrids' are small plants with large flowers in mixed colors. 'Pacific Giant' is a seed strain with large mixed-colored flowers.

# RODGERSIA

*Rodgersia pinnata*  Saxifragaceae

Rodgersias are bold perennials with pinkish red flowers and large, pinnately compound leaves. These moisture-loving plants grow from stout, fibrous-rooted crowns.

*Rodgersia pinnata*

**Flower color** The small rose red flowers are carried in 1–2-foot (30–60-cm) plume-like clusters.

**Flowering time** Late spring and early summer.

**Height and spread** 3–4 feet (90–120 cm) tall; 4 feet (1.2 m) wide.

**Temperature requirements** Zones 4–7.

**Position** Prefers constantly moist, humus-rich soil. Thrives in partial to full shade. Must be protected from hot afternoon sun in warm zones.

**Cultivation** Rodgersias form huge clumps from large crowns that can remain in place for years. Be sure to provide at least 3–4 feet (90–120 cm) of room around each of the plants.

**Propagation** Divide plants in fall or spring. Sow seed outdoors in fall or indoors in spring.

**Pest and disease prevention** No serious pests or diseases.

**Landscape uses** Plant rodgersias in bog and water gardens or along streams. Combine them with hostas, irises, astilbes, ferns, ligularias and primroses.

**Other common names** Rodger's flower.

**Other species** *R. aesculifolia*, finger-leaved rodgersia, has palmately divided leaves and creamy white to pure white flowers. Zones 4–7.
*R. sambucifolia*, elder-leaved rodgersia, is similar to *R. pinnata* but with white flowers. Partial shade. Zones 4–7.

# ORANGE CONEFLOWER

*Rudbeckia fulgida* Compositae

Orange coneflowers are cheery summer daisies with oval to broadly lance-shaped, rough, hairy foliage on stiff stems. Plants grow from fibrous-rooted crowns.

**Flower color** The daisy-like flowers have yellow-orange rays (petal-like structures) and raised dark brown centers.

**Flowering time** Mid- to late summer.

**Height and spread** 1½–3 feet (45–90 cm) tall; 2–4 feet (60–120 cm) wide.

**Temperature requirements** Zones 3–9. Extremely heat-tolerant.

**Position** Average, moist but well-drained soil. Full sun to light shade. Good drainage is important.

**Cultivation** Orange coneflowers are tough, long-lived perennials. They spread outward to form large clumps. The edges of the clumps are the most vigorous. Divide the plants every two to four years and replant into soil that has been enriched with organic matter.

**Propagation** Divide in spring or fall. Sow seed outdoors in fall or spring or indoors in late winter.

**Pest and disease prevention** No serious pests or diseases.

**Landscape uses** Plant orange coneflowers with other daisies, sedums, phlox, bee balms and

*Rudbeckia fulgida*

chrysanthemums. They combine well with ornamental grasses.

**Other common names** Black-eyed Susan.

**Varieties** *R. fulgida* var. *sullivantii* is a stout grower with wide leaves. 'Goldsturm' is a popular compact cultivar of this variety. The variety speciosa (also known as *R. neumanii*) has narrow leaves and smaller flowers.

# CANADIAN BURNET

*Sanguisorba canadensis* Rosaceae

The tall bottlebrushes of Canadian burnet bloom in late summer atop stout stems clothed in pinnately divided leaves with oblong leaflets. Plants grow from thick, fleshy roots.

**Flower color** The fuzzy, white flowers lack petals. They are tightly packed into dense spikes.

**Flowering time** Late summer and early fall.

**Height and spread** 4–5 feet (1.2–1.5 m) tall; 4 feet (1.2 m) wide.

**Temperature requirements** Zones 3–8. Plants do not tolerate excessive summer heat.

**Position** Evenly moist, humus-rich soil. Full sun to partial shade.

*Sanguisorba canadensis*

**Cultivation** Mulch plants to help keep the soil cool and moist. Plants form stout clumps with age. Divide overgrown clumps.

**Propagation** Divide in spring. Sow seed outdoors in fall.

**Pest and disease prevention** No serious pests or diseases.

**Landscape uses** Plant at the rear of the bed or border with phlox, monkshoods, asters, boltonia and ornamental grasses.

**Other species** *S. obtusa*, Japanese burnet, grows to just 3–4 feet (90–120 cm) with drooping rose-pink flower clusters.

# LAVENDER COTTON

*Santolina chamaecyparissus* Compositae

Lavender cotton is a compact, semi-woody shrub with small, white, woolly, pinnately divided leaves topped with yellow flowers in summer. Plants grow from fibrous-rooted crowns.

**Flower color** The button-like yellow flowers are held above the foliage on thin stalks.

**Flowering time** Summer.

**Height and spread** 1–2 feet (30–60 cm) tall; 2 feet (60 cm) wide.

**Temperature requirements** Zones 6–8.

**Position** Prefers average, well-drained soil. Thrives in full sun. Plants tolerate drought, poor soil and salt.

*Santolina chamaecyparissus*

**Cultivation** Plants need winter protection in cold areas. Cut back in early spring to promote strong healthy growth.

**Propagation** Layer in spring. Take cuttings in summer.

**Pest and disease prevention** No serious pests or diseases.

**Landscape uses** Use lavender cotton to edge walks and beds or to configure intricate knot garden designs. Combine it with other perennials that need good drainage like pinks, rock cresses and sedums.

**Other species** *S. virens*, green lavender cotton, is similar but has deep green foliage.

# PINCUSHION FLOWER

*Scabiosa caucasica* Dipsacaceae

Pincushion flowers are old-fashioned perennials that are regaining the popularity they had in Victorian gardens. The stems are loosely clothed in lance-shaped to three-lobed leaves.

**Flower color** The unusual soft blue flowers are packed into flat, 2–3-inch (5–7.5-cm) heads. The flowers increase in size as they near the margins of the heads.

*Scabiosa caucasica*

**Flowering time** Summer.

**Height and spread** 1½–2 feet (45–60 cm) tall; 1–1½ feet (30–45 cm) wide.

**Temperature requirements** Zones 3–7.

**Position** Average to humus-rich, moist but well-drained soil. Full sun to light shade. Sensitive to high temperatures. Will not tolerate wet soil.

**Cultivation** Pincushion plants form good-sized clumps in one to two years. There is a tendency to become overcrowded; divide if this occurs. Remove fading flowers to promote continued bloom.

**Propagation** Divide in spring. Sow fresh seed outdoors in fall or indoors in late winter.

**Pest and disease prevention** No serious pests or diseases.

**Landscape uses** Plant in groups to increase their visual impact. The airy flowers seem to dance above low, mounded plants like phlox, pinks and yarrows. They combine well with bee balms, daylilies and columbines.

**Cultivars** 'Alba' has white flowers.
'Butterfly Blue', of uncertain parentage, is long-blooming with lilac-blue flowers.
'Clive Greaves' has large lavender-blue heads.
'Miss Wilmot' is creamy white.

# SHOWY STONECROP

*Sedum spectabile*  Crassulaceae

Showy stonecrops are late summer perennials with clusters
of pink flowers atop thick stems clothed in broad, gray-green
leaves. Plants grow from fibrous-rooted crowns.

**Flower color**  Small bright pink
flowers are borne in 4–6-inch
(10–15-cm) domed clusters. The
pale green buds are attractive in
summer and the brown seed heads
hold their shape all winter.

**Flowering time**  Mid- to late
summer.

**Height and spread**  1–2 feet
(30–60 cm) tall; 2 feet (60 cm)
wide.

**Temperature requirements**
Zones 3–9. Plants are heat-tolerant.

**Position**  Prefers average to
humus-rich, well-drained soil.

Thrives in full sun. Once
established showy stonecrop is
extremely drought-tolerant.

**Cultivation**  Clumps get quite
full with age and may fall open.
Divide overgrown plants.

**Propagation**  Divide from spring
to midsummer. Take cuttings of
nonflowering shoots in summer.
Sow seed in spring or fall.

**Pest and disease prevention**
No serious pests or diseases.

**Landscape uses**  Plant in formal
borders, informal gardens and rock
gardens. Combine with yarrows,
purple coneflowers, cranesbills,
coreopsis and ornamental grasses.

**Cultivars**  'Brilliant' has rose pink
flowers.

**Hybrids**  Several hybrid cultivars
are available. 'Autumn Joy' is a
stout sedum with dark flowers.
'Ruby Glow' has 1-foot (30 cm)
sprawling stems with purple-
tinged leaves and ruby red flowers.

*Sedum spectabile*

# LAMB'S-EARS

*Stachys byzantina* (syn. *S. lanata*) Labiatae

Lamb's-ears are eye-catching foliage plants with basal
rosettes of elongated, densely white, woolly leaves.
These sun-loving plants grow from slow-creeping stems.

**Flower color** Small, two-lipped
rose purple flowers are carried on
woolly flower stalks. Many people
consider the flowers unattractive
and remove them.

**Flowering time** Early summer.

**Height and spread**
6–15 inches (15–37.5 cm) tall;
12–24 inches (30–60 cm) wide.

**Temperature requirements**
Zones 4–8. Plants are sensitive to
hot, humid weather.

**Position** Well-drained, sandy or
loamy soil. Full sun to light shade.
Intolerant of heavy, soggy soil.

**Cultivation** Lamb's-ears form
dense broad clumps of tightly
packed foliage. Divide overgrown
clumps to control their spread.

**Propagation** Divide plants in
spring or fall.

**Pest and disease prevention** In
wet, humid weather rot may occur.
Cut back affected plants. Proper
siting is the best defense.

**Landscape uses** Looks equally
attractive in formal and informal
gardens. Plant at the front of
formal gardens or combine in
cottage-style gardens with irises,
coral bells, alliums and sedums.

*Stachys byzantina* (syn. *S. lanata*)

**Cultivars** 'Primrose Heron'
has soft, primrose yellow foliage
in spring.
'Sheila McQueen' has larger,
less-woolly leaves and grows well
in warmer zones.
'Silver Carpet' is a neat, compact
cultivar that is mostly listed as
nonflowering but will flower in
some gardens, depending on the
site and the conditions.

# Stoke's Aster

*Stokesia laevis* Compositae

Stoke's aster is attractive in foliage and flower. The broad, lance-shaped leaves are deep green with a white midvein. The leaves form a rosette from a crown with thick, fibrous roots.

*Stokesia laevis*

**Flower color** The 2–3-inch (5–7.5-cm) daisy-like flowers have ragged blue rays and fuzzy white centers.

**Flowering time** Summer.

**Height and spread** 1–2 feet (30–60 cm) tall; 2 feet (60 cm) wide.

**Temperature requirements** Zones 5–9.

**Position** Average to humus-rich, moist but well-drained soil. Thrives in full sun to light shade. Established plants tolerate poor, dry soil.

**Cultivation** Plants can grow undisturbed for many years. Divide in spring or fall as necessary.

**Propagation** Divide in early spring. Sow seed outdoors in fall or indoors in winter after stratification. To stratify, mix seed with moist peat moss or seed-starting medium in a plastic bag. Close the bag with a twist-tie and place it in the refrigerator for four to six weeks. Then sow the mixture as you would normal seed.

**Pest and disease prevention** No serious pests or diseases.

**Landscape uses** Combine in formal and informal landscapes with columbines, verbenas, phlox, goldenrods and various ornamental grasses.

**Cultivars** 'Alba' has white flowers.
'Blue Danube' has 5-inch (12.5-cm) lavender-blue flowers.
'Klaus Jelitto' has 4-inch (10-cm), deep blue flowers.

# FOAMFLOWER

*Tiarella cordifolia* Saxifragaceae

Foamflowers are elegant woodland wildflowers with fuzzy flowers and rosettes of triangular, three-lobed hairy leaves. Plants grow from fibrous-rooted crowns and creeping stems.

**Flower color** The small, starry white flowers are borne in spike-like clusters. They are often tinged with pink.

*Tiarella cordifolia*

**Flowering time** Spring.

**Height and spread**
6–10 inches (15–25 cm) tall; 12–24 inches (30–60 cm) wide.

**Temperature requirements**
Zones 3–8.

**Position** Prefers evenly moist, humus-rich, slightly acid soil. Thrives in full shade but will tolerate partial shade.

**Cultivation** Foamflowers spread by creeping stems to form broad mats. Divide the plants to control their spread.

**Propagation** Remove runners from the crowns or stems in summer and treat them as cuttings if they lack roots of their own. Sow seed in spring.

**Pest and disease prevention**
No serious pests or diseases.

**Landscape uses** Foamflowers are consummate groundcovers. Their tight foliage mats discourage weeds under shrubs and flowering trees. In woodland gardens combine them with bulbs, ferns and wildflowers like fringed bleeding heart and bloodroot as well as hostas and irises. Use them to cover unattractive terraces.

**Varieties** *T. cordifolia* var. *collina* (also listed as *T. wherryi*) is a clump-former with many pink-tinged flower spikes in each rosette.

## COMMON SPIDERWORT

*Tradescantia* x *andersoniana* Commelinaceae

Common spiderworts have satiny flowers that open in the morning and fade in the afternoon. They are borne in clusters at the tips of the stems. Plants grow from thick, spidery roots.

**Flower color** The 1–1½-inch (2.5–3.5-cm) flowers have three rounded blue, purple or white petals.

**Flowering time** Spring and early summer.

**Height and spread** 1–2 feet (30–60 cm) tall; 2 feet (60 cm) wide.

**Temperature requirements** Zones 3–9.

**Position** Moist but well-drained, average to humus-rich soil. Full sun to partial shade.

**Cultivation** After flowering plants tend to look shabby. Cut them to the ground to encourage new growth. Plants in dry situations go dormant in summer.

**Propagation** Divide in fall. Self-sown seedlings often appear.

**Pest and disease prevention** No serious pests or diseases.

**Landscape uses** Plant in informal gardens with bellflowers, columbines, hostas and a variety of ferns. In formal gardens combine them with tulips and spring-blooming perennials.

**Cultivars** A few cultivars of common spiderwort are available. 'Blue Stone' has rich medium blue flowers. 'James C. Weguelin' has sky blue flowers. 'Pauline' has orchid-pink flowers. 'Red Cloud' has maroon flowers. 'Zwanenberg Blue' is purple-blue.

*Tradescantia* x *andersoniana*

# NETTLE-LEAVED MULLEIN

*Verbascum chaixii* Scrophulariaceae

Nettle-leaved mullein has thick flower spikes and stout stems with broadly oval, pointed leaves. The species has yellow flowers; the cultivar 'Album' has white flowers.

**Flower color** The small, five-petaled yellow flowers are tightly packed into dense clusters.

**Flowering time** Summer.

**Height and spread** 2–3 feet (60–90 cm) tall; 1–2 feet (30–60 cm) wide.

**Temperature requirements** Zones 4–8.

**Position** Average, well-drained soil. Full sun to light shade.

**Cultivation** Plants spread slowly and seldom need division.

**Propagation** Sow seed outdoors in fall or spring or indoors in spring. Take root cuttings in late winter or early spring. Plants often self-sow but are not vigorous.

*Verbascum chaixii*

**Pest and disease prevention** No serious pests or diseases.

**Landscape uses** Grow nettle-leaved mulleins in the front or middle of formal borders or in rock gardens. Plant in informal borders with fine-textured perennials like thread-leaved coreopsis, cranesbills and meadow rues. In informal garden they make an excellent contrast to mounded perennials; combine them with catmints and ornamental grasses. They also grow well in pots.

**Cultivars** 'Album' has white flowers with purple eyes.

**Other species** *V. olympicum*, olympic mullein, has broadly oval, pointed, silver gray hairy leaves and yellow flowers. Zones 6–8.

# Rose Verbena

*Verbena canadensis* Verbenaceae

Rose verbena has deeply lobed leaves and circular, flat flower clusters at the ends of the stems. Plants grow from fibrous-rooted crowns but also root along the trailing stems.

**Flower color** The tubular lavender to rose pink flowers have flat, five-petaled faces.

**Flowering time** Late spring through fall.

*Verbena canadensis*

**Height and spread** 8–18 inches (20–45 cm) tall; 12–36 inches (30–90 cm) wide.

**Temperature requirements** Zones 4–10.

**Position** Poor to humus-rich, well-drained soil. Full sun. Plants are heat- and drought-tolerant.

**Cultivation** Plants spread quickly to form broad clumps. Prune or divide plants that overgrow their position.

**Propagation** Take stem cuttings in summer.

**Pest and disease prevention** Powdery mildew may cause white blotches on the foliage. Spray infected plants with wettable sulfur to control the spread of the disease.

**Landscape uses** Rose verbena is an excellent "weaver." Use it to tie mixed plantings together at the front of the border. The stems will cover bare ground between yuccas, mulleins and ornamental grasses.

**Hybrids** A number of lovely hybrids is available in a full range of colors from white and yellow to pink, rose, red, maroon, lavender and purple.

**Other species** *V. bonariensis* (syn. *V. patagonica*), Brazilian vervain, is an upright plant with sparse foliage and rounded clusters of violet flowers. Zones 7–9.

# SWEET VIOLET

*Viola odorata* Violaceae

Sweet violets are beloved for their delicate, fragrant, early-season flowers. They produce rosettes of heart-shaped leaves from creeping, fibrous-rooted rhizomes.

**Flower color** The deep purple or blue flowers have five petals. Two point upward and three point outward and down. The two outfacing petals have fuzzy beards.

**Flowering time** Spring.

**Height and spread** 2–8 inches (5–20 cm) tall; 4–8 inches (10–20 cm) wide.

**Temperature requirements** Zones 6–9.

**Position** Moist, humus-rich soil. Sun or shade. Widely tolerant of varying soil and moisture.

**Cultivation** Violets are prolific spreaders and make themselves at home in any garden.

**Propagation** Divide plants after flowering or in fall. Plants often self-sow.

**Pest and disease prevention** No serious pests or diseases.

**Landscape uses** Violets form attractive groundcovers under shrubs and flowering trees. In informal gardens plant them with bulbs, wildflowers, hostas and early-blooming perennials. Violets attract butterflies.

*Viola odorata*

**Cultivars** 'Deloris' has deep purple flowers.
'White Queen' has small white flowers.

**Other species** *V. sororia*, woolly blue violet, is similar but has hairier foliage. 'Freckles' has pale blue flowers flecked with purple centers. 'Priceana' has white flowers.

# ADAM'S NEEDLE

*Yucca filamentosa* Liliaceae

Adam's needle produces tall, oval clusters of bell-like white flowers and rosettes of sword-shaped, blue-green leaves. It grows from a woody crown with fleshy roots.

*Yucca filamentosa*

**Flower color** Nodding creamy white flowers have three petals and three petal-like sepals that form a bell.

**Flowering time** Summer.

**Height and spread** 5–15 feet (1.5–4.5 m) tall (5 feet [1.5 m] is average); 3–6 feet (90–180 cm) wide.

**Temperature requirements** Zones 3–10.

**Position** Average to humus-rich, well-drained soil. Thrives in full sun to light shade.

**Cultivation** Adam's needle plants thrive for years with little care. After flowering the main crown dies but new side shoots keep the plant growing.

**Propagation** Remove young sideshoots from the clump in spring or fall.

**Pest and disease prevention** No serious pests or diseases.

**Landscape uses** The spiky, evergreen clumps of Adam's needles add a dramatic focus to any planting. The showy clusters of white summer blooms are a bonus! Plant in dry borders or rock gardens as features or in seaside gardens for an added accent. Contrast the stiff foliage with the soft or delicate foliage of plants like lamb's-ears, sedums and verbenas.

**Cultivars** 'Bright Edge' has yellow-variegated leaves.

277

# PART FIVE

# FLOWERING TREES, SHRUBS & VINES

# TREES, SHRUBS AND VINES IN YOUR GARDEN

L ike all flowering plants, the key to success with flowering trees, shrubs and vines is putting the right plant in the right place—a place where the soil, sun, moisture and temperature conditions match the growing requirements of the plant you've selected. A camellia planted in Massachusetts, for instance, quickly becomes a casualty of the first cold winter. A staghorn sumac planted in waterlogged soil rapidly shows signs of distress. Even subtle influences can affect your plants. For example, the heat reflected from a white or light-colored wall can burn the foliage of trees and shrubs in the summer—and even broad-leaved evergreens in the winter.

# USING TREES IN THE LANDSCAPE

Species with a slow-to-medium growth rate, like oaks, generally require less maintenance than fast-growing ones.

The biggest investment in your landscape—in both time and money—is the selection, purchase and planting of trees. Trees dominate the landscape with their size and their effects on the surroundings. A landscape with trees has psychological benefits, too, by making you feel rested and peaceful.

**Defining trees** By horticultural definition, trees are woody plants with one main stem or trunk. Trees generally have a mature height ranging from 15–100 feet (4.5–30 m) or more. A small tree is defined as one that generally doesn't exceed 25–35 feet (7.5–10.5 m) in mature height. A medium-sized tree matures at about 50–65 feet (15–19.5 m) and a large tree matures at approximately 75–100 feet

(22.5–30 m) or taller. Growing conditions, climate, competition with grass and other plants, mechanical or animal damage and pollution can prevent a tree from reaching its mature height.

**The uses of trees** These versatile plants frame views, develop patterns for your landscape and unify your color design. To get the most out of the trees you select, consider the following features and what they can add to your design. Read the instructions that come with the plant to find out whether it is deciduous or evergreen. If all leaves drop each fall, with new leaves each spring through summer, the tree is deciduous.

**Beauty** Trees serve as backdrops for other plants or garden features and as focal points, like large, living sculptures. You can use them to screen unwanted views and give you privacy. Your trees establish the walls and ceilings for your outdoor rooms. You can use them to soften the architecture of your house or to call attention to it.

**Livability** By shading your house, trees keep things cool, reducing energy bills. (Don't plant evergreen trees for summer shade, though; they'll block the sun in winter, preventing passive solar heating of your house.) You can use trees as a windbreak, to intercept and buffer prevailing winds. If winter winds are your bane, needle-leaved evergreens are

*Trees can be used as backdrops, screens or features in your yard.*

the best choice for a windbreak. If you live near the coast, choose salt-tolerant species to filter the sea winds. Patios or play areas become more usable during hot summers when shaded by trees. Trees also reduce glare. Plus, many trees have edible fruits that can feed your family or attract wildlife.

**Consider growth rates** Trees grow at different rates, ranging from less than 1 foot (30 cm) per year to several feet (about 1 m) per year. Fast-growing trees, such as poplars and willows, are often short-lived, surviving only 20–30 years; their wood is also more susceptible to damage.

# CHOOSING TREES

**As well as considerations of height and flower color, you will need to think about the shape of your new trees and the way that they grow.**

### Look below the surface

Before you plant, consider what your new tree is like under the ground as well as above. Shallow roots cause mowing problems and can buckle pavements. Other problem trees have roots that seek water and invade water lines, septic tanks and swimming pools. Willows are notoriously thirsty trees, a good quality if you need a tree for a poorly drained area, but a tree to avoid within 100 feet (30 m) of any water pipes.

### Consider form and function

When you select trees for your yard, use your landscape plan to help you decide what shape of tree to select and how each tree will function in the landscape.

**Specimen trees**  Specimen trees are showy in some way. They may put on an eye-catching display of flowers in spring, like a flowering crab apple or blaze with autumn color, like the red maple 'October Glory'. Or they may have unusually colored leaves, such as purple smoke tree or bright berries, such as American mountain ash. Select a specimen

**UNDERGROUND LIFE**
Remember to think about how the tree will grow below, as well as above.

*Mimosa is a deciduous tree with fluffy pink flowers borne in mid-summer.*

**Shade trees** Shade trees may have showy features, but it's their cooling effect that's most important. A tree with a round or vase shape is ideal for use as a shade tree. Decide the location of a new shade tree with care: Make sure the shadow of the tree will shade the area you intend it to and not block out valuable sources of light. If you want filtered shade or want to be able to grow grass under your tree, use a tree with small, fine leaves, such as a thornless honey locust, not one with a dense canopy of large, overlapping leaves, such as a Norway maple.

tree with multiseasonal interest. A saucer magnolia is very showy for a couple of weeks during the spring when in flower, but it fades into the background the rest of the year. A kousa dogwood, on the other hand, bears showy flowers in spring, raspberry-like red fruits in fall and attractive bark in winter.

**Street trees** Street trees are tough species that withstand the difficult growing conditions along the street. They're tolerant of heat and pollution, grow well in poor soils and can stand drought. Their roots must grow in very limited spaces and their crowns must fit under overhead utility lines. Street trees have to be neat: Look for trees that don't have messy fruit that can stain concrete and cars, falling twigs that can cause damage or large leaves that can block storm sewers. Despite these requirements, a number of attractive and adaptable trees are available for roadside planting. Among small trees, consider a golden-rain tree with its rich yellow mid-summer flowers. Suitable medium to large trees include thornless honey locust with its greenish spring flowers and Japanese pagoda tree with its creamy, fragrant fall flowers.

# USING SHRUBS IN THE LANDSCAPE

Shrubs are hardworking plants in any landscape. They provide practical solutions to your landscaping requirements and offer beauty and fragrance. One of the most creative and ornamental ways to use shrubs in a landscape is in mixed plantings, combining deciduous and evergreen species, interplanting shrubs that bloom at different seasons or adding flowering shrubs to a perennial border to create year-round interest.

### SHRUB SHAPES

You can choose from a variety of shrub shapes or create your own shapes with careful pruning.

**Defining shrubs** Shrubs are woody plants with multiple stems, ranging from a few inches (centimeters) tall to approximately 15 feet (4.5 m) at maturity. Occasionally an individual shrub is trained to a single tree-like stem, called a standard. And large shrubs are sometimes "limbed up," by removing the lower branches, into small trees. Like trees, shrubs can be deciduous, evergreen or semi-evergreen. Deciduous shrubs, including such favorites as roses and spireas, often have attractive flowers. For heavy flower production, plant them in full sun.

**Evergreens** Evergreen shrubs have leaves year-round, though you will notice that each year some of the oldest leaves drop off and are replaced by new leaves. Shrubs with wide, often thick, leaves, such as camellias and rhododendrons are called broad-leaved evergreens. Shrubs with thin, narrow leaves, such as junipers are classified as needle-leaved evergreens. A few shrubs are semi-evergreen, holding some of their leaves well into winter. Glossy abelia, for example, is evergreen in the south and semi-evergreen farther north.

**Double action** Some shrub genera include both deciduous and evergreen species. Hollies are a good example. When the deciduous hollies, possum haw and winterberry, drop their leaves in the fall, large clusters of bright red berries are revealed. Their berry display is generally much showier than that of many of the evergreen hollies, such as Chinese holly and English holly, whose berries are often hidden by their leaves. Other shrub genera with

*Flowering shrubs like camellias can provide a dramatic show during their bloom season.*

both deciduous and evergreen species include viburnums, rhododendrons and azaleas.

**Seasonal attractions** In your landscape, shrubs can be utilitarian, but they can also be a focal point. Look for shrubs with multiseasonal interest—especially for use as accents or specimens. Oak-leaved hydrangea, for

instance, has interesting oak-leaf-shaped leaves that turn purple in fall. Its showy clusters of off-white flowers dry on the plant and persist well into the winter. The fruit on shrubs such as pyracanthas and viburnums provide food for birds, while the plants serve as protective cover. Fruiting shrubs are also excellent for attracting wildlife.

# CHOOSING AND USING SHRUBS

You can use shrubs to define the border of your property, hide an exposed foundation on your house or block an unwanted view. These useful plants can create privacy, show people where to walk or just provide an attractive show throughout the year. They also filter noise, break the force of the wind and provide shade.

*Evergreen camellia*

sitting area from an area designed for active play or to wall utility areas off for trash or storage. You can also use shrubs as a backdrop for plantings of flowers. But if you use shrubs in this manner, look for ones that will complement but not compete with your flowers. Choose green shrubs like boxwoods or junipers, for example, and avoid those with showy blossoms of their own.

**Screens and hedges**  Shrubs are the perfect choice for hedges and screens, to block unattractive views, sights and sounds. To calculate how many shrubs you need to buy for an effective hedge or screen, determine the mature spread of the species you've selected. Figure on spacing the shrubs closer together than their mature spread so that they'll form

**Specimens**  Shrubs make excellent specimen plants. Use them to call out a special feature in your yard such as the beginning of a path or the end of a border or patio. For specimens, look for shrubs that are attractive for as many months as possible. Many

viburnums, for example, have attractive spring flowers, summer fruit and good fall color.

**Backdrops and walls**  You can use shrubs to mark the garden rooms or the parts of your landscape—to screen a quiet

*Mix trees, shrubs and wildflowers for a charming effect.*

**Groundcovers** Shrubs are an excellent substitute for grass in areas where lawns don't grow well, where mowing is difficult or where you want less maintenance. Planted in a well-mulched bed, low-growing junipers or rockspray cotoneaster will form a low-maintenance cover on a steep hill. Where soil erosion is a problem, use shrubs with creeping underground stolons, such as red-osier dogwood or shrubs with arching stems that root when they touch the ground, such as winter jasmine.

**Size up your selections** If you want your shrubs to stay short, regular pruning will keep them in bounds. But a more practical, less time-consuming approach is to choose shrubs that mature at the height you need. There are dwarf or miniature cultivars of many popular shrubs, including 'Bronxensis' forsythia, which matures at 2 feet (60 cm) in height. Dwarf cultivars of many trees—especially spruces and arborvitae—are also commonly used as shrubs. Look for plants with names like 'Prostrata', 'Nana', 'Compacta', 'Densa' and 'Pumila', but don't stop there. Be sure to verify mature height before you buy; compact forms of some trees and large shrubs may still be much larger than you want at maturity.

*Shrubs like barberries offer both fruit and flowers.*

an unbroken line. For example, if a shrub has a mature spread of 5 feet (1.5 m), plan to space the plants 3–4 feet (0.9–1.2 m) apart, depending upon how large they are when you buy them and how quickly you want a solid screen or hedge. Divide the total hedge length by the spacing you select to determine the number of shrubs to buy.

# USING VINES IN THE LANDSCAPE

**Vines are often used simply for the beautiful flowers and foliage they bring to the garden. But vines have functional uses as well: They are fast-growing and quickly lend an established look to the landscape. They can also soften or hide the harsh architectural lines of buildings, create or define garden spaces, provide privacy, screen unsightly views or noise, cover up ugly masonry and break up the monotony of long fences and walls.**

**SPRING SCENT** Wisteria is a deciduous, vigorous climber that brings spring color and heady scent to your garden.

**Defining vines** While all vines twine or climb, keep in mind that there are three basic types of vines: annuals, herbaceous perennials and woody perennials. Most vines are fast growers, although some of the woody perennials may take a year or two to get established. Annual vines, such as common morning glory, climb a lamppost or trellis in a hurry, making a good show in a single season. You'll need to replant annual vines each year, although some will self-sow. Some vines grown as annuals in the north, including black-eyed Susan vine, are perennial in warm climates. Herbaceous perennial vines, such as crimson starglory, die back to the ground every winter and regrow in spring. Hardy woody vines include such familiar species as clematis, honeysuckles and wisteria. Most hardy woody vines are deciduous, dropping their leaves each fall but leaving a woody stem from which new leaves, flowers and fruits grow the following year. Others, including wintercreeper euonymus and English ivy, are evergreen.

**How vines climb** Vines either trail along the ground or climb appropriate supports. If you want your vines to climb, you'll need to know how they do it. Then you can choose an appropriate support for the vine you have in mind. Some vines, such as passionflowers and sweet peas, climb by means of tendrils that grasp any objects they touch. These vines soon blanket a trellis or pergola, with little training from you. Vines that climb with tendrils need supports thin enough for their tendrils to grasp. Some tendrils will coil around supports themselves, while others will loop around supports, then twine around themselves.

Other vines, such as wisterias, climb by twining their entire stems around supports. Twining vines need no encouragement to wrap themselves around a pole or porch post. These vines wrap themselves around slender supports, like wires, railings or other vines, as well as around large objects like columns and tree trunks. English ivy, wintercreeper euonymus and climbing hydrangea use adhesive aerial rootlets along their stems to cling to wood, brick, stone or other materials. Virginia creeper and Boston ivy bear tendrils that end in adhesive disks, which attach themselves to surfaces.

**Vines that need help** A few plants, like climbing roses, are often classified as vines even though they have no natural way to attach to a support. To help this type of vine climb, either weave its stems back and forth through a fence, trellis or arbor or tie its stems loosely to the support until it has established itself.

*Most flowering vines make a dramatic statement with their vibrant colors and shapes.*

# CHOOSING VINES

You can find a vine for any type of soil—fertile or poor, wet or dry—and any exposure from full sun to deep shade. Just as with trees and shrubs, the best course is to match the plant to your site rather than trying to alter your conditions to suit the plant. Most vines are adaptable plants and accept a wide range of growing conditions. A few vines require special conditions. Clematis, for example, need sun for good flower production but do best with cool roots, so plant them in full sun but shade their roots with a groundcover, low-growing perennials or an organic mulch.

*You can guide young vines around a support.*

**Climbing vines** Climbing vines will soften the look of a raw new fence or quickly screen an unsightly view. A hot, sunny porch becomes much more inviting when a trellised vine adds dappled shade. Vines trained on upright supports can fit in spaces too small for most trees and shrubs. They can be used as a vertical accent in flower or herb gardens or to mark the corners of an outdoor living area. Many vines also do well in containers on a deck or patio or in a courtyard garden.

**Deciduous vines** Deciduous vines growing on the south and west sides of your house will shade the walls in summer, reducing your home's energy needs. Where banks are steep or grass is difficult to grow, evergreen vines make excellent groundcovers. Some vines, such as grapes and Chinese gooseberry, provide edible fruit for you or for welcome kinds of wildlife.

### Climbing supports for vines

If you want your vines to grow upright, begin training them on supports as soon as you plant them. Use a structure big enough to support the mature plant and put it in place before you plant the vine.

*Wisteria needs a strong support.*

Buy or build freestanding supports that are constructed of sturdy, durable materials. Wood is a traditional and attractive choice for fan-shaped trellises, lattice panels, graceful arbors or other supports. For longevity and durability, choose cedar or another naturally rot-resistant wood or keep the support structure painted. Wire fencing framed with two-by-fours is a low-cost option that will give a vine years of sturdy support. Use galvanized or plastic-coated fencing to prevent rust. Copper or aluminum wire and tubing can also be fashioned into rustproof supports.

**Training vines** Use string to guide young vines to the structure you want them to climb. It doesn't have to be a special gardening material; household string is fine or you can use strips of soft fabric (as long as it won't break down in

*A striking combination of clematis, grapes and yellow-leaved hops.*

wet weather). Fasten one end of the string or fabric to the support and tie the other end around a rock or a stick. Place the rock at the base of the plant or dig the stick into the ground nearby, making sure to avoid the vine's rootball. Remove the string when the vines begin to twine or cling.

# GROWING TREES, SHRUBS AND VINES

When you start to shop for trees, shrubs and vines, look for the best plants you can find. They are a long-term investment and it's well worth the effort to find good-quality plants. Be careful when buying from discount, grocery and hardware stores. The plants may be in bad condition because they often receive minimal care. Proper planting is a critical step if your trees, shrubs and vines are going to flourish in your landscape. Your new plants won't grow well if you handle them improperly or if you prepare a poor planting site. You have put time into carefully planning your landscape and matching individual plants to each site. Now take the time to do a good job of planting.

# SELECTING AND BUYING PLANTS

Always look for healthy, vigorous plants, with leaves of proper size and color (unless plants are dormant). Buds should be plump and firm, and the bark on the stems should be undamaged. Inspect all plants for signs of insects and diseases; if the leaves are spotted or chewed, or if the stems have indentions or cankers, don't buy them. And be sure the plant is labeled with species and cultivar names so you know exactly what you are buying.

*Good quality plants have vigorous growth.*

## Buying bareroot stock

Bareroot plants are just that—they're dug from the field and sold with bare roots. Bareroot plants are less expensive than other nursery stock; they may cost half as much as the same plant grown in a container. Bareroot plants offer another advantage: After planting, the roots will easily adjust to your garden's soil, whereas the roots of container-grown plants have to make the transition from the nursery soil to yours. Most deciduous trees, shrubs and vines can be successfully grown from bareroot stock. Don't buy large trees or any evergreens bareroot; their roots can dry out easily, causing damage that's hard to overcome. Buy and plant bareroot stock when it's dormant, which is generally from late fall to early spring. If you can't plant immediately, temporarily "heel in" your plants by laying them along a shallow trench in a shady, protected area and covering their roots with soil.

### Buying balled-and-burlapped stock

Balled-and-burlapped (B&B) plants are often the most expensive and the soil ball makes them heavier to handle. Be sure the root ball is large enough to support and anchor your plant. Properly handled root balls should be well wrapped, firm and moist. Avoid lifting B&B plants by the trunk and handle them carefully or the root ball might break apart and damage the roots. Since B&B stock comes with soil, plants have to make the transition from the nursery soil to yours. The difference in soil type can cause uneven water distribution, either soaking the root ball or leaving it drier than the surrounding soil.

### Containerized stock

Not to be confused with container-grown plants, containerized or processed-balled plants are initially dug bareroot. Their roots are then packed or potted in organic matter or potting medium, not field soil. As with bareroot stock, most of the roots are left behind in the field. When you buy, check inside the packing or slip the pot off; if there are only a few large, cut roots but no fine, small roots, don't buy the plant. The nursery didn't hold it long enough for new roots to grow; the plant will be slow to establish.

### Buying container-grown stock

Unlike containerized plants, container-grown plants are grown from the start in a container. Since you get all of the root system, transplant shock is minimal. You can set container-grown stock aside until you're ready to plant (keeping it watered)

*Balled-and-burlapped stock, dug from the field with a ball of soil around the roots.*

without fear of damaging it. When you shop for a container-grown plant, gently slip it out of the container to inspect the root ball. Well-cared-for plants have many roots showing on the outside of the ball. The roots should be white or light tan in color; brown or black roots are probably diseased or rotting from overwatering.

# PREPARING THE PLANTING SITE

Most trees, shrubs and vines are planted one by one in individual holes. But before you plant, you should think about creating planting areas, not just digging holes. You'll want to prepare a large enough growing area so the roots of your new plants can spread easily for at least a few years, until they get well established.

*Most flowering shrubs thrive in ordinary soil.*

**Soil improvement** Average garden soil is fine for most trees, shrubs and vines—especially if you've picked ones that are well adapted to the site. But if you have less-than-ideal soil or you suspect a nutrient deficiency, a soil-improvement program may be in order. In an area where topsoil has been removed, you will definitely need some preparation.

**Planting hole preparation**
Dig the planting hole before you remove your stock from its container or wrapping to prevent the roots from drying out. Make the hole as wide and as deep as necessary to accommodate the roots of the plant without crowding. Angle the sides of the hole to about 45–60 degrees so that it's wider at the top. Dig your planting hole no deeper than the depth of the root ball—or slightly shallower in heavy soils. The last step is to loosen the soil around the hole, so the roots of your new plant will be encouraged to spread out from the planting area. To do

this, fluff up the soil 2–5 feet (0.6–1.5 m) out from the hole with a spading fork or rotary tiller. You can also dig a layer of organic matter, such as compost, into the soil in this area to enrich it, reduce weeds and keep it moist.

### DEALING WITH PROBLEM SOILS

Planting naturally well-adapted species is the best way to handle problem soils, particularly those with slow drainage. Building raised beds and filling them with improved soil is an option for shallow-rooted vines and even some small shrubs. But the roots of trees and many shrubs and vines will soon outgrow the beds. If your soil is extremely sandy or clayey, save your raised beds for flowers and vegetables and choose species of trees, shrubs and vines that are compatible with your soil conditions.

### PLANTING BENEATH TREES

For easier planting and maintenance, group plants into larger beds, rather than separate holes. When adding fertilizers to the soil beneath established trees and shrubs, be careful not to apply fertilizer to the roots of the trees; it could cause damage.

### PLANTING SMALL SHRUBS

Small container-grown trees and shrubs are easy to buy and plant. Fall and spring are ideal planting times, but container-grown stock will adapt to a new home almost any time the ground isn't frozen. If you plant during hot weather, remember to keep the soil evenly moist to promote root growth and avoid heat stress.

# PLANTING TECHNIQUES

You can plant anytime the ground isn't frozen. Plant bareroot stock when it's dormant, from late fall to as early in spring as possible. Balled-and-burlapped stock does best when planted in the cooler months of spring or fall. You can plant container-grown stock anytime during the growing season, but if you plant during summer, be sure to pay extra attention to watering.

*Azaleas and other shrubs perform best when planted properly in well-prepared soil.*

### Planting bareroot stock

Before you plant, soak the roots of bareroot trees, shrubs or vines in water overnight and plant the stock the next day. Don't soak the roots too long or they will begin to decay.

### Planting container-grown and containerized stock

Slip your new plants from their containers and remove any paper or cardboard labels or tags and any wires. Add durable, weatherproof labels near each plant or mark the names on your landscape plan. Inspect the roots of your plants and prune any that are broken, soft and mushy or diseased, cutting back to healthy tissue.

### Planting B&B stock
Remove any rope, twine or nails from B&B stock. If your balled-and-burlapped

**PREPARING TO PLANT**
After preparing the hole for planting, remove the plant from the pot. If it won't come easily, tap around the base of the pot with a stick. Prune away broken or circling roots.

**PLACING THE PLANT**
Once you've placed the plant in the hole and made sure that it's set straight, you can backfill half the hole. Water the soil and finish backfilling.

stock is wrapped in synthetic material, wait until the plant is in the hole, then snip the wrapping into pieces, removing as much of it as you can. If the root ball begins to shatter, cut slits in the remaining material and leave it in place.

**How to plant**  Keep a firm, level area of soil in the bottom of the hole on which to set the plant and dig a few inches deeper around it so that extra water can drain away from the roots easily. Now set the plant into the hole. (If you're

planting bareroot stock, build a cone of soil in the hole and settle the plant on top of the cone, spreading the roots over it.) Start refilling or backfilling, with the soil you removed when you dug the hole. Backfill half the hole, then water the soil to remove large air pockets. Once the water drains away, finish backfilling and water again. With the leftover soil, build a well around the hole to trap and hold water over the plant's roots.

**Staking**  Staking holds trees and shrubs in place while their roots grow out from the root ball into the surrounding soil. Trees taller than 8 feet (2.4 m) or top-heavy trees with a large crown or top in relation to the size of the root ball benefit from the support of stakes that prevent them from falling over. If staking is necessary, use one or two stakes for small trees, two or three for large trees.

# CARE AND MAINTENANCE

Maintaining your landscape doesn't have to be an exhaustive or expensive undertaking. Preventing problems before they get started is a simple but important part of the plan—and one that depends on you. Be alert to signs of stress that might be a result of pests or diseases. Perform any maintenance as soon as you see that it's needed and you will keep your labor and expense to a minimum.

*Keep a special bin for your compost scraps.*

**Composting** Making and using compost is at the heart of any successful organic garden. Compost makes a great soil amendment and fertilizer and it's also an ideal way to recycle yard wastes and kitchen scraps.

**Mulching** A thick layer of organic mulch around trees, shrubs and vines cuts down on all other maintenance chores. Mulch is a labor-saving way to control weeds and it also helps retain moisture and improve your soil, encouraging healthy root growth. The variety of mulches means you can use it as a design feature in your garden beds.

**Watering** New trees, shrubs and vines require regular watering to keep the soil around them evenly moist for at least one full year after

**PEST PROTECTION**
To prevent damage from gnawing rodents, such as mice or rabbits, you can install a loose-fitting plastic or wire guard around the trunks of your new trees and shrubs. Apply the guard to a height of about 18 inches (45 cm). If your area gets deep snow, wrap the trunk to a higher level.

planting. When rainfall is inadequate during the growing season, you will need to provide supplemental irrigation.

**Feeding** Most trees, shrubs and vines don't need much in the way of supplemental fertilizers. In fact, a layer of compost applied over the soil to the drip line will offer all the added nutrition most plants need. If your soil is low in nutrients, plants may grow slowly, have few flowers or have leaves that are small and pale. In these cases, if mulching doesn't help, you may need to apply fertilizers.

**Controlling weeds** Weeds are an eyesore and compete with your plants for nutrients, water and light. In addition, they can harbor all kinds of pests and diseases. Use mulch as the basis of your weed-control program and whenever possible, pull weeds while they're young. Don't dispose of them into your compost bin.

**Controlling pests and diseases** Keeping a watchful eye for insects, diseases or pesky animals doesn't take much time, but it goes a long way toward protecting your landscape investment. When problems arise, you can take care of them with safe organic methods.

**USING THE NEWS**

If your mulch supply is limited and your weeds are rampant, newspaper makes an excellent weed barrier. Lay it down in sections, several pages thick and cover it with organic mulch to smother weeds. The organic mulch keeps the newspaper from blowing away and also covers the unattractive paper. The newspaper will gradually decompose over the next year or two, adding organic matter to the soil.

# A PRUNING PRIMER

**Proper pruning can promote healthy growth on ailing plants, improve the form of poorly shaped ones, show off the natural beauty of good-looking plants and encourage the production of more or better fruits or flowers. By taking the time to learn the proper techniques, you'll be amply rewarded with a healthy, attractive landscape.**

*Hedge clippers are handy for shearing.*

**Why should you prune?** There are many reasons you may want or need to prune. Judicious pruning at planting time defines the shape of your new trees, shrubs and vines. As your new plants grow, they will occasionally need pruning to correct structural problems that develop, such as branches that rub or grow at tight angles or to remove vertical water sprouts and suckers. Maintenance pruning is also necessary to remove damage caused by weather, animals, people or insects and diseases. You may need to direct growth, especially of fast-growing vines or control the height or spread of your plants. Some vines, especially vigorous growers like trumpet creeper and wisteria, need heavy pruning to keep them a manageable size and to increase the number of flowers.

**When to prune** There are times when you need to ignore the season and pick up the pruners, however. If damage from storms, equipment or disease occurs, you should prune immediately, removing all damaged wood. Otherwise timing is critical to successful pruning.

- Spring pruning stimulates a flush of vigorous growth. It's a good time for heavy pruning because plants will recover fast.

- Summer pruning is a good time for tidying up, but avoid heavy pruning, which can stress plants in hot weather.
- Fall is a good time to make thinning cuts, removing branches back to a main stem. Don't prune back branch tips in fall because the tender new growth that results can be easily damaged by freezes.
- In winter, dormant plants are easy to prune since the lack of leaves makes it easy to see the plant's structure.

**Pruning tools** The pruning tools you'll need depend on what kinds of plants you will be trimming. Hedge clippers are the traditional choice for formal hedges. Pruning shears are best for stems and twigs. As the diameter of the branches increases, switch to loppers, which work well on branches that are finger-sized or larger. When loppers aren't large enough, use a pruning saw.

**Pruning cuts** Pruning basically comes down to two types of cuts: thinning and heading. A thinning cut removes branches where they join the stem. Be sure to cut just outside the branch collar—the raised or otherwise distinct area at the branch base. Cuts that are flush to the stem, removing the collar area, don't heal (close) well.

Heading cuts stimulate regrowth. Save them until the end of the pruning job. A nonselective heading cut slices off branch tips in midstem, bringing on a thick flush of uniform growth. Selective heading snips off the tip of a branch back to a bud or side branch. Cut slightly above a bud pointed in the direction in which you want new stems to grow. In general, prune above buds that face outward, not inward.

Start with a cut from underneath.

Finish by sawing off the stub.

# LANDSCAPE CHARTS

### Plants for Flowering Hedges

A flowering hedge can provide seasonal or year-round interest. Flowering shrubs generally look best when you let them grow in their natural arching or spreading forms, without extensive pruning.

✿ *Abelia* x *grandiflora* (glossy abelia): Semi-evergreen. Lightly fragrant pale pink flowers in spring and summer. 4–6 feet (1.2–1.8 m) tall. Zones 6–10.

✿ *Chaenomeles speciosa* (flowering quince): Deciduous. Single or double red, pink or white flowers in spring; yellow fruit ripen in fall. 4–10 feet (1.2–3 m) tall. Zones 4–8.

✿ *Deutzia* spp. (deutzias): Deciduous. White flowers in summer. 2–10 feet (0.6–3 m) tall. Zones 4–9. (Height and hardiness vary among species.)

✿ *Forsythia* spp. (forsythias): Deciduous. Yellow flowers in early spring. 6–8 feet (1.8–2.4 m) tall. Zones 4–9.

✿ *Hibiscus syriacus* (rose-of-Sharon): Deciduous. White, pink, red or violet flowers in summer. 8–15 feet (2.4–4.5 m) tall. Zones 5–9.

✿ *Hydrangea paniculata* var. *grandiflora* (peegee hydrangea): Deciduous. Large clusters of creamy white flowers in late summer. 4–10 feet (1.2–3 m) tall. Zones 4–8.

✿ *Philadelphus coronarius* (sweet mock orange): Deciduous. Fragrant white flowers in late spring. 6–8 feet (1.8-2.4 m) tall. Zones 4–9.

✿ *Potentilla fruticosa* (shrubby cinquefoil): Deciduous. Lemon yellow flowers in late spring and again in summer to fall. 2–4 feet (0.6–1.2 m) tall. Zones 2–8.

✿ *Prunus laurocerasus* (cherry-laurel): Evergreen. Fragrant white flowers in spring. 10–15 feet (3–4.5 m) tall. Zones 6–9.

✿ *Rosa* spp. (roses): Deciduous. Shrub, grandiflora and floribunda roses come in a range of colors. Height and hardiness vary among species.

✿ *Spiraea* spp. (spireas): Deciduous. White flowers in spring. 3–6 feet (0.9–1.8 m) tall. Zones 4–9. (Height and hardiness vary among species.)

❀ *Syringa* spp. (lilacs): Deciduous. Fragrant white, pink or purplish flowers in spring. 5–20 feet (1.5–6 m) tall. Zones 3–7. (Height and hardiness vary among species.)

❀ *Viburnum* spp. (viburnums): Deciduous or evergreen. White flowers in spring or summer. 5–12 feet (1.5–3.6 m) tall. Zones 3–8. (Height and hardiness vary among species.)

### Fast-Growing Vines

Don't overlook the value of flowering vines and climbing plants in your outdoor living spaces. These versatile plants can help you to solve various problems in your yard.

❀ *Aristolochia durior* (Dutchman's-pipe): Deciduous. Twining vine with dark green heart-shaped leaves and pouched flowers in summer. Zones 4–8.

❀ *Clematis maximowicziana* (sweet autumn clematis): Deciduous. Twining woody vine with fragrant white blooms in late summer into fall. Zones 5–9.

❀ *Ipomoea* spp. (morning glories): Annual. Twining vine with trumpet-shaped blue, white or pink flowers from summer into fall.

❀ *Mina lobata* (crimson starglory): Annual in most climates. Twining vine with lobed leaves and showy clusters of red buds and orange-and-yellow flowers.

❀ *Passiflora* spp. (passionflowers): Dramatic purple, pink or white flowers from summer to fall. Climbs by tendrils. Zones 7–10. (Hardiness varies among species.)

❀ *Thunbergia alata* (black-eyed Susan vine): Annual. Twining vine with heart-shaped leaves and orange-yellow flowers in summer.

### Plants with Multiseason Interest

When you only have room for a few trees and shrubs, you need to choose the plants that will provide the greatest effect for the space they take up. Listed here are some flowering deciduous trees and shrubs that can provide attractive features in more than one season. The plants are listed by botanical

**Growing Trees, Shrubs and Vines**

name, followed by the common name, flower color, special features and hardiness zones. A hardiness zone map is on page 311.

✿ *Abelia* x *grandiflora* (glossy abelia): Lightly fragrant pale pink flowers in spring through summer; glossy green leaves turn reddish in fall. Zones 6–10.

✿ *Amelanchier* spp. (serviceberries): White flowers in spring; red to black berries in summer; yellow to red fall color. Zones 3–8.

✿ *Berberis* spp. (barberries): Small yellow flowers in spring; red to black berries in late summer into winter; red or purple fall color. Zones 4–10. (Hardiness varies among species.)

✿ *Callicarpa* spp. (beautyberries): Pinkish purple flowers in late summer; bright purple berries in fall and winter. Zones 5–9.

✿ *Chionanthus virginicus* (white fringe tree): White flowers in early summer; females produce blue berries in summer; yellow fall color. Zones 5–8.

✿ *Cladrastis lutea* (American yellowwood): Fragrant white flowers in late spring; yellow fall color; smooth gray to tan bark. Zones 3–8.

✿ *Cornus florida* (flowering dogwood): White flowers in spring; red berries in late summer to fall; reddish fall color. Zones 4–9.

✿ *Cornus kousa* (kousa dogwood): White flowers in late spring; red fruit in late summer; red fall color; peeling bark. Zones 5–9.

✿ *Cornus mas* (cornelian cherry): Yellow flowers in early spring; red berries in late summer; peeling bark. Zones 4–8.

✿ *Cotinus coggygria* (smoke tree): Airy masses of pale pinkish flowers in summer; yellow orange or reddish purple fall color. Zones 5–8.

✿ *Eucalyptus* spp. (eucalyptus): Yellow, red or white flowers in summer to fall; aromatic bluish leaves; peeling bark. Zones 9–10.

✿ *Fothergilla* spp. (fothergillas): White flowers in spring; bright yellow to orange-red fall color. Zones 5–9.

- *Hamamelis* spp. (witch hazels): Yellow orange or reddish flowers in fall or early spring; yellow to orange fall color. Zones 5–9.

- *Hydrangea quercifolia* (oak-leaved hydrangea): White flowers in summer; burgundy red fall color. Zones 5–8.

- *Itea virginica* (sweetspire): White flowers in late spring to early summer; bright red to purplish fall color. Zones 5–9.

- *Lagerstroemia indica* (crape myrtle): White, pink, red or purplish flowers in summer; peeling bark. Zones 7–10.

- *Magnolia stellata* (star magnolia): White flowers in spring; red seeds in summer. Zones 5–9.

- *Malus* spp. (crab apples): White or pink flowers in spring; red or yellow fruit in summer. Zones 4–8.

- *Oxydendrum arboreum* (sourwood): White flowers in summer; bright red fall color. Zones 5–9.

- *Parrotia persica* (Persian parrotia): Yellow orange and scarlet fall color; gray-and-white mottled bark. Zones 5–10.

- *Prunus serrulata* (Japanese flowering cherry): Small white flowers in spring; yellow fall color; peeling reddish brown bark. Zones 5–8.

- *Pyracantha* spp. (firethorns): White flowers in late spring to summer; red fruit in fall. Zones 6–9.

- *Rosa rugosa* (rugosa rose): Fragrant white, pink or red flowers in summer; orange-red fruit in late summer. Zones 3–10.

- *Stewartia* spp. (stewartias): White flowers in summer to fall; yellow, red or purplish fall color; showy peeling bark. Zones 5–9. (Hardiness varies among species.)

- *Viburnum* spp. (viburnums): White flowers in spring or summer; red to purple fall color. Zones 3–9. (Hardiness varies among species.)

# PLANT HARDINESS ZONE MAP

A hardiness zone map enables you to match the climate where you live with flowering plants that will thrive there—the key to success in any garden.

**Using the map** Plants grow best within an optimum range of temperatures. The range may be wide for some species and narrow for others. Plants also differ in their ability to survive frost and in their sun or shade requirements. This map of the United States and Canada is divided into 10 zones. Each zone is based on a 10°F (5.6°C) difference in average annual minimum temperature. Some areas are considered too high in elevation for plant cultivation and so are not assigned to any zone. There are also island zones that are warmer or cooler than surrounding areas because of differences in elevation; they

have been given a zone different from the surrounding areas. Many large urban areas are in a warmer zone than the surrounding land. The zone ratings indicate conditions where designated plants will grow well and not merely survive. Many plants may survive in zones warmer or colder than their recommended zone range. Remember that other factors, including wind, soil type, soil moisture, humidity, snow and winter sunshine may have a great effect on growth. When buying a flowering plant, have a look at the zone information listed on its tag, or refer to the guide in this book.

|  | |  |
|---|---|---|
| Zone 1 | | Below -50°F (Below -45°C) |
| Zone 2 | | -50° to -40°F (-45° to -40°C) |
| Zone 3 | | -40° to -30°F (-40° to -34°C) |
| Zone 4 | | -30° to -20°F (-34° to -29°C) |
| Zone 5 | | -20° to -10°F (-29° to -23°C) |
| Zone 6 | | -10° to 0°F (-23° to -18°C) |
| Zone 7 | | 0° to 10°F (-18° to -12°C) |
| Zone 8 | | 10° to 20°F (-12° to -7°C) |
| Zone 9 | | 20° to 30°F (-7° to -1°C) |
| Zone 10 | | 30° to 40°F (-1° to 4°C) |

**FIRST PORT OF CALL**

It's important to choose flowering
plants that grow well in your area.
The Plant Hardiness Zone Map is
your first port of call when deciding
what plants to buy. Then other
considerations can come into play,
such as the microclimate of your yard.

# GLOSSARY

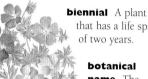

**annual** A plant that has a life span of one year or less.

**biennial** A plant that has a life span of two years.

**botanical name** The name, usually based on Latin, that is given to a plant to specify its genus and species. The genus is the first word and the species is the second word in the name.

**container-grown stock** Plants that have been grown from the start in a container.

**cultivar** A variety of plant that has been produced from a mother plant by cultivation rather than by natural propagation. The name of the cultivar is set in single quotes after the botanical name.

**cutting** A section taken from the stem of a plant in order to reproduce the plant. Many flowers are easily propagated from cuttings.

**deadheading** Pinching off spent flowers before they can form seed so that the plant will produce more flowers in an attempt to make more seed.

**division** The propagation of a plant by removing a section from the root and replanting it.

**forcing** Providing a condensed version of winter indoors so that plants will bloom early.

**half-hardy** Plants that can withstand a touch of frost near the beginning or end of the growing season.

**hardy** A plant that can survive climactic extremes, especially cold, heat and dryness, throughout the growing season.

**hybrid** The offspring of two different species of plants. In the botanical name, an "x" indicates that the plant is a hybrid.

**layering** The propagation of a plant by means of burying one of its still-attached, long, flexible stems into the soil next to the plant. This encourages roots to form at each buried leaf node.

**mulch** A material that is used to cover the surface of your garden soil in order to keep the soil warmer in winter and cooler in summer, to retain moisture and to hinder the growth of weeds. Mulch can be an organic material, such as compost, grass clippings or shredded leaves, or an inorganic material, such as black plastic and landscaping fabric.

**naturalizing** Planting in random, natural-looking drifts; commonly done under trees, in woodlands and in large, grassy areas.

**nursery bed** A temporary growing area.

**overwintering** Growing plants indoors during winter.

**perennial** A plant that has a life span of more than two years.

**pH** A measure of the alkalinity or acidity of soil based on a scale of 1 (strongly acid) to 14 (strongly alkaline).

**propagate** To reproduce a plant.

**rhizome** The underground runner or stem of a plant.

**sepal** The outermost part of the flower; usually a green, cup-like structure.

**taproot** The strong, tapering central root of a plant that grows straight down in search of water and nutrients.

**tender** A plant that originates from tropical or subtropical climates and that cannot tolerate a degree of frost.

**topography** The lay of an area of land, such as hills, valleys and slopes.

**umbel** A section of a plant in which a few flower stalks spread from a common center; called a simple umbel when each stalk ends in a single flower; called a compound umbel when each stalk bears another umbel. The flowers are generally very small.

**var.** Plants that develop a natural variation in the wild are called varieties; the varietal name is included as part of the botanical name after the abbreviation "var.".

# INDEX

Index

Entries in *italics* indicate illustrations and photos.

## A

Abelia, glossy 306, 308
Adam's needle 209, 217, 277, *277*
Ajuga 211, 213, *213*, 221, *221*
Alyssum, sweet 31, 36, 42, 43, 50, 51, 67
Amaranth, globe 60, 88, *88*
Anemone, Japanese 209
Annuals 29, 312
    caring for 64–7
    cut flowers 48–9
    fragrant 50–1
    growing from seed 56–61
    true 30–1
    types 32–3
Aphid *69*, 154
Aster
    China 76, *76*
    New England 179, 183, 209
    Stoke's 271, *271*
Astilbe 179, 213
Azalea *300*
Azure monkshood 220, *220*

## B

Baby's-breath
    annual 89, *89*
    perennial 183, 244, *244*
Balled-and-burlapped (B&B) stock 297, 300–1
Balloon flower 209, 261, *261*
Baneberry, white 213
Barberry *289*, 308
Bareroot stock 190, 197, 296, 300
Basil 52
Basket-of-gold 183, 217
Bean
    castor 37, 44, 67, 105, *105*
    scarlet runner 44, 45
Beardtongue, common 258, *258*
Beautyberry 308
Beds and borders 34–5
Bee balm 179, 181, 215
Begonia 39, 60
    tuberous *122*, 125, 126, 137, 152
Bellflower 183, 229, *229*
Bergenia *21*, 213, 227, *227*

Biennials 61, 312
Black-eyed Susan vine *44*, 108, *108*, 290, 307
Blanket flower 179, 209, 217, 242, *242*
Bleeding heart 213, 236, *236*
Bluebell, Virginia 255, *255*
Boggy sites 214–15
Boltonia 179, 209
Botanical name 312
Bugloss, Siberian 213, 215
Bugs 204–5
Bulbs
    caring for 150–5
    chilling 132–3
    container 136–7
    cut flowers 140–1
    fall 126–9
    indoor 130–3
    planting 146–9
    spring 118–21
    summer 122–5
Burnet, Canadian 266, *266*
Butterflies, plants for 178–9

## ACKNOWLEDGMENTS

Weldon Owen would like to thank the following people: Sarah Anderson, Lisa Boehm, Trudie Craig, Peta Gorman, Michael Hann, Aliza Pinczewski, Puddingburn Publishing Services (index)

TEXT Bonnie Lee Appleton, C. Colston Burrell, Susan McClure, Patricia S. Michalak, Nancy J. Ondra, Rob Proctor, Sally Roth, Alfred F. Schneider, Elizabeth Stell

ILLUSTRATIONS Tony Britt-Lewis, Stuart McVicar, Barbara Rodanska

PHOTOGRAPHS Heather Angel; Gillian Beckett; Thomas Buchholz; John Callanan; Brian Carter; Nigel Cattlin; Bruce Coleman Ltd; Corel Corporation; Jules Cowan; Eric Crichton; Michael Dirr; Thomas Eltzroth; Derek Fell; The Garden Picture Library: Lynne Brotchie, Linda Burgess, Christopher Gallagher, John Glover, Michael Howes, Lamontagne, Jane Legate, Zara McCalmont, Mayer/Le Scanff, Jerry Pavia, Gary Rogers, J. S. Sira, Brigitte Thomas, Mel Watson, Steven Wooster; Holt Studios International; Andrew Lawson; Stirling Macaboy; S & O Mathews; Clive Nichols; Nancy J. Ondra; Jerry Pavia; Joanne Pavia; Photos Horticultural; Rodale Stock Images; Tony Rodd; ⌐ita Sabarese; John J. Smith; Harry Smith Collection; Kim Taylor; David Wallace; Weldon Russell; Weldon Trannies

CONSULTANT EDITOR Geoffrey Burnie has 20 years' experience in horticulture. He is the author of several books on ⌐g and has been a consultant and contributor to *Better Homes and Gardens* magazine since 1983.